HOLLYWOOD
BLOCKBUSTERS

HOLLYWOOD BLOCKBUSTERS

The Anthropology of Popular Movies

David Sutton and Peter Wogan

BERG

Oxford • New York

English edition
First published in 2009 by
Berg
Editorial offices:
First Floor, Angel Court, 81 St Clements Street, Oxford OX4 1AW, UK
175 Fifth Avenue, New York, NY 10010, USA

Berg is the imprint of Oxford International Publishers Ltd.

Library of Congress Cataloging-in-Publication Data

A catalogue record for this book is available from the Library of Congress.

British Library Cataloguing-in-Publication Data

A catalogue record for this book is available from the British Library.

ISBN 978 1 84788 486 2 (Cloth)
978 1 84788 485 5 (Paper)

Typeset by JS Typesetting Ltd, Porthcawl, Mid Glamorgan
Printed in the UK by the MPG Books Group

www.bergpublishers.com

For Beth,
You always managed to convince me to watch that movie that I wouldn't
have gone to otherwise, and you were always right
— DS

For my sons, Zach, Liam, and Peter
You wanna' have a catch?
— PW

CONTENTS

ACKNOWLEDGMENTS

"You're gonna' need a bigger boat." "That rug really tied the room together." "Bonasera, Bonasera, what have I ever done for you to treat me so disrespectfully?" These and other movie lines have become so interwoven into our conversations over the past ten years of writing this book that, like a transformative fieldwork experience, they have become part of who we are. We barely imagined when we first presented a short conference paper on *The Godfather* in 1999 that we would spend the next decade engrossed in the anthropological analysis of blockbuster movies, but we're glad we did. Though the joys of collaboration are underrated and underreported in academia, we are grateful to have had this opportunity to work together so closely on our joint passion for interpreting American culture and applying anthropological ideas in novel contexts. We will argue in this book that blockbuster movies are like enormous, collective dreams, touching on the psyches of millions of people at the same time. Certainly writing about these movies has fulfilled a dream of ours, and we owe thanks to a number of colleagues, friends, and relatives for their faith in this project.

Berg editors Anna Wright and Tristan Palmer, as well as the anonymous Berg reviewers, deserve special thanks for their help in conceptualizing this project and seeing it to fruition. For their astute observations and helpful suggestions about specific chapters, we're also deeply grateful to Lee Drummond (*The Godfather*), Michael McKernan (*Field of Dreams*), Elizabeth Bird and Bahram Tavakolian (*Jaws*), and the audience members that responded to our presentations at Southern Illinois University, the American Culture Association meetings, and the American Ethnological Society meetings (*The Godfather, Field of Dreams, The Big Lebowski,* and *Jaws*). Sutton presented an early version of our *Godfather* chapter at the University of Michigan, and would like to thank Carol Bardenstein and the Humanities Center participants for taking the time to read and comment in detail on it.

Others helped, too. Our mothers, as always, were guiding influences. Nancy Wogan proofread the entire manuscript with her usual sharp editor's eye (and exclamation points!), while Connie Sutton provided a careful critique of many of the chapters, and she and Antonio Lauria expanded our ideas through their reflections on Mead's "Studies of Culture at a Distance" project. Frank Miller helped us think through the cover design, Kailey Bunch provided excellent proofreading, and the journal *Anthropology and Humanism* kindly allowed us to reprint parts of an article that we originally published on *The Godfather* (Sutton and Wogan 2003).

Sutton's colleagues also added important insights. Sutton had an ongoing dialogue about *The Godfather* and Mafia movies with Antonio Lauria and Nick Doumanis. Anthony Webster was particularly helpful in thinking through ideas about entextualization, reported speech, and other linguistic notions. Special mention goes to Leonidas Vournelis, for his eagerness to explore an anthropological approach to popular culture more generally (one of these days, *The Anthropology of South Park*), and his many valuable suggestions on particular chapters. Kenneth Routon and David Anthony also provided valuable suggestions on *The Village* chapter.

Wogan's colleagues were also encouraging at critical junctures. In 1999 Wogan shared some of his ruminations about *The Godfather* with Jerry Gray, an Economics Professor at Willamette University, where Wogan had just joined the faculty. Instead of saying, "You can't do this kind of thing, you're an *anthropologist*," Gray invited Wogan over to his house to watch *The Godfather*. When the film was over and Wogan elaborated on some of his ideas, Gray, as well as two other senior colleagues, Spanish Professor Patricia Varas and Rhetoric and Media Studies Professor David Douglass, let Wogan know that he was onto something and should keep pursuing it. Obviously he took this advice to heart, and he's grateful for the generosity of these senior colleagues.

Wogan turned some years later to his cousin Andy Knipe, to test out his and Sutton's theories about *Field of Dreams*. Wogan actually did this with some trepidation, knowing that Knipe was a true baseball aficionado and not one to mince words. Fortunately, Knipe agreed that *Field of Dreams* remains one of the best movies ever made, and he confirmed that we were on the right track. Andy Knipe died of Lou Gehrig's disease before this book could be published, but Wogan still expects to see him come walking through a cornfield someday, as he told him in their last conversation.

Our students also made this book come about. Sutton discussed and debated *The Village* with a number of his graduate students, both in and out of seminars, and equally appreciates the insights of his gender seminar into *The Big Lebowski*. He has used *The Godfather* in virtually all of his classes, and has noticed how it even awakens the interest of some of the guys sleeping in the back row. He is also grateful to his honors class on "The Social Life of Things" for lengthy discussions and written responses to some of the interpretations of *Jaws* that we develop here. Wogan has also benefitted from many lively discussions about blockbuster movies with his students, especially those enrolled in "Survey of Anthropological Theory," "Visual Anthropology," and "Warfare, Violence, and Peace." These discussions taught him that you *can* go to another level, especially when you have faith in each other.

Finally, we want to thank our families. Maria McIvor, Wogan's wife, and Beth Rowe, Sutton's wife, have helped us work through all these ideas, with Beth and Maria taking the phone out of our hands sometimes and setting us straight when we were stuck on a point. And even without explicit discussion, our kids have given us new ways of viewing these movies. For example, Wogan's sons took to *Field of Dreams* right away and never let go. Even when they saw this movie for the first time, four years ago, they got it. Peter, five years old at the time, couldn't quite understand how a cornfield could talk, but he said, "That voice is cool," and then he hid behind the couch and whispered, "If you build it, he will come." Liam (age 7) marveled that the credits simply stated, "The Voice—As himself," and asked who "himself" was and why he didn't have a name. And Zach (age 9) did a perfect imitation of Terence Mann sarcastically asking Ray Kinsella, "Want some cookies?" Many, many viewings later, they still want to watch *Field of Dreams* again, and continue to quote it at the dinner table and on car rides.

It has been a particular pleasure for Sutton during the years of working on this book to see his older son Sam go from being a star-struck, young movie fan to a movie critic always wanting to discuss the latest viewing, a video maker, a screenwriter, and an aspiring all-around contributor to our collective dreams. His younger son Max has become curious about the movie project, but still wonders why we didn't include a chapter on Indiana Jones. We hope that we have provided something that will inspire the younger generation to carry on our love of quoting and interpreting movies.

1 INTRODUCTION

At a time when just about everything, from the mundane to the spectacular, has been subjected to an anthropological lens, why have anthropologists been so cautious about extending their insights to popular Hollywood movies? And what might be the rewards of an approach to these movies that is unabashedly anthropological?

This book employs current anthropological concepts to illuminate American blockbuster movies, such as *Field of Dreams*, *Jaws*, and *The Godfather*.[1] While most mass media suffer ever-faster spin cycles and increasingly fragmented audiences, these films have enjoyed remarkable, enduring popularity. They have become so deeply woven into the cultural fabric that lines from them—"If you build it, he will come"; "You're gonna' need a bigger boat"; "Make him an offer he can't refuse"— have been incorporated into our everyday language. Clearly these films continue to fascinate and appeal to American audiences, making them tantamount to the myths and sacred narratives that anthropologists routinely study in other parts of the world. If anthropologists were to find a culture that spent as much energy on myths as Americans do on Hollywood movies—constantly watching and talking about them, gossiping about their heroes—they would create a cottage industry exclusively devoted to unpacking the meaning of those myths. Strangely, though, few anthropological studies have even considered Hollywood movies. We propose to do something about this.

Though scholars in film studies and cultural studies offer plenty of excellent interpretations of film texts, we believe that anthropology has something to add. In calling for anthropological readings, however, we are not trying to erect new disciplinary boundaries. In fact, we believe such boundaries impede the scholarly enterprise, and we intend to engage with the work of non-anthropologists in the pages that follow. Nonetheless, there are ways of approaching problems that still tend to be typical of anthropology: a focus on topics such as kinship, gift exchange, and ritual, and a comparative perspective on human societies, systems of meaning, and modes of everyday activity. We will try to show that these anthropological approaches can provide fresh angles on familiar Hollywood movies, and, more generally, on American society and cultural processes.

ORIGINS OF THIS BOOK

We see our project very much in the anthropological tradition of making "the strange familiar and the familiar strange." Unfortunately, anthropologists have tended to shy away from the latter half of this promise; anthropologists too often focus on the "strange," without using the understanding gained through fieldwork and cross-cultural training to comprehend such seemingly mundane, familiar phenomena as Hollywood movies.

In fact, this book began in the wake of our own reverse culture shock. When we returned to the U.S. over ten years ago after doing extended fieldwork in other countries, we started to see ostensibly trivial aspects of American culture in a new light, including movies that touched on themes we had been investigating while abroad. Wogan had been studying literacy practices in highland Ecuador, examining the ways in which a local indigenous group used writing as a symbol for government and Catholic Church power (Wogan 2004b). In this state of heightened sensitivity to literacy symbolism, he happened to watch *The Godfather* and couldn't help noticing images of writing in this movie, such as a bandleader's contract and FBI badges. He began to view these literacy images as a subtle, deeply critical commentary on the American state, capitalism, and social relations. At roughly the same time, Sutton also watched *The Godfather* and noticed interesting parallels to his own field research on food practices and gender in Greece (Sutton 2001). For the next few years, we watched *The Godfather* repeatedly, compared notes, discussed the film in our classes, and continued honing our analysis, until we finally felt compelled to publish an article on it (Sutton and Wogan 2003). That experience alerted us to the anthropological possibilities offered by blockbuster movies.

Over the past decade, we have expanded our discussions to include other films, read widely in the literatures on visual anthropology and media studies, and incorporated movies into our undergraduate teaching and field research projects. Certainly there was no shortage of films to analyze, but we only focused on those that seemed particularly complex and interesting from an anthropological point of view. The result is this book.

ETHNOGRAPHY, ANTHROPOLOGY, AND BEYOND

We have to stress that this book is *not* an ethnography, unlike most other recent anthropological work on mass media, which has focused on the production, circulation, and reception of various media texts worldwide.[2] While we recognize the value of these ethnographic media studies, our own aims here are different. This book provides a textual reading of Hollywood movies,[3] rather than an ethnographic analysis of their production or reception by specific audiences.

We have cast our analysis at the level of "American society" in full recognition that this is a broad, semi-fictionalized construct. We do this as a tentative first step, a way to get people thinking about these texts. But we also know there is ultimately no such thing as American society and no interpretation that will apply to all Americans; there are only specific audiences responding to specific films in specific contexts. Like most other anthropologists, we take as a given that "culture" is inchoate, an ever shifting amalgam of contradictory values and practices, and that any claims to the unified coherence of "culture" are always political and value-laden.[4] To understand the social and personal meaning of films, then, ethnographic studies must be done with specific audiences. Toward that end, we will present some results of our own ethnographic studies in the Conclusion, and suggest ways that others could ethnographically study audience responses to the issues raised in this book.

We believe this is a reasonable order. Creating textual readings is an important first step before undertaking ethnographic research on audience responses, just as other fieldwork projects start off with provocative, tentative theories rather than blindly poking in the dark. For example, Elizabeth Traube, while admiring Janice Radway's research on audience uses of romance novels (1984), notes that research can also fruitfully begin with textual readings:

> An ethnographer who took this latter route could search for correspondences between patterns embodied in mass cultural narratives and the more loosely structured stories that people tell about their lives, their narrative constructions of personal and collective identity. In the process, of course, the ethnographer would probably come to revise the original textual analysis. On the other hand, I suspect that preunderstandings of mass entertainment culture would help to elucidate the fictions through which people live their lives. (1989: 275; see also 1990: 378; 1992)

Elizabeth Bird is a particularly good example of an anthropologist who has combined textual readings with creative ethnographic approaches, as seen in her book-length studies of supermarket tabloids, television scandals, and other mass media phenomena (1992, 2003). Resisting notions of "ethnographic purity" and "more ethnographic than thou" attitudes, Bird points out that traditional participant-observation is not necessarily feasible or relevant when studying a dispersed audience, nor is it always necessary when the investigator is a member of the culture being studied; in such cases, the "fieldwork" has started years before the textual analysis itself (Bird 2003: 7–10).

The value of textualist approaches needs to be stressed because the proper relationship between anthropology, ethnography, and mass media remains a matter of contention. Anthropologists and cultural studies scholars still debate where their respective disciplinary boundaries properly lie, with some anthropologists insisting on the superiority of fieldwork (e.g. Geertz 1998; Nugent and Shore 1997) and some scholars of cultural studies even condemning each other for supposedly corrupting "true" anthropological ways of doing ethnography (see Bird 2003: 6; Peterson 2003: 126–7). As anthropology has moved away from the study of discrete, bounded communities and more toward multi-sited ethnography, the definition of ethnography and anthropology itself has come up for debate. Clifford Geertz refers to this debate as "the most critical issue facing cultural anthropology in these postcolonial, postpositivist, posteverything times. This is the value, the feasibility, the legitimacy, and thus the future of localized, long-term, close-in, vernacular field research—what [James] Clifford at one point lightly calls 'deep hanging out'..." (Geertz 1998: 69). In our own publications, we have found ourselves on both sides of this debate. Our previous work on Greece and Ecuador has been based on long-term fieldwork (Sutton 1998, 2001, 2008; Wogan 2004b), and we have even argued for the value of extended fieldwork over the "thinness" of certain multi-sited ethnographies (Wogan 2004a) and auto-ethnographies (Wogan 2007). At the same time, we have contributed publications that are more theoretical and multi-sited, and less strictly tied to fieldwork (Sutton 2006, 2007; Wogan 2004b, 2006).

This debate over fieldwork applies with particular force to media studies. Although anthropologists today are more willing than ever before to study mass media, many still do not know what to make of anthropological studies of mass media that are not rooted in traditional fieldwork. Lila Abu-Lughod, for example, accepts that "anthropologists cannot dispense with 'textual analysis,' the equivalent of symbolic analyses of rituals and myths that have illuminated so much" (1997: 112), but she sees such textual interpretation as subsumed within a larger ethnographic project, and she is critical of research on media for using "a notion of ethnography that little resembles the anthropological ideal" (1997: 111). On the other hand, Kath Weston questions "nostalgia for ethnography," which she sees as consistent with a more general longing for "real anthropology." As she puts it:

> The flag-planting approach asks anthropologists to stake an exclusive claim to particular methodologies or concepts, all, of course, in the name of saving the discipline. Ethnography becomes a distinctive anthropological practice with a long academic pedigree, and pity the poor sociologist who has only lately discovered it. Culture is "our" concept, and damn any cultural-studies type who tries to claim it for his or her own. (Weston 2008: 130)

Another commentator sums up this way: "The debate continues to revolve around the binary of textualism versus social context" (Schein 2008: 210). We can't hope to resolve these fundamental, meta-theoretical debates (nor can any single intervention), but we want to note at the outset that anthropology itself remains contested terrain, so where one stands on textual, anthropological readings of mass media will depend on how one defines anthropology in general.

These debates also demonstrate, however, that anthropology is in flux and new possibilities are opening up. Not only do we now have important precedents like Bird and Traube, but there is growing interest in the anthropology of mass media and a constant pushing of the discipline's boundaries. In fact, we will demonstrate later in this chapter that there is a small but expanding literature on the anthropology of feature films. Textualist approaches, in particular, have now established a place for themselves, as noted by Mark Allen Peterson in his comprehensive review and assessment of the field: "Although the formal features of texts ... cannot in themselves validate particular meanings, the close reading of texts is likely to remain significant to the anthropology of media" (2003: 119).[5]

Furthermore, the interpretations we provide in this book are not entirely text-internal. In fact, the entire textualism *vs.* ethnography distinction starts to crumble under closer inspection. Having lived our entire lives in the U.S. (more than 45 years each), our interpretations are based on an intimate understanding of the society in question. Like other anthropologists, we've been doing ethnography based on participant-observation: participating in social routines, observing others' behaviors; talking to people; thinking systematically about what we are seeing, hearing, and experiencing. We are at least as familiar with the U.S. as the fieldworker who spends a couple years in another culture and struggles to learn the language(s) spoken there. Our work is one of those cases Bird talked about: the fieldwork started long before the textual readings were created. At a time when anthropology is giving more serious attention to "the native point of view" (while also recognizing the blurriness of any claims to insider status), it would make sense to valorize such native understandings of Western anthropologists themselves. From this perspective, our film interpretations are textual *and* ethnographic.

Thus, rather than insisting on a strict, traditional definition of ethnography that pits it and textualist readings against each other, we believe that a mixture of the two will be most fruitful, and we suggest that multiple, flexible approaches to mass media will prove to be enlightening. In fact, we welcome exchanges with cultural studies, film studies, and other fields, and are excited by the possibilities of such interdisciplinary dialogue. Most readers will know the language, culture, and texts we talk about here, so they will be well positioned to contribute to this discussion. This is a refreshing change of pace for us. Cultural anthropologists almost always work alone, without other anthropologists at their field sites; they almost never publicly share their field notes and other unprocessed "data"; and their publications often draw for evidence on languages only known by a handful of other anthropologists. As a result, there is relatively limited opportunity to play with, and push back against, anthropologists' interpretations of specific texts.[6] By comparison, analysis of Hollywood blockbusters is more transparent, open to discussion and debate, and we find such transparency invigorating.

We especially hope that our interpretations will encourage other investigators to explore these blockbuster films through ethnographic research with specific audiences. Toward that end, in the Conclusion chapter we review the literature on the ethnography of audience responses, describe some of the results of our own ethnographic work on student reactions to films, and suggest other ways that these issues could be further explored ethnographically. Such ethnographies are indispensable because no single reading can ever be the final word on these movies. Other researchers would undoubtedly come up with different interpretations of the films we examine, while ethnographic research would inevitably bring out audience-specific, alternative perspectives, which is exactly as it should be when dealing with complex social phenomena like blockbuster movies. It would be especially interesting to see how some of these blockbusters are perceived in countries like Canada and the United Kingdom, where they have also enjoyed great popularity. We refer throughout this book to the U.S. only because that is the society we know best, but we believe that this type of analysis can be pursued elsewhere with good results. Ideally, such audience research will be integrated with studies of media production, as well as the more general "social space" of media (Larkin, cited in Abu-Lughod 1997: 111).

For now, though, this book will stand or fall on its ability to say something thought provoking and original about these blockbuster films, American society, *and* certain anthropological concepts. Rather than merely using film to illustrate anthropological concepts, we try to give new insights into anthropology and American society. For example, the notion of polytemporality has been suggestively explored in changing notions of gender and in commodity production in recent works (Taussig 2008; Weston 2002). We will suggest in Chapter Four that the concept of polytemporality gains considerable nuance when applied to a Hollywood blockbuster, especially when combined with approaches drawn from contemporary linguistic anthropology and pitted against common American notions of time. In other words, we try to expand anthropological theories and concepts. We're doing what others do with ethnographies and empirical studies; the difference is that our case material consists of blockbuster movies.

At the same time, our readings of these films should be useful in the classroom as illustrations of anthropology's insights, which is why we try to state our arguments in accessible language. In fact, we have found that films are particularly effective for the teaching of anthropology, since they give students direct access to the data and thereby provide them with opportunities to create their own original interpretations and to challenge the authors. In the Conclusion, in the process of discussing an ethnographic project, we summarize a full, three-week unit on the teaching of *Jaws*. Whether with students or scholars, we welcome anything that broadens the discussion.

ANTHROPOLOGY AT THE MOVIES: A BRIEF HISTORY

How have anthropologists interpreted and analyzed popular movies in the past? While there is not a large body of literature on this subject, it is important not to ignore past approaches, as we do not wish to reinvent the wheel, but, rather, to build on the strengths and avoid some of the pitfalls of the work of previous anthropologists. This brief review considers most of the major works which have analyzed

Hollywood movies, and notes our own points of overlap with and divergence from these authors.[7]

Anthropological interest in popular movies began with Margaret Mead and her colleagues during the Second World War under the rubric of the *Study of Culture at a Distance* and the Columbia University Research on Contemporary Cultures (RCC) project. This was the first suggestion that anthropology take movies (and other elements of Western popular culture) seriously. Indeed, there are indications (Beeman 2000) that Mead may have been an early influence on the field of cultural studies, as she presented this approach in a series of lectures to the nascent "Birmingham School" in the early 1950s. While these readings were based in the now discarded paradigms of national character studies and the "culture and personality" school of anthropology, they should not be dismissed out of hand. They were an early attempt to claim an approach to movies that was not based in filmic or aesthetic criteria, but, rather, in what insights such popular products—in tandem with interviews and other methods—could give to the key thematic concerns of particular cultural groups.[8] Indeed, movies were seen in some ways as superior to literature for this kind of cultural analysis because they were identified as collective products, oriented toward a popular audience.[9]

The methodology for a thematic analysis of movies for the RCC project was laid out most extensively by Martha Wolfenstein (Wolfenstein 2000 [1953]; Wolfenstein and Leites 1950). She drew from previous analysis of folklore (inspired by Boas and Benedict) and mythology (inspired by Freud and Joseph Campbell) to suggest an approach that focuses on recurrent elements at the level of character, gesture ["the image of a man leaning his head on a woman's bosom" (2000: 294, 297)], and plot structure to mine national cultural differences in the resolution of common psychic issues, such as Oedipal conflict or reaction to the primal scene.[10] She was careful to note, however, that we cannot draw a direct connection between themes in movies and cultural attitudes, noting that there may be a complex relationship between fantasies and real-life confrontations of these issues, and that "It is necessary to have independent evidence on both topics" (304).

More promising, for our purposes, is Gregory Bateson's extended reading of the Nazi propaganda film *Hitlerjunge Quex,* which he developed as part of his work for the Office of Strategic Services during the Second World War (1980).[11] Bateson noted that the popularity of the film with Nazi audiences justified treating it not merely as "an individual's dream or work of art," but, rather, as a myth. He approached it with "the sort of analysis that the anthropologist applies to the mythology of a primitive or modern people" (1980: 21). While Bateson also gave considerable weight to issues of family and personality, he contextualized these concerns within a much broader analysis of the film, looking at such things as notions of time and historical consciousness, political and other key symbols, rituals and rites of passage, and elements such as age grades (as a replacement for the family among young Nazis). He combined all these elements in analyzing the multiple ritual/symbolic deaths of the main character that lead to the ultimate rebirth of the Nazi movement. Instead of seeing family conflict as a direct expression of shared psychological dispositions, Bateson grounded it in social structural concerns and correlative ritual and symbolic processes; in many ways we can see Bateson's movie analysis as an extension of the sort of issues that he developed in his groundbreaking ethnography of the Papua New Guinean Latmul tribe's *Naven* ceremonies (1958 [1936]).

In spite of these promising beginnings, the thread of popular culture analysis was cut as anthropology moved away from national character studies in the 1960s and 1970s. Indeed, aside from several studies by RCC participant John Weakland on the films of communist China (1966a; 1966b), there was almost no analysis of popular movies in anthropology until the late 1980s and early 1990s.[12] Weakland's work, while on some levels sharing all of the problematic aspects of the earlier *Study of Culture at a Distance Approach*, does add one or two interesting new elements. Weakland's most extensive work, *Chinese Political and Cultural Themes: A Study of Chinese Communist Films* (1966a), was published by the U.S. Naval Ordnance Test Station as part of their Studies in Deterrence series and distributed to military research facilities across the country. Framed in the mode of "know your enemy," Weakland saw his role as explaining elements of Chinese culture so as to both predict Chinese reactions to U.S. foreign policy and to understand the significance and resonances of statements made by Chinese political leaders. While reiterating the argument for the superiority of movies to novels and other creative products as materials for cultural interpretation, Weakland's study made two additions to earlier approaches. First, he suggested that films are useful for study because they allow for the comparison and contrast of verbal and visual behavior, that is, what characters say as opposed to what they do, thus drawing from traditional anthropological methods of participant-observation: "This is highly important because the visual material is richer, and often less ambiguous, than the verbal, and because they can be compared; there may be highly revealing qualifications or inconsistencies between the two statements" (1966a: 6). Second, Weakland watched all the films in the company of one or more "native-born" Chinese informants (1966a: 12), and held discussions with them immediately subsequent to the viewing. In this sense, his was the first study to draw systematically on audience response (although he doesn't highlight this data in the body of his study).

Finally, similar to Bateson but extended over a range of movies, his study is an interesting precursor to more recent work, in that he focuses on political themes in Chinese films by looking at how they are often subtly embedded in larger cultural themes of the family, the position of women in society, the role of education, and the relationship of the individual to the group. He noted that, whatever the "propagandistic" messages of these films, they are "rooted in real problems of social interaction that inhere in Chinese cultural organization" (1966a: 44), thus raising the issue of the role of films in mediating cultural contradictions (discussed below). Though these early studies might seem problematic today, as much for their overly psychological interpretations as for the anthropologist's involvement with government and some of their assumptions about national identity, we can take from them the importance of thematic analysis and understanding films less as propaganda and more as myths confronting key cultural issues. They also offer, albeit without developing the concept, the idea of audience response as part of understanding popular movies.

With the publication in 1989 of Elizabeth Traube's *Dreaming Identities: Class, Gender and Generation in 1980s Hollywood Movies*, the long, dry spell in anthropological investigations of movies was broken. Traube's approach was informed by a general anthropological approach that sees myth and ritual as expressing and sometimes temporarily resolving key cultural tensions, contradictions and ambiguities. More generally, she was interested in situating movies within particular cultural-historical moments, noting, "On the assumption that mass cultural forms annex and disguise popular concerns, I abstracted a pattern from a set of commercially successful films intended for middle-class audiences, and tried to define the social conditions with which the pattern might resonate" (1990: 375). In analyses of movies such as *Ferris Bueller's Day Off* and the *Rambo* series, Traube explored cultural tensions between home and work, the individual and the organization, creativity and utilitarianism, and abstract *vs.* concrete loyalties. She looked at how these tensions were overlaid with gender and class assumptions in ways that reinforced but also challenged middle-class patriarchal ideologies typical of the 1980s. Traube also examined representations of the cultural Other in movies such as *Indiana Jones and the Temple of Doom*, which she saw as an attempt to justify neo-colonialist attitudes in the U.S. and deny history and political economic considerations in the understanding of non-Westerners. Thus, Traube's work represented a major advance on earlier approaches in bringing lines of tension within society clearly into focus (rather than subsuming them to "social structure"); in fact, hers was the first analysis to explicitly make gender a key analytic concept. In what follows we will draw on all of these aspects of her work.

Yet for all the attention Traube's book has justly received, it doesn't explicitly or extensively draw on anthropology. In *Dreaming Identities*, Traube does not refer to her own work on myth analysis in Eastern Indonesia (1985), and only makes reference to anthropology in passing (1992: 41, 133). Traube's use of feminist psychoanalysis and object relations theory, with its discussion of such topics as "sublimated version(s) of the female Oedipus complex, a displaced version of what would be appropriate in the conjugal family" (1992: 89), recalls the film analysis of Wolfenstein, Mead and Bateson, but she makes no reference to this work. Nor does she reference Mead or contemporary feminist anthropology in discussing issues such as "the institution of women's mothering as a key factor in gender development." We find this aspect of her work problematic and, in contrast, explicitly anthropological insights will be central to the approach we take in this book.

Unlike Traube, Lee Drummond, in his book *American Dreamtime: A Cultural Analysis of Popular Movies and their Implications for a Science of Humanity* (1995), provides a full-scale intervention into contemporary anthropological theory, so we can only provide a taste of his complex argument here.[13] Like Traube, Drummond draws on the notion of cultural contradictions expressed through movies as myths. Drummond cites Gregory Bateson's concept of schismogenesis (ironically, though, without citing Bateson's work on movies), which he refers to as "the representation of unresolvable dilemmas that lie at the heart of a cultural system, a representation that makes life bearable only by disguising its fundamental incoherence" (1996: 3). He also sees the movie-going experience in traditional Durkheimian ritual terms, as bringing people together in congregation in highly emotional and sensory-charged atmospheres (movie theaters) to create a sense of shared experience, even if different meanings are drawn from that experience. But, unlike Traube, Drummond focuses less on people-movies, and more on movies that ask questions about what it is to be human by challenging the boundaries between human and animal, organic and technological. Thus, his focus on movies such as *Jaws*, *Star Wars*, and *E. T.* is guided by a desire to explore movies that, while still dealing with traditional issues like family, are distinctive in offering new perspectives on previously neat separations of human, animal, and machine: movies that ask us to imagine new meldings of bodies with technologies and human with non-human. The "mythic ambivalence" of *Star Wars* is to present its viewers with a full panoply of positive and negative human–machine combinations, from the totalitarian vision of the Death Star, to the machine–human Darth Vader, to the "spontaneity, loyalty and affability" of R2D2, who seems more human than many of the stick-figure human characters in the movie (178). In short, Drummond uses his movie analysis to develop an approach to culture and society which, though grounded in structuralism and semiotics, also presciently anticipates much recent work on human–technology and human–environment interactions. We draw on Drummond's ideas about irresolvable dilemmas specifically in several of the chapters that follow, and we devote an entire chapter to *Jaws*, one of the films he analyzed. We take Drummond as a more general inspiration in his use of movies not simply as material for a particular analysis but as *phenomena* and *experiences,* the understanding of which—like good ethnography—aids in the development of anthropological ideas and concepts.

Both Drummond and Traube, in their different ways, treat movies as sources of key cultural categories. This is also the approach taken by Louise Krasniewicz in her clarion call, "Round up the Usual Suspects: Anthropology Goes to the Movies" (2006). Like us, she bemoans the dearth of anthropological studies of popular movies, and calls for an approach that focuses on movies as cultural myth/ritual. She notes:

> For anthropologists, movies must engage with the habitual patterns of a culture that is always looking for ways to address its existential questions. These patterns are persistent categories, cultural themes, interpretive strategies, integrated sets of symbols and world-views that members of that society see as normal and natural. If movies didn't relate to these patterns, even in a contradictory or incomplete way, we would have less reason to see them and use them. (2006: 12)

Note that, in these lines, Krasniewicz seamlessly links the notion of themes/patterns with that of categories, implicitly tying together the earlier approach of Bateson et al. with these more recent, structuralist-influenced analyses. Krasniewicz is particularly interested in thinking about categories from the perspective of the metaphor theory of George Lakoff, noting, for example, the role of prototype metaphors such as "mother" and how they serve to refract kinship experiences that fail to match the prototype, a theme that she provides a short, suggestive analysis of for the movie *The Birds*. She also explores[14] the way movies spread beyond the screen to become integrated in the culture through language, toys, and other commodities which allow for "creative retellings and reenactments of [the movies which spawn them]" (2006: 12).

The past decade has seen the beginnings of a more serious engagement with Hollywood movies, as called for by Traube, Drummond and Krasniewicz, along with the growth of media anthropology and studies of the production and reception of movies in non-Western contexts, as noted above. The focus of these analyses has tended to fall into two major categories: (1) a focus on movies that deal with biotechnologies and human-machine interrelations; and (2) an interest in popular movies that raise questions of representation, particularly in terms of images of other cultures and anthropologists. Unfortunately, these studies have not always explicitly engaged with each other or other relevant anthropological material.

In the first category, for example, Anne Allison (2001) looks at the *Robocop* series, focusing on questions of "queer" bodies, disassembled by violence and reassembled by technology. Allison uses the concept of the Cyborg, "a fusion of artificial machinery and living (animal, human, or alien) organism that confuses prior identity borders" (2001: 241–2), to talk about the fragmentation of identity in contemporary society. Rather than seeing Robocop as a hypermasculinized subject meting out violence on others, Allison notes that Robocop is continually coming apart and being re-assembled, challenging notions of individual (male) agency through a sense of power that is always contingent on an assemblage of detachable parts. She sees this as an attractive image for contemporary postmodern times (particularly for children), given the fractured nature of family and other collective identities. But while she contextualizes *Robocop* within a particular historical moment, and in many ways her analysis parallels that of Drummond and Traube in suggesting the mythic aspects in imaginary resolutions of sociocultural tensions, her scholarly dialogue is strictly limited to film theory and technology studies. Even when making references to anthropologists' knowledge that bodily "borders always provoke a mixture of danger and pleasure, and border-crossing is steeped in rituals, tinged often with violence as in initiation rites" (2000: 248), all of her illustrative examples are drawn from other studies of movies.

Deborah Battaglia, also working on issues of biotechnology, situates her analysis of the film *Multiplicity* within current social concerns about new genetic tech-nologies, including cloning, and their implications for changing understandings of "life itself." She sees movies as "major cultural documents" addressing "popular debate about genetically engineered entities" (2001: 495).[15] While placing her analysis within a broad spectrum of films that deal with cloning and other forms of replication, Battaglia eschews a film studies approach to understanding cloning, noting that an anthropological perspective offers an understanding of replication based on social exchange theory and relational models of personhood (she refers to ideas about male parthenogenesis in Melanesia, as well as studies of personhood in India), rather than ego-centered concerns about boundary-maintenance (497, 505). She argues that there is a recognition in *Multiplicity* of the social relations that make us multiple, rather than individual, even if this multiplicity is "commodity driven" by the "fetishization of time in late-capitalist nightmarescapes" (512). Where Allison uses her analysis to comment on the debate on media and child violence, Battaglia sticks with a textual reading of the film as a commentary on contemporary times, though noting the possibility of diverse receptions and the need for ethnographic exploration (513). Unfortunately, there is no dialogue between Allison and Battaglia on their points of overlap, nor does either of them engage with Drummond's work.

Of those approaches in the second category, representations of "other" cultures in popular films, Steven Caton's book-length treatment (1999) of the film *Lawrence of Arabia* is one of the most extensive. Caton focuses his attention on the question of orientalism in the film, i.e., stereotypes of the Arab Other. While not using the concept of myth, he agrees with the basic notion that films are contradictory texts which may both support and challenge dominant ideologies. He illustrates the many ways that *Lawrence of Arabia* challenges orientalist stereotypes and contains multiple critiques of the colonial project, while not denying its hegemonic functions. In doing so, he gives multiple perspectives on the making, social context, and reception of one particular film. He also distinguishes between the "reception" and "reading" of movies, noting that anthropologists may study the reception of movies *in situ*, but "a reading is another matter ... and is not a straightforward empirical issue in any sense. It is largely a construction by a film analyst of the way in which a film *might* be apprehended from a particular spectator position. The most one can claim is that the construction is plausible, given what one knows about specific audience responses..." (Caton 1999: 21). We agree with Caton's distinction between reception and readings, and place ourselves in the latter category. As noted earlier, we are interested in audience reaction studies and incorporate our own into the Conclusion, but throughout the body of the book we are concerned with constructing plausible—though hardly definitive—readings of movies employing anthropological theories, approaches, and questions.

More specifically, we utilize Caton's argument that *Lawrence of Arabia* can be seen as an allegory of anthropology in that it is deeply concerned with the process by which one attempts to live with and, in some cases, befriend and know individuals and groups of people defined as Other. Somewhat similarly, Jonathan Gales and Elizabeth Bird (2005) look at the movie *Jerry Maguire* as a representation of anthropological knowledge and fieldwork relationships. Their readings, like Caton's, are impressive because the anthropological symbolism is not obvious to the casual viewer. We draw on these works in Chapter Five, where we look at *Jaws* as an allegory for anthropological understanding.

Other works also raise questions about filmic representations of the anthropologist. Richard Chalfen, for example, discusses the movie *Krippendorf's Tribe*, and suggests that despite its highly unflattering depiction of anthropology, it raises interesting issues of representation (Chalfen 2003; see also Chalfen and Pack 1999; Drummond 2000). Chalfen suggests that, intentionally or not, the movie opens up questions about the creation/invention of culture, the staging of cultural performance, and the idea that only non-Western people have a "culture"; questions that engage in interesting ways with the concerns of contemporary, postmodern anthropology.[16] Chalfen is quite helpful in our discussion of *Jaws*, especially since he considers a contemporary film that is specifically about a professional, academic anthropologist.

Finally, a number of anthropologists have written about representations of other cultures in feature films, often considering issues of orientalism, stereotypes, and racism, and how such images relate to ethnicity, social trends, and power relations in the U.S. (Bird 1996; Brown 1998; Pack 2000, 2001; Traube 1992: Chapter 1; Verrips 2001). A group of commentaries have coalesced around one particular film, *The Gods Must Be Crazy* (2004 [1980]), which represented the !Kung hunter-gatherers of South Africa and was the highest grossing foreign film in the U.S. at the time of its distribution (Tomaselli 2006: 172). These authors trace the multiple discourses of alienation, materialism, primitiveness, ecology and racism running through the film, contextualizing these readings in the larger body of work of the director, as well as in critical and popular reactions to the film (Gordon and Douglas 2000; Tomaselli 1990, 1992, 2002, 2006; Volkman 1986, 1988). All these works show encouraging dialogue with each other, and we draw on some of them in several chapters here.

PRECEDENTS AND VALUE ADDED

We draw two broad conclusions from this review. On the positive side, anthropologists have clearly used movie analysis to engage with complex cultural artifacts and develop their anthropological ideas, not simply to apply a watered-down anthropology to popular texts. We are in agreement with this approach and hope to show how anthropological ideas are enriched through their engagement with popular movies. On the negative side, almost all these previous authors, with the most notable exception of those writing about representations of other cultures, neglect or ignore the work of other anthropologists writing on movies, so there is no sense of building on this small (but recently expanding) tradition in the field.[17] We hope to rectify this omission, by engaging with the work of some of these authors in our subsequent chapters.

Of all the authors whose work we've reviewed, our approach is closest to that of Traube and Drummond, most obviously because they also provide book-length treatments of blockbuster Hollywood movies, with full chapters devoted to single movies (or, at most, a handful). More importantly, we share Traube and Drummond's view that movies can be usefully thought of as cultural myths: that movies explore (or exploit) key cultural contradictions and that their appeal lies in their ability to present these cultural contradictions for repeated consideration.[18] This is a guiding insight that we use throughout this book in our different takes on movies, such as *The Godfather* and *The Big Lebowski*.

Traube and Drummond have also inspired us as trailblazers who were willing to step outside of anthropological orthodoxy to suggest new insights into popular culture. We don't imagine that it takes the same courage to write anthropologically about Hollywood movies in 2009 as it did in the late 1980s and early 1990s, and for that, we are grateful to these pioneers. We especially appreciate Drummond for having shown that one can critically analyze blockbuster movies and still *like* them, a refreshing combination in academia, where critique is more valued than celebration. Given that any analysis of blockbuster movies remains hard to find in the pages of anthropology journals—reflecting its ongoing marginal status in the discipline—it remains important to renew Traube and Drummond's argument that anthropology and popular movies do mix and that they can be fruitfully brought together in the ongoing quest for understanding of cultural matters.

This book differs from Traube and Drummond, however, in an important respect. Where Drummond bases his readings on his particular version of structuralism and semiotics, and Traube explicitly uses critical theory and feminist psychoanalysis, we draw from a variety of contemporary anthropological approaches. That is, we are happily and unapologetically eclectic in our use of anthropology, and we believe that we can expand the purview of anthropological insight by drawing more diversely on contemporary anthropology. In the chapters that follow, we examine individual blockbuster movies in relation to "classic" anthropological topics such as gift-giving, boundaries, egalitarian societies, orality and writing, and knowing the Other. We develop our analysis by drawing, in different chapters, on recent anthropological concepts such as entextualization, counterpower, polytemporality, and the cultural construction of literacy.

We note one final difference with Drummond and Traube: we tend to be more eclectic in our choice of movies. While Drummond focuses on movies that deal specifically with the human-animal-technology nexus, and Traube tends to focus on "people" movies to explore themes of race/class/gender, we have chosen a more diverse range of movies. This diversity should help readers see the possibilities for applying insights to movies of their own choosing, such application being the ultimate test of the value of the approaches being developed here. Let us turn, then, to a preview of the movies discussed in the subsequent chapters.

SNEAK PREVIEW

The movies we consider, though eclectic, do have a few things in common. With one exception, all were major blockbusters, in most cases having enjoyed popular success in the U.S. for a few decades, as measured by box office records and incorporation as common reference points in American culture. Given the number of films that come and go every year, such enduring popular success is unusual, and we take it as an indication that a film may have tapped into a core tension within American culture. The one exception here is *The Village*, which did not enjoy the lasting popular success of the other movies. This is just the flip side of the same coin; we find this film interesting precisely because of its disjuncture with popular culture, and we make this disjuncture the focus of our analysis. Some might also say that *The Big Lebowski*, another one of our choices, is not technically a blockbuster, since it didn't do that well at the box office, but what it lacked in initial ticket sales, it has made up for in intense fan devotion, and its popularity seems to be growing with time. Also, as one of the most recent films considered here, *The Big Lebowski* is particularly popular with younger audiences, and worth including here so as to bring the analysis up to date. In all cases, we look at films that contain some ambiguity that calls for further thought, specifically through an anthropological lens. Finally, we personally like these films. Certainly other films could have been chosen, but, for all the above reasons, these films worked best for our analysis of movies as cultural myths.

In Chapter One we explore the overwhelmingly popular film *The Godfather,* truly a movie worthy of the term "myth" in the sense developed here: a narrative that explores key cultural contradictions. These contradictions revolve around the interplay between impersonal capitalism and the personal world of family relations, or the unresolved experiences created by the modern public/private dichotomy. We explore the way that these contradictions are played out in the film through images of food and writing. In doing so, we are drawing on previous anthropological analyses of the so-called "gift giving economy," as well as postmodern views of writing as "inauthentic" (Clifford 1988). We suggest that the power of the film lies not simply in its nostalgia for strong ethnic identity and patriarchal/family ties but, more importantly, in its exploration of ongoing dilemmas over how to reconcile the public and the private, business and personal realms.

Sports are often deeply revealing about a culture, as Clifford Geertz demonstrated in his famous analysis of the Balinese cockfight (1973). More recently, Bradd Shore (1996) has shown that baseball reveals a tension in the U.S. between individualism and group belonging, most dramatically represented in the confrontation of a lone batter (the individual) against nine fielders (society). In Chapter Two we extend this work, analyzing the symbolism of the baseball field in *Field of Dreams.* We show that foul lines, in the movie and baseball itself, create an image of precise control, which stands for social regulation—dictating how to "stay in line." Yet this social regulation is constantly undermined by the fuzziness of other lines. All this line play—juxtaposing precise and blurry lines, upending the seemingly precise ones— reveals a deep ambivalence about social control, as well as group belonging itself.

Both *The Godfather* and *Field of Dreams* are movies marked by a preoccupation with masculinity models, the different ways that male identity is performed, and the contradictory demands of these performances. In Chapter Three's analysis of *The Big Lebowski,* we enter a world where masculinities have multiplied and none can claim dominance. What is less clear is the way that these masculinity models relate to cultural time periods. In this chapter, we analyze the ways that these models are temporally emplaced. Drawing on cross-cultural explorations of historical consciousness and the anthropology of time, we argue that the film suggests a view of the present as made up not just of hegemonic and resistant masculinity models, but of multiple, coexisting, miscommunicating temporalities. But the real heart of this chapter looks at how these alternative temporalities and masculinities are explored through language use, through the process of "entextualization," in which words and phrases circulate through the movie that seem to be out of context and out of time. We relate this to the quotability of the film itself, a key aspect of its enduring cult appeal.

M. Night Shyamalan has made a number of blockbuster movies but his 2004 film *The Village* was panned by critics and, while it did well in theaters, it has had much less staying power than his earlier films and enduring blockbusters like *The Godfather*. Thus, in Chapter Four we take a somewhat different tack, arguing that the relative failure of *The Village* derives from a number of underlying, cultural assumptions. We argue that previous reviews of *The Village* reveal the ways that alternative political and social possibilities are imagined, or not imagined, in the contemporary U.S. Drawing on political anthropology, studies of stateless and egalitarian societies, and "anarchist anthropology," we show how *The Village* has been systematically misread as a post-9/11 fable on the uses of fear, rather than as a utopian experiment in mitigating the sources of inequality. This chapter argues that anthropologists need to do a better job of conveying what we know of small-scale societies and their viability in the so-called "modern world" and that *The Village* is an excellent place to start.

We continue this reflexive tack in Chapter Five, where we discuss another movie of indisputably mythic status, *Jaws*. We take up a question of interest to previous critics of the movie by asking: what does the shark represent? As with our discussion of *The Godfather*, we focus on a seemingly insignificant detail—the shark's eyes—expanding the discussion to include larger questions of the filmic representation of Otherness and the scientist/anthropologist.

In the concluding chapter, we suggest ways that our analysis can be extended to other films and aspects of popular culture such as television, and we call for ethnographic research to investigate how specific audiences have received and interpreted these films and other mass media. To indicate possibilities for such analysis, we include a discussion of some of the findings of our own research on audience responses to film, including a recent project on student responses to *Jaws*.

NOTES

1. We use the term "America" to refer to the United States, but in doing so we don't mean to slight Central and South America. Much of what we say about the U.S./America might also apply to Canada, the United Kingdom, and other places, as noted below. For the sake of conciseness, though, we stick with the term "America"; and for variety, we also use "U.S."
2. See, for example, Ginsburg, Abu-Lughod and Larkin (2002); Dickey (1993); Mankekar (1999); Askew and Wilk (2002); McCall (2002); Meyer (2003). For reviews of the literature on the ethnography of audience responses, see our Conclusion chapter, as well as Peterson (2003).

3. By "textual" we are referring to what are also known as "text-internal" interpretations. While movies share some qualities with literary works, they are obviously quite different in many ways, having powerful sensory/experiential components that make them closer to rituals (see discussion of Drummond below). In using the term "textual" we are not suggesting that movies should be treated primarily in linguistic/literary terms, but simply distinguishing our approach from more explicitly "ethnographic" studies. For a critique of the de-sensualizing aspect of the textual metaphor in anthropology, see Howes (2003).

4. On culture as "inchoate," see Fernandez (1986). On the issue of cultural wholes and fragments, see Clifford (1988), and, for a provocative, different view on the usefulness of positing cultural wholes, see Graeber (2001: 86–9).

5. Or to take a non-media example, note that recent changes in anthropological approaches to myth and ritual—seeing them as historically changing and historically contextual (e.g. Comaroff and Comaroff 1993; Fausto and Heckenberger 2007)—do not invalidate, but, rather, add to, more traditional approaches.

6. Of course, anthropologists do evaluate each other's arguments, based on evidence cited, plausibility, and concurrence with well-known theories and ethnographic work done in nearby areas (see Jacobson 1991). By comparison with readings of Hollywood movies, though, all such evaluations depend on more indirect sources.

7. For a more thorough discussion of some of these authors, we direct the reader to Peterson's book-length study of media and anthropology (2003).

8. While these groups were typically seen as national, Mead notes that the approach could equally be applied to any "society or subgroup" based on occupational, geographical, or other criteria (Mead 2000: 22). Indeed, she suggests a heuristic focus on "national cultures" when "the aim is to make recommendations on the *national level* or to make predictions about the behavior of individuals acting in *nationally* defined contexts" (2000: 24, emphasis in original).

9. Weakland writes that films are superior to other fictional material such as literature in "projecting important cultural views" because "they are a group rather than an individual product … [and] they are a mass medium of communication, aimed for a very wide and popular audience; they thus are likely to deal, relatively simply, with quite basic and general themes, not ones which are highly intellectual, specialized, or esoteric" (1966b: 6).

10. For example, Wolfenstein sees the primal scene as transmuted in French and American films into a plot element of a couple and an onlooker: "In the treatment of the onlooker and the couple, French films seem to re-evoke the feelings of disappointment of the child in order to inure us to them. American film plots tend to solve the problem by denying that anything painful has happened. The differences in themes are derived from the choice of different devices for resolving a common emotional problem" (Wolfenstein 2000: 303).

11. Excerpts were published during the Second World War and the essay was completed in 1945. It was also excerpted in *The Study of Culture at a Distance*, Volume 1 (see Wolfenstein 1953), but the full version was not published until 1980.

12. Two exceptions are short essays by Kottak (1982) on *Star Wars* as a structural transformation of *The Wizard of Oz* and by Karp (1976) on the Marx Brother's *Duck Soup* using notions of ritual drawn from Victor Turner. Boulanger (2004) more recently provides a short, suggestive analysis of *American Pie* as ritual, or "abortive rite-of-passage," drawing on both structuralism and Turner.

13. For an in-depth discussion of Drummond's approach, see Peterson (2003: 109–14).

14. This is more developed in her other work, writing with colleague Michael Blitz (2002).

15. Sarah Franklin explores similar issues in her analysis of *Jurassic Park*, noting, for example, that "the repeated invitation to witness the making of *Jurassic Park* provides a powerful analogy for the forms of public witnessing which surround the remaking of life itself. Now that biology has become increasingly technologized, geneticized and informatic, its literal reconstruction in the lab has become increasingly public and visible..." (2000: 216). As indicated in this quotation, however, her discussion focuses not so much on a reading of the movie itself, but more on the wider *Jurassic Park* phenomenon (museums, toys, theme parks), so we do not review it in depth here.

16. Sydel Silverman (2007) also has published a short essay, part of a larger project on the work of Hortense Powdermaker, that suggests that anthropology and Hollywood films parallel each other in their relationship to U.S. society in the period from the 1930s to the 1950s. She writes, for example: "The parallel in anthropology to the socially timid movies of Powdermaker's time and afterward was a dominant theoretical apparatus that underlined values, social cohesion, and timelessness" (2007: 526; see Powdermaker 1950).

17. This omission is more understandable in some cases than others. For example, given that anthropologists generally tried to ignore *Krippendorf's Tribe*, Chalfen (2003) did not have much to work with. Chalfen is certainly aware of the work anthropologists have done on film, and where relevant to his analysis, he cites other anthropologists.

18. In this regard we see them much as Geertz (1973) sees the Balinese cockfight: as a cultural art form. We are aware of the many criticisms of Geertz's approach, but we believe that such a view is appropriate as one way, though not the only way, of understanding and interpreting popular movies.

2 *THE GODFATHER*: THE GUN, THE PEN, AND THE CANNOLI

The Godfather came out in 1972, yet it remains popular to this day. What could explain this enduring popularity? Given the wildly expanded media options now available to audiences, it's remarkable that *any* film from the 1970s is still watched on a mass scale. And *The Godfather* isn't just watched out of historical curiosity, it's quoted in everyday life, especially by males, and consistently placed at the top of lists of all-time favorite movies. In a poll done by *Empire Magazine* in November, 2008, *The Godfather* was voted number 1 among the "500 Greatest Films Ever"; *Entertainment Weekly* named it "the greatest film ever made"; on Metacritic.com's list of all-time high scores, *The Godfather* placed number 1; and the phrase "I'm gonna' make him an offer he can't refuse" came in at number 2 on the American Film Institute's list of "100 Greatest Movie Quotes of All Time."[1] To take a more concrete example, President Barack Obama recently named *The Godfather* his all-time favorite film.[2]

What's going on here? What keeps Americans coming back to this film? If audiences just wanted to see violence, they could have their pick of any number of more violent films. Something more—much more—than simple lust for violence must account for America's ongoing fascination with *The Godfather*.

Good explanations have been provided by critics that explore the way this film deals with capitalism and family life, placing it in a long tradition of gangster films that focus on the vexing relationship between the individual and American society.[3] However, none of the previous critics has mentioned writing or food symbolism. By contrast, we see these symbols as crucial aspects of the film's commentary on American society, so crucial that they alter the film's basic perspective.

As noted in the Introduction, our interest in food and writing symbolism in *The Godfather* grew out of our own reverse culture shock after doing fieldwork in other countries (Sutton in Greece, Wogan in Ecuador). Upon returning to the U.S., we found that we could not stop thinking about certain cultural patterns that we had been studying while abroad. With this in mind, we wrote this chapter, focusing on "orality," which stands for food and a gift economy, and "writing," which stands for capitalism and its legal arm, the state.[4]

It is important to state from the outset that we do not assume that *The Godfather* tells us anything about actual Mafia, Sicilian, or Italian-American culture, only that it tells us something about American dilemmas concerning capitalism and family life, as played out against the fantasy space of ethnic "authenticity." Our premise here is that the film has fascinated audiences because of its ability to target strains and tensions in American culture over the proper role between family and business, or, more broadly, emotion and objectivity, the private and public realms. A central aspect of the film's appeal is that, like a good myth, it toys with viewer's ambivalent feelings about these complex tensions (see Drummond 1995).

Accordingly, we would never expect an audience to come away with a unanimous, untroubled interpretation of the film's meaning; there will be as many different interpretations as there are different opinions at any time about American capitalism, the state, and family life. We are not trying to offer a single, definitive interpretation, but only to uncover hidden symbolism that seems fundamental to the film, making it likely to figure in individual interpretations.

In this chapter, we follow the trajectory of *The Godfather*, analyzing key scenes that involve writing and/or food. We will also pause at various points to show how such symbolism plays into tensions in American society.

THE WEDDING SCENE: AN INITIAL OPPOSITION BETWEEN THE OLD AND NEW WORLD

In the opening wedding scene, writing is identified with mainstream American society, specifically the state and capitalist relations. While the Corleones are implicated in this society, we also see—through their disdain for writing, and their use of food and drink—that they belong to another cultural order.

For example, in the opening scene, FBI agents in the parking lot are shown writing down license-plate numbers on notepads, an FBI agent flashes his identification badge at Sonny, Don Corleone's son (James Caan), and the legislative and judicial branches of the government are represented through telegrams sent to the Don by senators and judges.

The most striking example, though, is the story of Don Corleone (Marlon Brando) making a bandleader "an offer he can't refuse." As the Don's son Michael (Al Pacino) tells the story, a bandleader denied requests to release the Don's godson Johnny (Al Martino) from a written contract, so "Luca Brasi held a gun to the bandleader's head, and my father assured him that either his brains or his signature would be on the contract." The Don's "offer" highlights a precise equivalence between guns and writing. Brains and pen ink are both made of viscous liquids that control life: without your brains, you're dead; and by signing a contract in ink, you "sign your life away." In other words, guns and pens can both be used to control life. The gun is also physically like the pen in that both are sleek, hand-held instruments. But these parallels only serve to highlight the film's showdown between these two types of power: the bandleader's written contract symbolizes the American legal, capitalist system and its ostensibly supreme power, but, when legal contracts run up against the brute force of the Sicilian Mafia, writing clearly loses. Inverting the saying about the pen being mightier than the sword, Don Corleone shows through this dramatic power play that, when push comes to shove, he is more powerful than the U.S. state and its written contracts.

Moreover, Don Corleone's style of power is different. Whereas the state's power is abstract (based on laws), mediated (communicated through writing, not face-to-face interaction), and inflexible (tied to the letter of the law), the Don's power is physical (the gun to the head), personal (the godfather–godson relationship), and flexible (sympathetic to changes in Johnny's circumstances). By the same token, two different kinds of intelligence are being contrasted in this brief story. Brains are commonly a metonym of school intelligence, as in the expression "he's a brain," but this literate intelligence is being devalued in the worst way by Don Corleone, as those brains are about to be splattered all over the written page.

The contrast between Old and New Worlds gets further developed in this first scene when we see how the Don forms bonds with his supporters. Rather than legal contracts, the Godfather's own "contracts" are sealed with gifts (usually food and drink), gestures, and verbal pledges—in short, a gift-giving economy. As we observe different visitors in the Don's office, we learn about the rules—the Do's and Don'ts—of this symbolic economy.

The undertaker Bonasera (Salvatore Corsitto) is particularly revealing as a negative example, a textbook case of everything you should not do when dealing with the Godfather. Bonasera comes to the Don because the American legal system has failed him: the two boys who beat and raped his daughter have been freed by the courts with nothing more than a suspended sentence. Bonasera therefore turns to the Don for vengeance, but he makes a crucial mistake when he asks, "How much shall I pay you?" In response, the Don gets up and, after a long pause, he says, "Bonasera, Bonasera, what have I ever done to make you treat me so disrespectfully?" The Don is deeply offended by Bonasera's attempt to invoke a contractual relationship in which services are immediately rendered upon payment of a named cash amount. Presumably Bonasera makes this sort of *faux pas* because he has been overly Americanized (the movie opens with Bonasera saying, "I believe in America"), so the Don has to educate him on the conventions of this patron–client relationship. Rebuking Bonasera and reframing the relationship as one of long-term gift exchange and friendship, the Don says, "You don't ask with respect. You don't offer friendship. You don't even think to call me Godfather. Instead, you come into my house on the day my daughter is to be married, and you, uh, ask me to do murder, for money." The Don says "for money" in a tone of disgust, almost unable to utter the word "money." And then, after agreeing to grant Bonasera's request, the Don ends by saying, "Some day, and that day may never come, I'll call upon you to do me a service; but, until that day, accept this justice as a gift on the day of my daughter's wedding." Eschewing capitalist contracts, the Don prefers long-term gift exchange, with its idiom of generosity and friendship. Don Corleone is not simply a pay-for-service businessman.

Disregard for money is also expressed by the Don's eldest child, Sonny, who breaks a reporter's camera and then throws bills on the ground in a contemptuous gesture, suggesting that money is trash. No attempt is made to count the money, so we can assume that Sonny has thrown more money on the ground than the camera was actually worth and to count the money would be beneath him. Like his father, Sonny belongs to a world of honor, expressed in his statement to the FBI agent in the car: "Goddamn FBI, don't respect nothing." The clash of the two worlds is further highlighted by the juxtaposition of the wordless FBI agent flashing his badge and Sonny responding by spitting on the ground.

Both Sonny's actions and his father's set up a basic contrast between American capitalism and what Pierre Bourdieu characterizes as a "gift economy":

> The gift economy, in contrast to the economy where equivalent values are exchanged, is based on the denial of the economic (in the narrow sense), a

refusal of the logic of the maximization of economic profit, i.e., of the spirit of calculation and the exclusive pursuit of material (as opposed to symbolic) interest, a refusal which is inscribed in the objectivity of institutions and in dispositions. It is organized with a view to the accumulation of symbolic capital (a capital of recognition, honor, nobility, etc.) that is brought about in particular through the transmutation of economic capital achieved through the alchemy of symbolic exchanges (exchange of gifts, challenges and ripostes, women, etc.) and only available to agents endowed with disposition adjusted to the logic of "disinterestedness." (1997: 234–5)

Bourdieu's characterization, which recalls Max Weber on pre-capitalism and the formalist-substantivist debate in economic anthropology, may be problematic as an ethnographic generalization, but it aptly captures the contrast embodied in this film's social imagery.

Obviously this contrast should not be overdrawn. The Corleones are not opposed to money *per se*, nor are they a familial haven in a heartless world of capitalism.[5] In fact, the Corleones are committed businessmen. This becomes increasingly clear (*and* complicated) as the film progresses, but even in this first scene, viewers will immediately recognize that the Corleones are running a business: they meet in an office and make references to "jobs" and the "family business."[6] In fact, if the Corleones were not capitalistic to at least some degree, comparisons with mainstream America would be untenable. The Corleones are distant cousins, not extreme exotics. As such, the Corleones are capitalists with a difference: they value honor, kinship, and long-term gift exchange. They represent a culture in which counting money and naming cash values is considered anti-social behavior.

The correct model for interaction in this gift economy is provided during the wedding scene by the baker, who asks the Don to help his future son-in-law remain in the U.S. The baker never mentions money. After his request has been granted, the baker leaves the room saying, "And wait 'til you see the beautiful wedding cake I made for your daughter," showing that he participates in food exchange like the Don, who, of course, is providing food and drink for everyone at the wedding.[7] The Don has also specifically given the baker a drink, a drink that represents conviviality, as opposed to the drink Bonasera accepts as solace when he starts to weep.

Simply put, the undertaker represents death, while the baker represents life— both literally and as metaphors for social life and death, the forces that keep society alive and moving. Not only does the baker provide food, but he engages in the male-dominated gift exchange that leads to the social reproduction of the family:

he is visiting the Godfather to insure that his daughter will marry Enzo, an Italian boy who has been working in his pastry shop. In this sense, the baker and the Don (whose daughter is also getting married) both participate in the exchange of women that perpetuates social life and family honor in this traditional world; by contrast, the undertaker has been thwarted in his proper male role as benefactor and protector of female honor ("Now she will never be beautiful again").

As the baker's example shows, this symbolic gift economy also involves male exchange and nurturance through food—men feeding other men. Don Corleone is shown physically embracing his godson Johnny as he leaves his office, saying, "You look terrible, I want you to eat." These words follow the Don's lecturing Johnny on the importance of being a "family man," and also stand in contrast to the bandleader's exploitation. Nurturing other men and being a "family man" are all part of being a good businessman in this gift economy.

Returning to the bandleader's contract, we also see that speech performatives, rather than writing, do the work of cementing mutual commitments with the Don. For example, Luca Brasi (Lenny Montana) vows, "I pledge my never-ending loyalty, Don Corleone," and the undertaker says, "Be my friend, Godfather," after which he bends down and kisses the Don's ring to confirm their new relationship. Also, jumping ahead for a moment to a later scene with the heads of the Five Families, Barzini (Richard Conte) says, "We all know him [Don Corleone] as a man of his word," adding "Look, we are all reasonable men here. We don't have to give assurances as if we were lawyers." In other words, a man of his word can be trusted; not only does he abhor a lawyer's written contract, but even speech performatives can sometimes be dispensed with.[8] In this sense, a man's word approaches the most binding contract of all: kinship bonds, which are so strong that they do not require explicit expression.

But why would the intricacies of this symbolic gift economy fascinate movie viewers?

TENSIONS IN AMERICAN SOCIETY

The Godfather, in suggesting in this first scene that family values should carry over into the rational world of business decisions, taps into a number of major tensions in American society. Above all, the Corleones offer an appealing resolution to the split between public and private realms that capitalism demands and that anthropologists have studied at length (Carrier and Miller 1999; Hart 2005; Herzfeld 1992;

Hochschild 2003). Bourgeois ideology opposes the mixing of these two spheres. Work is supposed to be rational and efficient and the family is supposed to be the realm of strong emotion. Work is supposed to be about rational self-interest, the profit motive, not personal emotions. More broadly put, Americans are expected to separate objectivity and subjectivity in the workplace. The tension comes from the fact that it is extremely difficult to compartmentalize social relations in this way and trying to do so causes considerable strain.

These strains become evident when a boss feels guilty about firing a friend or when workers worry that they're making bad business decisions due to emotional concerns. The gift economy is, as it turns out, also present in American mainstream business: the dinners, lunches, and drinks with clients and colleagues, the talk on the golf course, the expense accounts, the entertaining hosted by spouses, etc. The problem is that, despite the ubiquity of these personal gift exchanges, rational interests and economic efficiency are still supposed to be the decisive factors. You cannot come to a corporate or bureaucratic meeting and say, "I gave John the contract because he's my friend and he took me to the Knicks game."

Perhaps most concretely, the split causes stress when work demands compete with family time, and when family members with differing occupations become distant from one another, both psychologically and geographically. Studies repeatedly show that Americans have for several decades been working longer and longer hours, cutting into their family time. The average American now works longer hours than he or she did 40 years ago (and more than medieval peasants), a problem that is especially acute for women who juggle commitments at home and the workplace (Schor 1991). Yet given the demand to separate work and emotion, Americans remain wary of family businesses, and very few—less than 4%, according to one poll—work in them.[9] Family and work remain pitted against one another.

The shift to an information economy over the past several decades has also created worker alienation, anxiety, and longing for more meaningful work, as seen in the popularity of the cartoon *Dilbert*, the movie *Office Space*, and the TV show *The Office*. Keith Hart notes, "Our language and culture contain the ongoing history of this attempt to separate social life into two distinct spheres" (Hart 2005: 4). Yet this separation comes at considerable cost; it's hard to separate personal feelings from rational business, and constantly trying (or pretending) to do so causes intense strain.

We argue that *The Godfather* plays upon this problem. The image of the Corleones in the film is compelling because it offers the possibility of reconciling capitalism and personalism, work and family, the public and the private realm. *The Godfather* offers a capitalism redeemed—capitalism with a sense of honor, family, and personal commitment, ostensibly bridging the split in industrial capitalism between the public world of markets and the private world of morality and strong emotion (see also Carrier 1990).[10] The movie plays on this contradiction between ideals and practice: the tension between an ideology that propounds the importance of objective, rational, efficient decision-making and actual practices based on subjective, committed personal relationships. In response, the Corleones offer the possibility of a cleaner, less dissonant reconciliation between American ideals and practice, between emotion and objectivity. This reconciliation will become questioned in the next stage of the film, where a now-famous distinction is made: "It's business, not personal." As of this first scene, though, the film shows viewers that "business" and "personal," especially familial emotions, can be smoothly integrated.

But the Corleones' "solution" does not, of course, remove the underlying tensions in American society, which is why the film continues to fascinate audiences. The ongoing concern over capitalism has been recently addressed by "socially conscious" companies, such as Ben and Jerry's or Smith & Hawken, but still has not been fully resolved.[11] James Carrier and Daniel Miller have, accordingly, recently called for anthropologists to engage in "a rearticulation of the private and the public through a clear understanding and portrayal of the consequences of each of these for the other" (1999: 43).

Against this background, the Corleones create an appealing image of ethnic unity, with its integration of business and family, and of meaningful work, where the stakes are clear and are often a matter of life and death. At the same time, the movie portrays a certain horror at the Corleones, reflected most prominently in Michael's girlfriend Kay's (Diane Keaton) open-mouthed shock at the story about the "offer he couldn't refuse." After all, these are Mafia men who break the law and engage in violence (e.g. the bloody horse's head, in a subsequent scene). We would argue that it is precisely this confusing combination—brutal men who nicely integrate work and family, objectivity and subjectivity—that makes it hard to wrap one's mind around the Corleones, and that such ambiguity adds to our fascination with the film.

Furthermore, the film consistently offers an image of extreme male solidarity. Indeed, deep love between fathers, sons, and brothers is expressed in the course of "business" relationships: a father and his sons work at the same business, sons try to save their father, and the father affectionately hugs and kisses his sons. When Michael is protecting his father in the hospital, he strokes his head, and holds his hand and kisses it, making tears spill down Don Corleone's cheeks. The Don also cries when he sees Sonny's corpse, and Tom Hagen sheds tears when Sollozo tells him that the Don has been shot. This male solidarity helps to answer Meg Ryan's question in *You've Got Mail*, "What is it with men and *The Godfather*?"[12] Tom Hanks could have answered: "*The Godfather* offers American males the hope that they can be rational *and* emotional at the same time."

Granted, the family business is decidedly patriarchal; the men run the business, women do not enter the office, and business is never discussed at the dinner table. Nevertheless, women are integrated into the family business in certain respects. For example, the Don's office is located in his home, where the men can quickly move back and forth from the office to the kitchen. Children play just outside the office, as we learn in the very first scene, when several children burst into the room just as Luca Brasi is finishing his pledge. Immediately after this, the Don walks out of his office into his own backyard to dance with his wife at a wedding that, as part of an ongoing gift exchange, is also ultimately part of his business. In this sense, work, family, and gender boundaries are less rigid than they might appear at first glance.

Writing is a particularly good symbol for all these tensions, since it elicits deeply ambivalent feelings in Western culture. Writing has long been associated with central aspects of modern Western identity: namely, Judeo-Christianity ("religions of the book"), science (which couldn't exist without detailed records), history (hence "myth" and "pre-history" mean historical consciousness without written records), and no less than "civilization" itself (as opposed to the illiterate and the "savage").[13] As one historian notes, "only early modern European civilization came to make its own ability properly to describe and understand the other, its own proper literacy, into the very definition of its own identity as against the rest of the world" (Harbsmeier 1985: 72). And these views continue into the present day, especially in assumptions about the connection between literacy and cognition. An educational anthropologist sums up as follows: "In the oral column go characteristics such as memory-based, empathetic and participatory, situational, and aggregative; in the literate column go the counterparts, such as record-based, objectively distanced, abstract, and analytic" (Collins 1995: 77).

These are the aspects of writing that usually get celebrated. But whenever westerners start to have doubts and misgivings about their society, writing is just as likely to come under fire, while its supposed opposite, orality, is elevated. As James Clifford (1986: 115–6) argues, writing has long been a symbol of civilization's inauthenticity: "Since antiquity the story of a passage from the oral/aural into writing has been a complex and charged one... Words and deeds are transient (and authentic);

writing endures (as supplementarity and artifice)." Thus, writing and orality are deeply conflicted, resonant symbols. Just as Clifford argues that this view entails nostalgia for a lost world of orality, we would argue that the appeal of the Corleones largely lies in nostalgia for an ethnic solidarity that has not succumbed to writing's "irretrievable loss" (Clifford 1985: 115)—nostalgia for a world where bonds are formed through food and drink, vows, and kinship, rather than impersonal legal contracts and corporate obligations.

In particular, many Americans believe, along with the Corleones, that written contracts do not mix well with family life. This belief underlies the outrage over pre-nuptial contracts, which represent the invasion of formal market principles into family life, one of the few domains supposedly exempt from these principles. Dependence on state contracts impugns family trust, the very basis of the "diffuse, enduring solidarity" of kinship (see Schneider 1980). By the same token, it would be simply unthinkable for the Don to ask his sons to sign a work contract. In short, the film dramatizes Americans' ambivalent feelings about writing and, by extension, capitalism and the state.

Having primarily emphasized this Old *vs.* New World opposition in the first scene, though, the film proceeds to explore the second-generation's attempt to bring the Sicilian and mainstream American worlds closer together. Once again, striking images of the oral and the literate come into play.

MICHAEL'S ATTEMPT TO COMBINE THE TWO WORLDS

The Don's son Michael is clearly identified with mainstream American society: he's a war hero, he went to college, and he doesn't work in the family business. As he tells his WASP girlfriend in the first scene, "That's my family, Kay, that's not me." In fact, he only learns about the attempted murder of his father from a newspaper headline, depending on the mediation of print rather than face-to-face interaction.

However, in this second stage of the film, it is precisely Michael's understanding of print media that allows him to propose an innovation on his father's methods, an innovation that sets him on course to become the Don's heir. Michael's proposal is offered in a crucial scene in which the sons and the *caporegimes* are debating how to respond to Sollozo (Al Lettieri), the drug dealer who has just tried for a second time to kill the Don. Sonny, the hot-headed eldest son and interim Don, wants to take revenge against Sollozo and his ally Tattaglia (Victor Rendina), but the Don's adopted son Tom Hagen (Robert Duvall), the voice of moderation, advises against any immediate action lest it cause an all-out war that can't be stopped. Tom clinches his argument by informing everyone that Sollozo is at least temporarily invulnerable because he's being guarded by a police captain named McCluskey (Sterling Hayden).

Sonny concedes to Tom, but then, to everyone's surprise, Michael proposes that he will kill both Sollozo and McCluskey. Sonny and the *caporegimes*, Tessio (Abe Vigoda) and Clemenza (Richard S. Castellano), start to laugh at Michael's seemingly outrageous proposal, and Tom looks away in disbelief. None of them understands what Michael has grasped: the power of print. Drawing on his understanding of literacy, Michael's solution is to kill the drug dealer and police captain, but then follow this up with newspaper stories about "a crooked cop who got what was coming to him," thereby putting a media spin on the killing and precluding retaliation from the state and the public. Michael's strategy was an innovative blend of guns and newspapers, a combination that was not envisioned by the others, who were still operating within the Don's own gun *vs.* pen opposition.

This shift is captured in the scene's seating arrangements. As the camera slowly zooms in, we see Michael seated directly between two figures: short-tempered Sonny, representing brute force, and sensible Tom, the adopted son of German-Irish descent. It makes sense that Tom, as a quasi-outsider, has until now been an intermediary with the outside world (reading the judges' and senators' telegrams, informing the police captain of the Corleones' legal rights). In this scene, Tom is even sitting at a desk with a typewriter and paper folders. Michael's proposal unites Sonny's gun and Tom's typewriter, bringing the Old and New Worlds closer together.

As we saw earlier, the mainstream American and Sicilian worlds were initially opposed, as in the story of the bandleader. Creating a similar binary opposition, Sonny says to Michael, "What do you think this is, the army, where you shoot 'em from a mile away? You gotta' get up close like this ... budda-bing! You blow their brains all over your nice Ivy League suit." In Sonny's view, Ivy League suits, just like written contracts, should remain clean and pure, unstained by blood and brains; the worlds of blood and suits are separate and opposed. Moreover, like the initial contrast between legal contracts and family connections, the difference is a question of impersonal *vs.* personal relations. Mainstream Americans interact at a distance, through written contracts and by shooting from a mile away, whereas the Corleones talk directly to each other and put a gun right up to their enemy's head. In fact, in the book on which the film is based, we find that Clemenza, who is of the Don's generation, even views handguns as overly impersonal and Americanized, compared with the more direct, traditional garrote (strangling rope): "The *caporegime*, Clemenza, took Sonny in hand and taught him how to shoot and to wield a garrote. Sonny had no taste for the Italian rope, he was too Americanized. He preferred the simple, direct, impersonal Anglo-Saxon gun, which saddened Clemenza" (Puzo 1969: 219).[14] Michael, however, sees a way to combine the Mafia's "up close and personal" style with the more distanced, mediated relationships of mainstream America, making the newspaper work for, rather than against, the family's violence.

Food symbolism also conveys the "before picture" of the traditional Old World gift economy that Michael is about to transform. Cannoli, a traditional Italian pastry (see Figure 2.1), comes up in connection with the killing of the Don's driver Paulie (John Martino), in a scene shortly before Michael makes his proposal to kill Sollozo and McCluskey. After Rocco (Tom Rosqui) shoots Paulie in his car, Clemenza says to Rocco, "Leave the gun, take the cannoli," referring to the box of cannoli that he had promised his wife he would pick up while at work that day. This line is often quoted by fans, presumably because it seems surprising and ironic that Clemenza's first thought, after participating in the killing of a man, is to remember his wife's demand for cannoli.

But something more significant is captured in the "Leave the gun, take the cannoli" line: another contrast between two rich symbols, much like the binary

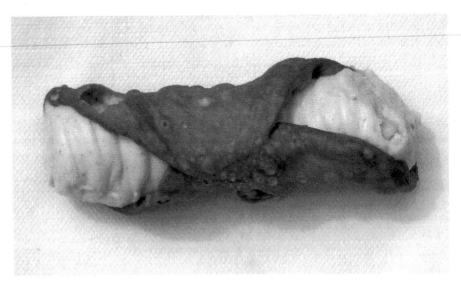

Figure 2.1. Traditional cannoli: fried pastry roll filled with sweetened and flavored ricotta cheese. (This one was not taken from a crime scene.)

opposition that Sonny creates between Ivy League suits and guns, and the one Don Corleone makes between contracts and guns. As in the latter case, the cannoli is being compared to the gun. The gun and cannoli both have a similar barrel shape (the word "cannoli" in Sicilian means "little tubes"), with a hard outer core and semi-hollow interior; and both are small enough to fit in one's hand, just like the gun and the pen in the story of the bandleader's contract.[15] Once again, a crisp symmetry, a poetic parallelism, is created between two objects. As in the Don's simple ultimatum to the bandleader ("either his brains or his signature would be on the contract"), the two halves of Clemenza's sentence use identical grammatical constructions: imperative/transitive verb (leave, take) + definite article (the) + noun/ direct object (cannoli, gun). However, this grammatical symmetry, together with the two objects' physical similarities, only serves to highlight functional differences: cannoli are harmless, whereas guns kill people; cannoli belong to the female world of cooking (life), whereas guns belong to the male world of killing (death). Or at least this is what viewers might expect, due to their assumptions about gender, family, business, and murder, and in light of the Don's earlier contrast between the gun and the pen, and Sonny's (albeit slightly later) contrast between guns and Ivy League suits. This sense that guns and cannoli don't mix is presumably why viewers find this line so ironic and incongruous.

In Clemenza's world, though, cannoli and guns *do* mix. The gun and the cannoli end up together in the back seat of Paulie's car; both are part of a day's work. Buying the cannoli may have even been part of Clemenza's dissimulation that this was just another normal day, so as not to arouse Paulie's suspicions. Before the shooting, Clemenza stops to urinate, and earlier he even jokes with Paulie, "Exterminate? That's a bad word ... Watch out we don't exterminate you." The opposition between guns and cannoli is also collapsed by the casual, matter-of-fact way Clemenza says, "Leave the gun, take the cannoli," without any indication that it's strange to put these two things in the same sentence. Importantly, Clemenza's alliance between the gun and the cannoli is perfectly consistent with the Don and Sonny's worldview. As we saw in the wedding scene, the Don accepts and provides food gifts while planning out violence; nurturance through food is the domain of men like the Don ("I want you to eat") as much as women. Clemenza, as an old-school figure, shares the Don's traditional outlook; in this world, men kill but also cross over into nurturing roles as part of a gift economy where family and business are blended together. Thus, Clemenza's "Leave the gun, take the cannoli" line further toys with American tensions over the split between the public and private sphere, suggesting that they don't have to be so rigidly separated.

The film plays with this same split in another food scene, right before Paulie's killing. When a package arrives, Sonny opens it, only to see a fish wrapped inside Luca Brasi's bulletproof vest. Bewildered, Sonny says, "What the hell is this?" Clemenza immediately answers: "It's a Sicilian message. It means Luca Brasi sleeps with the fishes" (meaning Luca Brasi was killed and tossed to the bottom of the river). Thus, food creates a substitute for writing; instead of a written note, the men get a package of fish. Granted, the fish package does not present the kind of clear-cut, binary opposition found in other scenes (the bandleader's contract, the cannoli, the Ivy League suit), and fish in the river are not prepared food like the cannoli or the wedding cake. But the fish still create a similar effect: instead of an impersonal, written message, the fish are "up close and personal," with a texture, sight, and smell that assaults the senses.[16] Once again, the film plays upon nostalgia for a lost world of orality, while complicating this sentiment with a dose of violence.

Clemenza's association with the Don's traditional world of food and violence is extended in a subsequent scene where Clemenza gives Michael pointers about cooking. With echoes in many subsequent Mafia films, Clemenza is shown making spaghetti sauce for a group of Mafia associates, narrating the recipe to Michael. Of course, it is significant that Clemenza is not teaching Michael any old recipe, but a recipe for spaghetti sauce, which is associated with authentic Italian traditions (like the garrote).

All of these food scenes reinforce the viewer's sense of a traditional Sicilian world. In utter contrast, Michael and the others are shown involved in a new kind of food consumption in a scene just before Michael's act of murder: while waiting for a phone call at Sonny's house, everyone sits around the table eating take-out Chinese food. This quick, non-Italian food is neither nurturing nor authentic, presaging the new, Americanized relations that are being ushered in by Michael's proposal.

BUSINESS, NOT PERSONAL

While the previous examples reinforce the sense of the Corleones' differences from mainstream Americans, the lines start to blur with the introduction of a Corleone axiom: "business, not personal." Tom uses this phrase in the same scene where Michael proposes to kill Sollozzo and McCluskey. In saying, "business, not personal," Tom is summing up the Don's philosophy so that he can win an argument with Sonny, who is threatening to start an inter-gang war:

TOM: Your father wouldn't want to hear this! This is business, not personal, Sonny!

SONNY: They shot my father. That's business? Your ass.

TOM: Even the shooting of your father was business, not personal, Sonny!

This exchange contradicts everything we thought we knew about the Corleones. Up until now, we had seen the Corleones treat business and personal as one and the same. We saw that the Don's business includes food exchange, nurturance, family relationships, and strong emotional bonds. But now we find out that the Don draws a strict line: at a certain point, decisions must be made for the benefit of the business, not to satisfy personal emotions. The Corleone family turns out to uphold the same mainstream American division between public and private realms that was discussed above. Sonny is the exception that proves the rule. Sonny doesn't grasp or like his father's philosophy (his response to Tom: "Well, then business will have to suffer, alright?"), but that's because he is uncouth and overly-emotional (he has sex with a bridesmaid during the wedding, speaks his mind when his father doesn't want to give anything away, and acts giddy about the war against Sollozo).

In short, the "business, not personal" philosophy flies in the face of all the poetic parallels we've been discussing, all the food and literacy symbols that serve to highlight the differences between Sicilians and mainstream Americans. What seemed like cultural difference has turned into sameness.

Perhaps viewers have latched onto this "business, not personal" line because it is an emotional balm for their own attempts to live with modern America's demand to separate emotion from business. Saying, "It's business, not personal" is equivalent to firing a good friend, or foreclosing on a sweet old lady's house, and saying, "It's my job, not me." Pointing to the exigencies of business at least partially assuages a guilty conscience for some people. If the Corleones, tough guys with deep, emotional stakes in their business, can separate business from the personal, the rest of us can and should as well. Certainly this is the way many people use this line, as seen by Tom Hanks' repetition of it like a mantra throughout *You've Got Mail*, as well as its use as the title of Keith Hart's book on the public-private split: *The Hit Man's Dilemma: Or, Business, Personal and Impersonal* (2005). But the repetition of this line in public discourse doesn't mean its philosophy is fully accepted; on the contrary, the line seems to need so much repetition because it has to paste over deeply troubling emotional and ethical issues.

The film itself does not actually take a clear stand one way or the other. When Michael subsequently proposes to kill Sollozo and McCluskey, he insists, "It's not personal, Sonny. It's strictly business." You don't have to be an anthropologist or psychologist, though, to realize that what people say is not always a good guide to their feelings and motivations. Michael is proposing to kill Sollozo, a man who *twice* tried to kill his father. He's also proposing to kill McCluskey, someone who punched him so hard that he broke his jaw. Not only that, McCluskey is a corrupt, Irish cop who doesn't like Italians ("I thought I got all you guinea hoods locked up," he says when he finds Michael and the baker's son in front of the hospital). As a returned war hero from the Second World War, Michael must be galled by this sort of bigotry and corruption in the country he just risked his life for. So is Michael's desire to kill Sollozo and McCluskey really "strictly business"? The context suggests otherwise.

The film therefore presents two contradictory possibilities: business and personal can be separated, but they can't. A legal contract (mainstream U.S.) and emotional attachments to a godson (Sicilian) are of two different cultural orders, but perhaps they're not, since the Corleones, like mainstream Americans, have to separate business and the personal. Part of what makes the film so effective as a myth is that it never calls direct attention to these contradictions, allowing the Don's gift economy and the "business, not personal" rule to coexist. It helps that these contradictions are hidden behind non-obvious symbolism, such as the bandleader's contract and cannoli. Perhaps most important of all, the Old World rules and actors' demeanors make it look like everything is clear-cut and seamless. The Don confidently hands out orders, without any equivocation or hesitation, and everyone seems to know their place within this strict cultural system. Even when Michael makes innovations, he does so with steely determination. It's easy to understand why Sarah Vowell, author and radio commentator, believes *The Godfather* is filled with moral certainty. She says about the "take the cannoli" line, "I loved Clemenza's command because of its lack of ambiguity" (2000: 58).[17] Others must be attracted to the film for the same reason, yet the opposite is also true: below the surface, the film is shot through with ambiguity—not narrative confusion but a subtle ambiguity that brilliantly plays upon tensions in American society itself.

Even Clemenza, who acts so matter-of-factly, is part of the film's contradictions. He's the first one to start laughing at Michael's proposal to kill McCluskey and Sollozo, yet in the next scene he tells Michael he approves whole-heartedly of the killing, going so far as to compare it to stopping Hitler. Clemenza tells Michael that these big gang battles "gotta' happen every five years or so, ten years, helps to get rid of the bad blood. Been ten years since the last one. You know you gotta' stop them at the beginning, like they should have stopped Hitler at Munich. They should never of let him get away with that." The Don's position is equally ambiguous. On one hand, Tom's reporting of his policy of separating "business and personal" implies that he wouldn't have had McCluskey and Sollozo killed; and, indeed, many scenes later, the Don turns his head away in disgust when he finds out that it was Michael who did this killing. On the other hand, he's hospitalized and absent while all these decisions are being made, so we never know for sure what he would have done.

As a result of all this ambiguity, viewers only remember and focus on certain things in the film, according to their own positioning. Some may sense the contradictions, but focus more on Michael's soft-voiced, reasonable tone, as well as his promise to use the respectable public sphere (newspapers), or they may be more taken with nostalgia for Don Corleone's gift economy. Others may see Michael as entirely motivated by family loyalty, love, and desire for vengeance, and view his talk of "business" as rationalization. And others may believe that business and the personal can be separated by Michael, Don Corleone, and Americans themselves. Even the same viewer may remember (consciously or not) different things at different times. Either way, the film succeeds in toying with the vexing American separation between the public and private sphere, business and the personal.

Even food symbolism is ambiguous at this middle point in the film. Sitting at a restaurant table with Sollozo and McCluskey, the two men he's about to shoot, Michael does not eat and barely speaks. By keeping his mouth closed to food and not touching the drink that Sollozo has handed to him as a gesture of truce, Michael resists the vulnerability of social interaction. By contrast, McCluskey's consumption of food in this scene shows his vulnerability. He gets shot by Michael while eating veal, a meat that is normally the privilege of power; by eating the veal so eagerly and unselfconsciously while he's supposed to be protecting Sollozo, McCluskey reveals that he has taken his power for granted. Similarly, Sonny is shown carelessly eating while his father asks for his opinion about the Sollozo drug business. Michael's resistance to food and vulnerable social relations in this restaurant scene is comparable to the way he remains impassive when, as noted above, Clemenza teaches him how to "cook for twenty guys," and the way he leaves his dinner unfinished when saying goodbye to Kay in the hotel, just before visiting his father in the hospital.

Though Michael's refusal of food and drink makes a clear contrast with McCluskey, it's unclear whether this refusal continues, or breaks away from, his father's ways. On the one hand, Don Corleone is also seen refraining from consumption in earlier scenes: he provides drinks for the undertaker, baker, and Sollozo, but doesn't drink anything himself. On the other hand, the Don's non-consumption could be due to his social role in these scenes since, as the host, his priority was to serve others and appear generous. According to this logic, Don Corleone might have accepted the proffered food and drink, as Sollozo seemed to be hosting the restaurant meeting (ordering the veal for McCluskey, handing Michael the wine). It's unclear, then, whether Michael's refusal to eat and drink is a departure from his father's ways. It makes sense, though, that Michael's relationship to food consumption remains murky in this scene: Michael is trying to combine some of the Old and the New, business and personal, and it's not yet clear where this move will take him.

In a significant jump-cut, the scene of Michael retreating from the bloodied bodies of Sollozo and McCluskey is immediately followed by the image of newspapers being printed and then men eating spaghetti. At least for a brief moment, Michael has managed to reconcile the two worlds: he has found a way to bring together food, writing, and violence.

THE MOE GREEN CASINO SCENE: INVERSION OF THE MOVIE'S INITIAL POSITION

After killing Sollozo and McCluskey, Michael goes into hiding in Sicily, where it seems likely that he will renew his ethnic roots. He improves his command of the Sicilian language, consumes "real" Italian food, and marries a Sicilian woman. As we realize by the end of the film, however, he can't easily recover his "homeland" or his father's ways. Michael's killing of Sollozo and McCluskey was a turning point in the Corleone family's trajectory. Once Michael started to use the New World system (symbolized by newspapers and Chinese food), the family was set on a path of ethnic self-destruction, moving toward the ideal-typical American business model of rational profit-making. This is confirmed in his determination to make the family "totally legitimate" within five years. The culmination of this movement occurs in the Moe Green casino scene, where the symbolic structures of the opening wedding scene are completely inverted.

Whereas in the wedding scene Don Corleone provides a party with food, drink, and music, Michael arrives at Moe's casino and coldly dismisses the women and musicians that his brother Fredo (John Cazale) has brought for a surprise party. Echoing his father's line from the wedding scene, Michael tells Fredo he is going to take over the casino by making Moe "an offer he can't refuse." But then Michael does something that would have been unthinkable for his father: he asks Johnny—the Don's *own godson*—to sign a stack of written contracts (taken out of Tom's briefcase), agreeing to sing at the casino for the next five years. Michael has completely inverted his father's ways. As noted above, the movie starts with celebratory food and drink, a story about the Don getting Johnny out of a legal contract, Johnny singing voluntarily for the party, and the Don embracing Johnny and telling him, "You look terrible, I want you to eat." Now the exact opposite occurs: Michael coerces Johnny into signing a legal contract, they sit at a dinner table with empty plates and untouched drinks, and everyone in the room is somber and joyless. Michael has entered the world of legal contracts and capitalism, precisely the world that his father had repudiated. Michael is both symbolically and literally leaving behind his father, taking the Corleone business to Las Vegas, a strange town several thousand miles away from his father's neighborhood and connections in New York. He is also shifting the very nature of the family business from food to money. Instead of the olive oil business, a symbol of Italian authenticity and a gift economy where greed at least seems secondary, Michael is moving the family into the casino business, inverting the first scene's sense that direct involvement with money is dishonorable.[18]

In other words, in the process of trying to become a legitimate American businessman, Michael has been forced to lose his Old World ways. Without the authenticating symbols of ethnic roots—food and a verbal contract—Michael is not a benevolent patriarch, but another corporate raider. Making Johnny sign a contract presages the horrific killings during the famous baptism scene that ends the movie. Johnny's contract marks the transition to a world where honor no longer guarantees a man's word. Violence no longer hides behind honor, but reveals itself at the heart of the American system of doing business. Indeed, this was foreshadowed in an earlier exchange between Kay and Michael, in which Kay claims that Michael is naive in thinking of his father as a typical powerful male. The Don, according to Kay, is unlike U.S. politicians and businessmen because these latter "don't have people killed." Michael's succinct reply is: "Who's being naive now, Kay?"

It is also important to note that on another level these oppositions were always blurred. Throughout, the Corleones have clearly been devoted to wealth-making (if not capitalist profit-making) in a cruel and efficient manner. At the same time, though, the film suggests, at least initially, that perhaps capitalism can be redeemed by a more humane, "honorable," personalized system of values that transcends "the bottom line" and the cold impersonality of the state and multinational capitalism.

The written and the oral are key symbols for this refracted image that plays upon contradictory ideas about business and family. Initially we are provided with the image of an authentic ethnic world where business can be personal and run on principles of honor, but ultimately we see that this combination can't hold up under the corrosive influence of mainstream society. *The Godfather* suggests that U.S. society is both like the Mafia in its quest for the consolidation of power and *worse than* the Mafia, since this power is unredeemed by a gift economy.

The movie closes with a triumphant Michael clearly identified with the written word: he is in his office, reading papers, and surrounded by books on the floor. When his sister Connie (Talia Shire) comes in crying about the murder of her husband, she slams down a newspaper on Michael's desk and screams to Kay, "Want to know how many men he had killed before Carlo? Read the papers, read the papers! That's your husband." Michael clearly belongs now to a world of the written word, with its distanced, mediated relations. Then, in a gesture befitting any contemporary U.S. politician, Michael denies everything to Kay, showing the devaluation of his own word. The final image is Michael's office door closing on Kay as she prepares a drink for him, the final rejected gesture of social connection that leaves the new Don in his office, cut off from his family and his father's Sicilian ways.

THEORETICAL DISCUSSION

Written and oral symbolism is woven into the film's fabric from the first to the last scene. It resonates with the writing-orality complex—including the nostalgia and sense of "irretrievable loss"—that Clifford has identified.

This is not a minor point. Writing and food symbolism affects the entire meaning of the film, leading to conclusions that are fundamentally at odds with those of earlier analyses. Previous scholars have claimed that the film's social critique lies in its revelation that American business is like the Mafia, but we argue that the critique comes from the opposite direction: the film shows that American business is *not enough* like the Mafia.

For example, Frederic Jameson argues that the film creates a critique of capitalism through the "pure Evil of the Mafiosi themselves" (1979: 146). Jameson locates this capitalist critique in "the substitution of crime for big business ... the strategic displacement of all the rage generated by the U.S. system onto this mirror image of big business..." (146). Glenn Mann echoes Jameson (useful qualifications notwithstanding) in his discussion of the film's "myth of the Mafia as evil" and its suggestion that the "Mafia's evil is society's evil as well" (2000: 115). Mann concludes that "The romanticization of Vito/Michael and the whole Corleone family deflects from the prosocial myth of the Mafia as evil and puts on hold the subversive myth of society as evil" (115).

On the contrary, we argue that the Mafia is not held out as "evil," but, rather, as an *appealing* image of what the world could be like. This romanticized image of the Mafia is a critique, but in the sense of what Clifford (1986: 114) calls a "critical nostalgia," a way "to break with the hegemonic corrupt present by asserting the reality of a radical alternative." To fantasize about lost worlds is to criticize the present, since "every imagined authenticity presupposes, and is produced by, a present circumstance of felt inauthenticity" (114), a point we develop further in our chapters on *The Village* and *Field of Dreams*. The image of the Corleones' gift economy presents just this sort of critical nostalgia—a world without legal contracts, a world based on strong emotional ties formed through food, drink, and kinship.

Our analysis is perhaps closest to that of John Hess (1975), but while Hess focuses on *The Godfather, Part II*, we have limited ourselves to the first movie in the trilogy, where the critique of capitalism is much more ambiguous. Our approach also has a strong affinity with that of Thomas Ferraro, who argues to good effect that previous scholars have mistakenly treated family and business as separate themes in the film. But as much as we agree with Ferraro's basic point, we cannot agree with his specific conclusion about the critique of capitalism offered by the film or Puzo's book: "Professionals often complain about taking work home with them, mentally if not literally. How much more frightening, then, is the alternative Puzo presents: when some Americans go home to papa, they end up confronting the boss" (Ferraro 1993: 38). Quite the opposite, we suspect that most people wish at some level that their work and family lives were *more* integrated. Even if this wish does not literally translate into desire for a family business (still not an option for many, given all the other economic and ideological forces mentioned earlier), there is at least enough ambivalence to make the Corleone image intriguing (cf. Hart 2005). As for Ferraro's excellent point about the importance of American valorization of ethnicity as a reason for the film's popularity, we would add that the film deals not only with ethnicity, but with what ethnicity symbolizes, including male solidarity and, more generally, ongoing dilemmas about reconciling "personal" and "business" lives.

More than thirty years after it was released, *The Godfather* remains extremely popular, something that can be said of very few films from the early 1970s. We suggest that one reason *The Godfather* is still watched, obsessively in many cases, is that it skillfully addresses vexing, unanswered questions in American culture about the proper boundaries between personal and impersonal relations.

NOTES

1. For these list results, see the following: http://www.afi.com/tvevents/100years/quotes.aspx#list; http://www.empireonline.com/500/99.asp; Burr (1999); and http://www.metacritic.com/film/highscores.shtml, accessed June 10, 2008

2. President Obama revealed this in an interview with Katie Couric. Elaborating, he said the undertaker scene "sets the tone for the whole movie ... I mean, there's this combination of old world gentility and ritual, with this savagery underneath. It's all about family. So it's a great movie" (Couric 2008). One could even speculate that Obama's attraction to ritual partly stems from the influence of his mother, who was a cultural anthropologist.

3. The best, most relevant previous analyses are the following: (1) Ferraro (1993); (2) Jameson (1979); (3) Hess (1976); and (4) Browne (2000). On the general relationship between gangster films and society, see Warshow (1975). Also, note that the director of *The Godfather*, Francis Ford Coppola, has even said that he consciously treated the Mafia as a symbol for U.S. capitalism: "I always wanted to use the Mafia as a metaphor for America. If you look at the film, you see that it's focused that way. The first line is "I believe in America." I feel that the Mafia is an incredible metaphor for this country... Both are totally capitalistic phenomena and basically have a profit motive" (quoted in Farber 1972: 224).

4. "Orality" is being used here loosely as a rubric for the various methods employed by the Corleones (gifts, food, gestures, speech performatives), not to reify the opposition between the written and the oral.

5. We obviously concur here with Ferraro's (1993) argument that, for the Corleones, business and family are one and the same.

6. For example, Tom says, "Who should I give this *job* to?" and the Don responds, "Give him [Carlo] a living, but never discuss the *family business* with him." The bodyguard Paulie's reference to cash values—he fantasizes about stealing the bride's wedding purse, which contains "twenty, thirty grand, in small bills, cash"—is an exception that proves the rule about attitudes toward money in this first scene: it foreshadows Paulie's later betrayal of the Don due to greed. The presence of the bridal purse itself does not contradict the Sicilian emphasis on gifts. As in U.S. culture, money can be converted into a gift if it is properly dressed up as such, i.e., by placing the money in a sealed envelope and putting all the envelopes in a special container (in this case, a white silk bag), without counting the money in public view. Luca Brasi, for example, would never just open up his wallet and hand the Godfather some bills for the bridal purse (see Carrier 1990).

7. To the extent that this mention of the cake seems like an over-eagerness to repay the Don's favor, it could be considered a violation of the usual rules of delayed gift exchange. Such telescoping can be partly attributed to the film's need to condense maximal information in this one scene. Moreover, the true, delayed repayment occurs later in the film when the baker's son-in-law risks his life to help Michael protect the Don at the hospital.

8. In this scene, the Don actually does make a promise, saying he "swears on the souls of his grandchildren." However, Barzini's implication is that the Don does not even need such a speech performative. The Don's disdain for writing is also strikingly clear in this passage from Mario Puzo's book: "The president [of the bank] always treasured that moment when he had offered to give Don Corleone a written document proving his ownership of the shares, to preclude any treachery. Don Corleone had been horrified. "I would trust you with my whole fortune," he told the president. I would trust you with my life and the welfare of my children. It is inconceivable to me that you would

ever trick me or otherwise betray me. My whole world, all my faith in my judgment of human character would collapse. Of course I have my own written records so that if something should happen to me my heirs would know that you hold something in trust for me" (Puzo 1969: 277).

9. According to a 1996 poll done by the Roper Center, only 3.7 percent (54 out of 1,435) people interviewed said they work for a "business owned in whole or in substantial part by a member or members of your family..."

10. Hart doesn't analyze gangster films in depth, nor do Carrier and Miller.

11. Carrier (1997) provides an analysis of the philosophy behind Paul Hawken's company Smith & Hawken, which derives from some of the tensions explored in this chapter. In particular, Smith & Hawken is posed as a response to the impersonal world of bureaucratic organizations and the systematic pursuit of monetary profit. Instead of written policy books and employee manuals, Hawken argues for employees who make moral decisions based on personal feelings: "You must give permission to your employees to do what they think is right... No policy book could cover all ... contingencies. Don't even try to concoct one. Our policy book says this: it has to feel right" (cited in Carrier 1997: 142).

12. The portrayal of Italian ethnicity was also one of the sources of the film's popularity, as argued by Dika (2000) and Ferraro (1993).

13. See Collins (1995), Derrida (1976), Harbsmeier (1985), and Street (1993). For examination of such language attitudes in the notion of "Imagined Communities," see Wogan (2001); and for comparison with highland Ecuador, see Wogan (2004b).

14. In the film, on the other hand, if not used in the way Sonny suggests, guns could act like bombs in twentieth-century wars, notable for their increasing distance and mediation, as documented by Bourke in *An Intimate History of Killing* (1999). Bourke, in fact, argues for a general nostalgia for "intimate," face-to-face combat in contrast to "the horrors of modern mechanized warfare" (1999: 48) in the accounts of U.S. and British soldiers during the Vietnam war and the first two world wars. The bayonet was seen as the weapon that could bring back the chivalric personal element in warfare seen to characterize the past, but which had been increasingly displaced in modern warfare.

15. A Freudian would say that the gun, pen, and cannoli all amount to the same thing: phallic symbols. There's certainly something to this interpretation. For example, at the exact same time that Rocco shoots Paulie, Clemenza urinates ("empties his own gun," you could say); and immediately afterward, Clemenza says to Rocco, "Leave the gun, take the cannoli." For our purposes, though, the Freudian perspective is not particularly useful, since it overlooks the crucial distinctions between these ostensible phallic symbols and their commentary on American society.

16. Perhaps the writing-food inversions even play on the Sicilian tradition of wrapping market-bought fish in newspaper, but only viewers familiar with this tradition could catch this symbolism.

17. We admire Vowell's work, and identify with her obsession with *The Godfather*. However, we suspect that she exaggerated her sense of the Corleones' moral certainty for comic effect, to highlight the contrast with her own college-student existence. Such a strategy seems consistent with the ironic style of her other writings and radio stories.

18. This inversion is highlighted in the first scene of *The Godfather, Part II*, also a family celebration, but in this case one in which Italian food and music have been replaced by standard U.S. fare (Uncle Leo asks for red wine and traditional music, and is given champagne cocktails, canapés, and "hickory-dickory-dock."). For an excellent analysis of this sequel, see Hess (1975).

3 *FIELD OF DREAMS*: FOUL BALLS AND BLURRY LINES

Field of Dreams (1989) seems to make just about everyone cry. Even men, or perhaps especially men, cry at this movie. When *Field of Dreams* first came out in theatres, men stayed in their seats after the credits rolled, tears flowing down their cheeks (Gehring 2004: 116; Winkler 2004: 704). Even tough guys cried. One of the producers reported that when the movie came out, "Arnold Schwarzenegger called to tell us that he couldn't stop crying ... [and] Ron Darling, who pitches for the Mets, told me it was the only time he had cried in a film" (Corliss 1989: 76). To this day, the ESPN website for "The Sports Guy" proclaims, "If you don't shed a tear watching *Field of Dreams*, you might have serious issues."[1]

But this is not just a "guy movie." Women also watch and cry at *Field of Dreams*, which helps explain why it was recently put in the Top 10 of a (unisex) list of "Best Movie Tearjerkers Ever."[2] The farm where *Field of Dreams* was made has even been converted into a pilgrimage destination for thousands of visitors each year, for men, women, and families, and the crying continues there, on the baseball diamond carved out of an Iowa cornfield.[3]

Clearly this film struck a nerve.

Yet, as strange as it sounds, we still don't understand exactly what role baseball plays in this movie, though baseball is its ostensible focus. Previous analyses of *Field of Dreams* have certainly considered baseball, but at a global level, with baseball as a whole symbolizing something else, such as religion, nation, gender, or the rural past (Aden 1999: 219–49; Altherr 2002; Boose 1993; Cooper 1995; Winkler 2004). But how do baseball's *inner workings*—the intricate rules and subtle feel of the game—structure this film? What is the meaning of the foul line that holds in the "ghost players," for example, and how does it relate to the cornfield wall? Why does one of the characters (Moonlight Graham) hold a glove, rather than a bat, when he steps over the foul line and turns back into an older version of himself? How are the film's magical moments similar to baseball's foul territory?

Granted, the film is ultimately not about baseball *per se*; it's about issues like family, mystery, religion, the 1960s, and race. Yet baseball is the vehicle through which these issues get expressed, and baseball presumably still reflects certain aspects of American culture, so we believe it's worth taking a closer look at the role of baseball in this film. Thus, we propose in this chapter to do with baseball and *Field of Dreams* what Clifford Geertz did with the Balinese cockfight (1973: 412–53), that is, treat a single sport as a ritual text that reveals deep cultural issues.[4] To do this, we will need to analyze baseball as we would any other ritual, by looking at minute ritual details, such as the use of space and time, the body movements of participants, and the symbolic objects.

We start this chapter, then, by putting one particular baseball phenomenon, the foul ball, under the microscope, looking for its larger ritual significance. Fortunately, Bradd Shore (1990, 1996: 75–100) has already provided an insightful framework for a ritual analysis of baseball, so we pick up where Shore left off. Then, in the second half of the chapter, we use this baseball analysis to shed light on *Field of Dreams*.

BASEBALL'S SOCIAL SIGNIFICANCE: LINES AS IMAGES OF SOCIAL CONTROL

Our approach here derives from our research outside the U.S. While studying literacy symbolism in the highlands of Ecuador, Wogan noticed the importance of a certain kind of lined paper, used in a witch's book that was said to kill victims. Wogan traced the symbolic origins of this witch's book back to other types of archival writing, such as birth certificates and baptismal records, noting that they all used the same kind of lined paper. He argued that "magical writing" like the witch's book provided an indigenous critique of state and church power (Wogan 2004b).

The more he thought about it upon return to the U.S., the less foreign the witch's book seemed. He started to realize how often lines are also used in the U.S. to enforce and symbolize social control. For example, lines of people marching in a parade evoke civic order; lines at the bank and supermarket organize turn-taking; and lines on paper determine where you write. Everyday expressions also clearly connect lines with social order. We say things like "He's way over the line," "Don't step out of line," and "Get in line." Similarly, a failed queue serves as a condensed image of social chaos, such as newspaper photos of people mobbing a bus or climbing over each other to get to scarce goods.

Through reflecting on these lines and further reading, Wogan realized that he was looking at a global phenomenon, based on Weberian imperatives of bureaucratic structures, such as states and religions. Tim Ingold, in fact, makes the connection between different kinds of "rulers" in his cultural history of lines: "A ruler is a sovereign who controls and governs a territory. It is also an instrument for drawing straight lines. These two usages ... are closely connected. In establishing the territory as his to control, the ruler lays down guidelines for its inhabitants to follow... As in the territory so also on the page, the ruler has been employed in drawing lines of both kinds" (2007: 160).

Wogan also began thinking about the way lines mark off playing space in various sports, such as the boundaries of tennis and volleyball courts, football and baseball fields, shuffleboard squares and bowling alleys. These lines determine where players can and cannot go, what is acceptable and unacceptable behavior, what falls inside and outside the special, regulated space of the game. Making the connection to his fieldwork, Wogan thought of these sports lines like the laws of society: they regulate behavior, and get interpreted and enforced by judges and police (or umpires and referees).

Then baseball entered the picture. Once Wogan's sons were old enough to play catch, he started spending more and more time watching baseball, both on Little League fields and television. This experience piqued his curiosity about the meaning and logic of baseball's rules, particularly rules about foul territory. The more he looked at baseball, the more it seemed like a strange ritual, so, for insight, Wogan turned to Sutton, a life-long baseball fan and father of sons who also loved baseball. Inspired by Shore's work, together we sensed that more could be said about the cultural significance of baseball's lines. Our analysis of baseball continued off and on for about five years. During this period, we watched *Field of Dreams* numerous times, often with our sons, and thought about its depiction of baseball lines. The upshot is this chapter.

Before we can get to our analysis of *Field of Dreams*, we have to take a close look in the next section at the lines that mark off the foul territory on a baseball field. As in any anthropological analysis of ritual, the pay-off here will come through intense focus on seemingly trivial details, so we hope readers will bear with us and trust that this is going somewhere. The good news is that you don't have to be a baseball fan to follow this discussion. In fact, non-fans may have a certain anthropological advantage here, insofar as they are positioned to see this game with the freshness of a cultural outsider.

BASEBALL'S AMBIGUOUS BOUNDARIES

As in other sports, the lines in baseball delimit the field of play: what's "fair" and what's "foul" (often called "out of bounds" in other sports). As regulators of the playing space and acceptable activity, lines in almost any sport serve as good symbols for social control and authority. The lines in baseball are particularly interesting; they seem unstable and ambiguous, reflecting American unease with social control itself.

To be specific, baseball's white, foul lines run from home through first base and third base and into the outfield. Everything inside these lines is fair territory; everything outside the lines is foul territory (a ball hit there does not advance the batter to a base) (see Figure 3.1).

But a foul ball (a ball hit into foul territory outside either of the foul lines) is not exactly out of bounds, at least not in the way you find in other sports, such as basketball. Strangely, a foul ball is both in bounds and out of bounds simultaneously. When a ball falls in foul territory, the batter doesn't run, and the defensive players are not required to field it; in this sense, the ball is out of bounds. At the same time, though, the foul ball *is* in bounds: it gets counted as a strike; if it's caught by one of the defensive players, it counts as an out; and after it's caught, a base runner can try to advance to the next base. The foul ball is technically out of play, but very much in play at the same time; it's called foul, but treated fair. The ambiguity is so deep that baseball fans don't even agree whether a fielding error should be counted in foul territory.

Probably because the foul line can make such a critical difference in baseball, many professional players deliberately avoid stepping on this little white line when exiting the field, as if to recognize that it is powerful, even sacred. Amazingly, though, this line gets thrown out the window every time someone hits a foul ball. When a ball goes into foul territory, the limits of the playing field suddenly shift from the area inside the foul lines to the area outside the foul lines (i.e., the grass in front of the dug-outs, up to the stands, even into the stands, if the player can get there in time). What seemed like the limit of the field (the foul line) doesn't matter anymore; the ostensible out-of-bounds line gets suddenly erased. In fact, foul balls seem to throw baseball's entire boundary system—and social control itself—into question.

The foul ball is, in a word, liminal, caught between two states of being.[5] Put differently, having a foul territory is like having two out-of-bounds lines or two play

Figure 3.1 The foul line, which runs from home through
1ˢᵗ base. Everything to the right of this line is foul territory;
everything to the left of the line (up to the 3ʳᵈ-base foul
line) is fair. Wogan's sons are seen here: Peter (age 9,
running to 1ˢᵗ base); Zach (age 13, catching the foul ball);
Liam (age 11, watching in 1ˢᵗ-base coaching box).

frames. The white foul lines are normally treated reverentially as the boundaries of
the playing space; but when a ball goes slightly outside those boundaries, the playing
space suddenly expands, to include the area between the foul lines and spectator
seats ("foul territory"). Foul territory says, "Here's the line … Oh, no, we changed
our mind—here's the line!"

Of course, lines may be transgressed in other sports, such as the crossing of the
touchdown line in American football, but baseball takes line transgression to an
extreme. Can you imagine a football field with two sets of out-of-bounds lines, or
a basketball player being allowed to chase the ball out of bounds and then shoot a
basket while standing behind the player's bench? It's hard to imagine such things,
since these sports have fixed, stable lines; in baseball, on the other hand, lines are
there to be transgressed.

Even in the case of football, there's a difference: the end zone is a scoring boundary, and therefore most comparable to baseball's home run wall, not the foul lines. Football's sidelines are the real counterpart to baseball's foul lines, yet they lack their amorphous, shifting quality. The end zone is not even perfectly comparable with the home run wall. Other than a field goal, the only way to score in football is to cross the end zone line; crossing that line is therefore an expected part of the game, accounting for the lion's share of the points in a game. However, hitting a home run is a relatively rare way to score in baseball. Similarly, the football field is bound by clear lines. The foul lines in baseball, by contrast, are not marked on the ground past the foul pole; beyond that point they must be projected in the mind's eye, and could theoretically go on forever. Lines are also clearly marked inside the football field (yard lines), but not in baseball's playing field. The closest thing to an internal baseball line would be the runner's base path, but this line is wide and not marked by paint or chalk. Lines are much more central to football: in every single football play, the goal is to cross the touchdown line or get a first down by progressing to the next ten-yard line, and the football referees must constantly measure the lines to verify whether this has happened. In football, lines are clearly established, whereas in baseball the lines constantly shift and blur.

Some lines in baseball also get set up only to be blurred. For example, the lines that make up the on-deck circle often get ignored; the batter's box lines immediately get muddled once the game starts; the base path, not marked by chalk, is open to interpretation and routinely gets transgressed when runners round the bases; and the base coaches often step outside the coaching boxes (Healy and Healy 1993: 120–1).

The point is not that baseball is superior to other sports or absolutely unique. Rather, it is that baseball's blurred lines have important social meaning: they reflect an ambivalence about social control, since lines (and their enforcers, the umpires) are clear representatives of society's regulative function, as noted above. Social control is first created and then resented and overthrown in baseball. This is not to say that baseball reflects an intrinsic, non-changing American character, but, rather, that for some Americans, some of the time, baseball's rules resonate with a certain ambivalence about social control. Our analysis of foul balls dovetails, in other words, with Shore's central point that "because baseball is a game that throws into question the relationship between individual freedom and social regulation, rules themselves have a distinctive place in the sport" (1996: 86).[6]

BLURRING SPECTATOR AND PLAYER BOUNDARIES

A specific subset of foul balls—ones that fall near the spectators in the stands—reveals another blurring of lines: namely, the break-down of the distinction between player and spectator. When a foul ball falls close to or in the stands, it is no longer clear where the professional player's space ends and the spectator's begins. Often a fielder reaches into the stands in an attempt to catch the ball, while the fans in the front rows reach out over the edge of their seats, sometimes several feet onto the ostensible playing field, to catch the ball. The fielder and fans are united in that moment in the same frantic pursuit. The desire of the player to make an out is matched only by the fans' desperation to get a celebrity token, a piece of "contagious" magic from a real professional game. Player and spectator motivations are different (especially if the fan supports the team at bat), but their physical actions are the same, and their bodies are brought into close proximity, even direct physical contact. In these moments, baseball fans become players in a way that goes well beyond the type of fan identification with athletes found in other sports (see Figure 3.2).

Moreover, this blurring of the fan-spectator distinction reveals ambivalence about social belonging in American culture. To understand why, we have to consider Shore's core insight that baseball represents the individual–society tension in America, where conflicting desires to be an individual and a group member exist at the same time (1990, 1996: 75–100). Shore locates this ambivalence in the very structure of a baseball game: a lone batter confronting nine fielders. This playing arrangement actually seems strange when compared with other American sports, where the competition is always between two teams composed of equal numbers of players: "*Of all American field sports, only baseball never directly confronts a team against a team*" (Shore 1996: 82, emphasis in original). This unique structure is a clue to baseball's social significance. By having one offensive player oppose a full defensive team, baseball enacts a showdown between the individual (the lone batter) and society (the fielders working together in a finely-tuned synchronization of mind and body). A batter gets a hit by himself, but no fielder gets an out by himself; getting a hitter out on a ground ball requires one or more throws between different fielders, and even a lone fielder who catches a "pop fly" needs the pitcher and catcher. Perhaps because he is so outnumbered, the hitter has some advantages: for instance, a tie at the bases goes to the runner, and a ball hit on the foul line is considered fair. Individualism and group belonging are juxtaposed, as players alternately fill these offensive (individualistic) and defensive (social) positions.[7]

Figure 3.2 Player merging with fans. During the 2005 World Series, Chicago White Sox first baseman Paul Konerko competed with the crowd to get this foul ball. He didn't make the catch, but apparently a fan did. Photo courtesy of Associated Press, photographer David J. Phillip.

Extending Shore's interpretation, we would argue that foul balls in the stands highlight baseball's individual *vs.* society tension. After all, seeing the fans in the stadium—30,000 to 40,000 unrelated people from various walks of life—is as close as any of us will ever get to seeing American society at large. In a very palpable sense, the fans *are* society in that moment. Thus, when fans merge themselves with the defensive players by chasing foul balls, they dramatize Shore's point that the defensive players (the group of nine) represent society. Fans chasing foul balls make manifest what was already latent in the structure of play. Every foul ball that goes into the stands plays out the individual-society tension that lies at the heart of baseball.

FOUL BALL'S IMPORTANCE

If at this point you're thinking that too much is being made of foul balls, we have to stress that they are a central part of the baseball experience. Foul balls occur in almost every at-bat, and stadium viewers have to constantly watch out for them— otherwise, they could be seriously injured, or even killed, by one. More positively, foul balls are exciting for fans. As noted earlier, most fans would love nothing more than to catch a foul ball, an authentic souvenir of a live game. Even if only a few fans ever succeed in catching one, it's a possibility that animates everyone's experience (see Figure 3.3).

Figure 3.3 Fans trying to get a foul ball. Note the women's hands raised high, ready to receive a gift from heaven, and the mixture of excitement, fear, and wonder in the faces of onlookers. Photographer Nate Billings took this photo during a college baseball game between Missouri and Texas Tech, May 23, 2009. Published on NewsOK.com, copyright 2009, OPUBCO Communications Group.

Andrew Knipe, in one of his "rants" on Ed Randall's *Under the Lights* radio show, captures the intense emotional investment that fans put into the foul ball:

> Were you ever lucky enough to catch a foul ball at a baseball game? How many stitches did you take? More than on the baseball itself?
>
> How much beer, mustard … and in some ballparks … sushi did you wear recovering the prized horsehide sphere? Was it worth it? Sure hope so!
>
> …Just last week a buddy of mine … mending from a near fatal motorcycle accident … went for a foul ball and came away with more injuries than he got on the Harley.
>
> It's as if sound gets warped to a disturbing groan and time gets suspended in an over cranked, slow-motion movie sequence. You look up at the pop up, tossing your cardboard food tray like you're Jorge Posada tossing his mask aside.
>
> Unlike "Georgey" [Jorge, the catcher], you misjudge it. The ball rolls under a seat in front of you and stops just inches from your shoe.
>
> You look down at the MLB logo and the official writing, printed there clearly for you to gaze at in delight.
>
> Your finger tips swing back slightly like eagle claws on a salmon … like a cheetah on a gazelle … and out of nowhere some lady with a porcupine haircut and mitts like Ray Nitschke strips you of it and jumps in joy with a savage laugh and a toothless grin.
>
> You come up with "stugots." Frighteningly funny but true.[8]

With all this emotion, adrenaline, and risk of physical injury, is it any wonder that when a foul ball goes into the stands, a loud "ahhhhh!" spontaneously rips through the crowd as thousands of people gasp in unison? There is something deeply moving about such a moment of collective emotional expression, comparable to the unisonance of singing a national anthem but perhaps even more remarkable for its spontaneity (Anderson 1991: 145).[9] Some of the loudest crowd noise erupts when a foul ball lands in the second or third level, eludes the grasp of four or five fans' outstretched hands, then falls to the level below. During these suspenseful moments, fans turn to watch others frantically scrambling for the ball, to see who will emerge victoriously, the ball raised high above their heads like a trophy. Fans even develop a sudden solidarity for those around them; if they can't get the ball themselves, they at least don't want it to fall to the level below.[10] During a televised game, the camera will invariably cover some of these scrambles for the foul ball; these dramas are simply too integral to the game to be ignored. In fact, the gasps of the crowd are so loud at these times that you can often hear them over the voices of the TV and radio commentators.

And sometimes, when fans in the first rows interfere with a fielder trying to catch a fly ball, these struggles for the ball can alter the outcome of an entire game. The most famous recent case is the "Steve Bartman incident," which occurred during the playoffs for the World Series in 2003. To appreciate the importance of this one foul ball, we have to keep in mind what was happening at this point in the playoffs. The Chicago Cubs were leading the series 3–2 against the Florida Marlins. If the Cubs won the next game, Game Six, they'd go to the World Series for the first time since 1945, and have a chance to win it all for the first time since 1908, ending the single longest drought in baseball history. For the long-suffering Cubs fans, Game Six was absolutely crucial.

It seemed they didn't have too much to worry about. The Cubs were winning this game 3–0 in the 8th inning. If the Cubs could just get five more outs, to end the 8th and 9th innings, they would be going to the World Series.

Then the incident occurred. A Marlins' player hit a foul ball near the left-field wall. The Cubs left-fielder, Moises Alou, ran over and tried to catch the ball, which would have created another out and brought the Cubs within just four outs of the World Series. However, a Cubs fan, Steve Bartman, instinctively reached down to catch what he thought was going to be a foul ball, and he knocked the ball away from Alou, preventing the out. Then the batter, given "another life," got a hit, and subsequently everything fell apart for the Cubs. The Marlins went on to stage a major comeback and won the game. Not only that, the Marlins went on to win the next game as well and went to the World Series, while the broken-hearted Cubs stayed home (see Figure 3.4).

After that fateful moment in Game Six, Cubs fans became furious with Bartman. They blamed him for costing the Cubs that game and, with it, their chance to win the Series for the first time since 1908. As replays of the incident ran on TV and Bartman's name quickly spread online, Bartman became vilified, perhaps the most hated man in Chicago. Police cars were parked outside his house to protect him and his family, and the Illinois governor even suggested that he enter the federal witness protection program. Others came to his defense, pointing out that he was being unfairly scapegoated for the loss, which was really due to the players' subsequent mistakes; they noted that Bartman, a lifelong Cubs fan, had just reacted instinctively, the way any fan would if a foul ball came near them. Eventually emotions cooled and Bartman came out of hiding. And, in an act of purification, the fateful foul ball was

Figure 3.4 The Bartman incident, as seen from a Cub fan's point of view. Drawing by Sam Rowe-Sutton.

sold at auction, publicly blown up, and boiled and eaten in pasta sauce at a Chicago restaurant. Some fans (especially outside Chicago) now laugh at the incident, seeing the hostility toward Bartman as an over-reaction, but to this day many Chicago fans still blame Bartman for keeping them out of the World Series, and baseball fans across the country know Bartman's name and what happened.

Not every foul ball has this much impact, but the Bartman incident demonstrates how crucial a foul ball can be to a game's outcome.

FIELD OF DREAMS

So how does the preceding analysis of the foul ball help illuminate the meaning of *Field of Dreams*?

The short answer is that *Field of Dreams*, like baseball itself, pulls off magic tricks and liminal moments by juxtaposing clear lines with imprecise ones. But to understand what this really means, we have to carefully watch what the movie does with lines, and this requires more close attention to detail because the film's plot does not, at first glance, revolve around lines.

INITIAL IMAGES OF LINES

Field of Dreams tells the story of Ray Kinsella (Kevin Costner), an Iowa farmer who hears a mystical voice say, "If you build it, he will come." Ray interprets this message to mean that if he converts his cornfield into a baseball field, Shoeless Joe Jackson, one of the 1919 Chicago White Sox players banned from baseball because of their plot to "throw" the World Series in a gambling scam, will return from the dead to play there. Ray proceeds to build the field, with the support of his wife (Amy Madigan) and against the advice of his "yuppie" brother-in-law Mark (Timothy Busfield), who is concerned that Ray's farm will fail. Shoeless Joe (Ray Liotta) does show up, emerging from the cornfield to play baseball on the field. Most of the film then concerns Ray's journey at the behest of the mystical voice, first to find 1960s author/radical Terence Mann (James Earl Jones), and then an obscure player named Archibald "Moonlight" Graham (Frank Whaley and later Burt Lancaster), and bring them back to play on his field. The movie's dénouement has Mark accepting the validity of the dream and Ray reconciling with his dead father (Dwier Brown), as they have a father-son game of catch on the field.

In an early scene, after Ray has finished building the baseball field, we see precise, fresh chalk lines in the infield. The camera shot is from behind home plate, focusing on the white lines of the batter's box and infield, which shine in contrast with the brown dirt and green grass that surround them. These straight white lines create an aesthetic of order; as Ray and wife Annie admire the field, Ray says, "It's pretty, isn't it?" Early on the film presents an image of linear precision: the beauty of straight lines on a clean sheet of paper.

Lines next appear a few scenes later, when Shoeless Joe Jackson arrives on the field. After playing ball with Ray, Shoeless Joe walks right up to the end of the field to meet Ray's wife Annie and daughter Karin (Gaby Hoffman). The camera zooms in on his feet so we can see that the tips of his cleats stop exactly at the point where the dirt meets gravel, i.e., the line of the grandstands (as we see in later scenes, the gravel comes up to this projected grandstand line and runs along the bottom of the first row of bleachers). This grandstand line clearly separates player from spectator, with Shoeless Joe on one side of it and Ray, his wife, and daughter on the other.

Music and dialogue also emphasize the fixity of this line. As the camera zooms in and Annie and Ray glance down at Joe's cleats, we hear ominous, eerie music, a stark contrast with the light piano notes that follow. A few moments further into the scene, Annie asks Shoeless Joe if he'd like to come inside; as he replies, "Uh, thanks, but I don't think I can," he, and then Ray and Annie, once again glance down at his cleats, imprisoned at the edge of the gravel.

However, later in this same scene, Shoeless Joe treads a very different kind of line where the outfield meets the cornfield—what would normally be the home run wall. As Shoeless Joe enters the cornfield, his body slowly disintegrates before our eyes, like a body gradually dematerializing and getting "beamed up" in *Star Trek* (see Murray 1981: 85). This cornfield "line" is completely permeable. The grandstand line holds Shoeless Joe in and emphasizes his corporality (as Karin says when looking at him on the other side of the grandstand line, "You seem real to me"); by contrast, the cornfield line lets his body escape and emphasizes his ethereal, ghostly nature.

The film presents a striking contrast, then, between fixed infield lines—the grandstand and foul lines—and the flexible, porous home-run wall. Indeed, the cornfield contains within itself this same contrast. Up close, the rows of corn make separated, straight lines; it is only when viewed from a distance, from home plate, that those lines blur together. This sort of juxtaposition, of fixed and blurred lines, is exactly what we find in the real game of baseball: a clear, straight foul line, surrounded by an amorphous, expansive foul territory. Seeing Shoeless Joe's cleats stop at the foul line makes us think the line can't be crossed, so we're that much more in awe when Shoeless Joe evaporates into the cornfield. In other words, one of the central magical elements of the film, the ghost players' entrance and exit through the cornfield wall, is essentially the magic of baseball's boundary lines. In both the movie and the game, lines are juxtaposed and then transgressed.

LATER IMAGES OF LINES

We see this transgression of lines even more clearly toward the end of the movie. For about four-fifths of the movie, we never see Shoeless Joe or any other ghost player cross over the grandstand line, so we assume that, within the film's fictional logic, that line is inviolable. But then, in a later scene, we find out that this line *can* be crossed: when Ray's daughter falls from the bleachers and starts choking, the young

Moonlight Graham crosses the grandstand line and instantly becomes his elder self, Doc Graham. It's precisely the earlier emphasis on the fixity of this grandstand line that makes the crossing of it by Doc Graham so surprising. Even within the film's magical world of time travel, viewers were not prepared for Doc Graham's moving into the present at the grandstand line; the film creates and then breaks apart its own construction of reality. The fixity of the grandstand line was an illusion, an elaborate set-up for this final magic trick.

Yet this is precisely the trick of foul territory in any baseball game. As argued above, foul territory mocks the fixity of the foul lines, and the balls that go near the grandstands blur the boundaries between spectator and player. Thus, when Moonlight Graham crosses the line, he does so as a fielder, not a batter; right before he crosses the grandstand line, he is holding a glove, which he drops on the ground and exchanges for his leather doctor's bag on the other side of the line. It would not have made sense if Moonlight Graham had been holding a bat before crossing that line, since the batter represents the lone individual, while the fielders represent society. Leather baseball gloves and doctors' medical bags both symbolize society, and the same is true of Doc Graham; he is the town doctor who devotes his life to his local community and receives its affection in return. It makes sense, then, that Moonlight Graham's transformation into his elderly, social self occurs at the grandstand line, the place where players blur with spectators, and where the metaphor of fielders as society becomes literalized.

Another fundamental frame shift occurs in this scene. When Doc Graham saves Karin, Mark is finally able to see the ghost baseball players, and we find out that people other than Ray, his family, and Terence Mann can see them, too. This change makes possible the film's final image of cars streaming into Ray's field, thereby completely rearranging the private-public line maintained throughout the film. Until this point, we were under the impression that Ray was pursuing a private dream, literally in his own backyard (albeit with Mr. Mann brought in to help interpret it), but after Mark sees Moonlight Graham cross that grandstand line, we realize that Ray's dream is an inherently public one. His field can be seen by others, and it will heal the soon-to-arrive masses, not just Ray. Moonlight Graham's crossing over the grandstand line is therefore the film's ultimate blurring of lines: a frame shift that retroactively makes a private obsession into a public act of healing.

Once again, sharp lines are established and then transcended.

SOCIETY—INDIVIDUAL TENSIONS

If baseball is a ritual that enacts the tension between individualism and collectivism, *Field of Dreams* reworks that ritual into a myth, a sacred narrative shot through with the same underlying tensions.

Thus, Ray Kinsella loves his family, yet he builds a baseball field that almost bankrupts them and then abandons them for a long road trip. Even toward the end of the movie, Ray tries to cross the cornfield into the afterlife; he stays in this world only after Shoeless Joe and Terence Mann remind him that he needs to be with his family. Ray is a middle-aged man struggling to reconcile his self-centered, youthful dreams with his family obligations. Like baseball itself, he is driven by conflict between the individual and society.

In the end, the movie finds a way for Ray to have both. His baseball field turns out to be financially profitable, so he gets to pursue his individual dreams and still support his family. In fact, the baseball field allows him to reconcile with the society beyond his family. Ray is initially alienated from his local community; he's not from Iowa, his in-laws and neighbors think he's crazy, and he can barely stand them himself. Yet as much as Ray rejects this town, he also wants to be a part of it. He wants to keep his house, and he protests to his brother-in-law that he's actually a pretty good farmer. Realizing these more public impulses, the baseball field transforms his private backyard into public, communal space, as we see in the film's final shot of cars arriving at Ray's farm.[11]

This community is not just one Iowan town, but the entire nation, as represented by Ray's father. When Ray leaves home, he rejects his father and his vision of the country; whereas Ray's father fought in the First World War, Ray went to Berkeley and "majored in the Sixties," presumably including the anti-war movement. When Ray tells Terence Mann that he once insulted his father by saying he could "never respect a man whose hero was a criminal," he could just as easily have been referring to ex-president Richard Nixon as Shoeless Joe Jackson. But by building a baseball field for Shoeless Joe and the other exiled White Sox players, Ray reconciles with his father—in the famous closing shot of them playing catch—and, thereby, the nation.

This is not just classic baseball; it's classic mythology. After setting up a narrative about vexing social dilemmas, the myth offers tidy, gratifying solutions. In this case, the solutions derive from a mythical image of baseball as an unchanging, pastoral tradition, the one thing truly capable of uniting all Americans.

A similar mythical resolution occurs to the other main characters. Terence Mann has retreated from public life, ever since they "killed Martin [Luther King, Jr.] and

Bobby [Kennedy]." He stopped writing novels and he shuns society. By the end of the film, though, he has rediscovered his role as a public intellectual, a chronicler of the times:

RAY: You're going to write about it [what you find in the cornfield]?

TERENCE: That's what I do.

Like Ray, Terence goes from recluse to healer of the social wounds left by conflicts over Vietnam and race relations.

Doc Graham goes through a similar transformation, only inverted. When Ray encounters him in Chisholm, Minnesota, Doc is an elderly town doctor, the epitome of a community leader. Ray presents Doc with the chance to go back in time to his youthful self, known as Moonlight Graham, so that he can play in the major leagues (he had left the majors after only half an inning, never having even gotten to bat). Doc, however, makes a firm decision to stay in the present, with his beloved wife and local community:

DOC: I was born here, I lived here, I'll die here, but no regrets.

RAY: Fifty years ago, for five minutes, you came this close. It would kill some men to get that close to their dream and not touch it. They'd consider it a tragedy.

DOC: Son, if I'd only gotten to be a doctor for five minutes, now that would have been a tragedy.

Doc is quite decisive here—"no regrets"—yet, magically, when we see his younger self, Moonlight Graham, hitchhiking by the side of the road in the film's present time, his decision gets reversed. Ray and Terence pick him up and take him back to Ray's field, where he finally fulfills his dream of playing major league baseball. This is a remarkable switch, even within the film's logic of time travel. We never find out how it is that Doc's mind and heart say one thing (he wants to stay with his community in the present), while his body does something else (goes back in time and leaves the community in pursuit of unfulfilled baseball dreams). He says he is unequivocally committed to his family and community, yet he pursues his more individualistic desires at the same time. This is the magic of baseball and myth: it dramatizes a dilemma, such as the tension between the individual and society, and then finds a satisfying—albeit illusory—way to resolve this dilemma.

CRITICAL RESPONSE

Rather predictably, critics have complained that *Field of Dreams* romanticizes baseball and doesn't give attention to the sport's nasty history of segregation and racial injustices (Boose 1993; Freuhling Springwood 1996; Rudd and Most 2003: 241). Although we agree that more treatment of racial issues would have been welcome, we believe that the critics have unfairly dismissed what the film accomplished in its portrayal of race relations.

Critics overlook a crucial point: an African American, Terence Mann (played by James Earl Jones), is a very strong, if not the strongest, character in the entire film. Terence Mann speaks authoritatively in Jones's trademark majestic voice, and he is both a sensitive writer (a novelist, software writer, and journalist) and a tough male figure (hence the name Terence *Mann*). He's not just a sidekick figure but, rather, a central part of the story. Mann's character is also entirely the product of the film's screenplay adaptation. In the book on which the film is based, W.P. Kinsella's novel *Shoeless Joe* (1982), there is no Terence Mann (instead, Ray searches for writer J.D. Salinger), nor any other central African-American character. Yet somehow the critics ignore or downplay all this in their efforts to condemn the film's racial politics.

Perhaps the critic who comes closest to recognizing the importance of Terence Mann's character is Lynda Boose, who says, "The narrative finally integrates the black male at the margins of its white-male bond..." (1993: 98). But even this half-sentence of begrudging recognition of Mann's character gets cancelled out by Boose's more extensive critical comments, such as the following:

> And so James Earl Jones (looking a bit embarrassed for affirming racial privileges that his role demands he seem oblivious to) leaps down off the bleachers and, speaking as Man(n), pleads for Ray not to sell the field because it and its players represent the space that allows "all" Americans to return to the dreams of their childhood—dreams that are embodied, of course, in an all-white, all-male baseball team on which no black players (let alone) women would have been allowed to play. (1993: 97)

Nowhere in her critique does Boose, nor any of the other critics, acknowledge Mann's strength of character. And Boose is factually incorrect: at least one black player, Jackie Robinson, *was* "allowed to play" on a team (the Brooklyn Dodgers) with one of the white ghost players seen on screen (Gil Hodges).[12]

In fact, Jackie Robinson is a crucial figure in the film, though one that, like Terence Mann, gets overlooked by critics. Everything hinges on Terence Mann's feelings about Ebbets Field, as expressed in the magazine interview that Terence gave (and which Ray finds during his library research):

> As a child, my [Terence Mann's] earliest recurring dream was to play at Ebbets Field, with Jackie Robinson and the Brooklyn Dodgers. Of course it never happened. The Dodgers left Brooklyn. They tore down Ebbets Field. But even now, I dream that dream.

This quote contains powerful symbols that structure the entire film, so it's worth spelling out its meaning. The key is to remember who Jackie Robinson was, namely, the baseball player that "broke the color barrier" at Ebbets Field in 1947, when he joined the Brooklyn Dodgers and became the first African American to play in the major leagues. Robinson endured horrible abuse at Ebbets from fans and even fellow players, who initially didn't want an African American player in their league. Terence Mann's quest to return to Ebbets Field and play with Jackie Robinson, then, calls up this entire painful history. At the same time, Ebbets Field offers hope that this racial wound might finally be healed. We find out at the end, when Terence Mann crosses into the cornfield, that his pain, the pain that must be "eased" and that sent Ray on his odyssey, is racial pain:

TERENCE: Ray, there's a reason they chose me [to go into the cornfield, the afterlife], just as there's a reason they chose you and this field. I gave an interview.

RAY: What are you talking about?

TERENCE: The one about Ebbets Field, the one that sent you to Boston to find me.

Thus, Jackie Robinson and Ebbets Field provide a racial subtext that structures the entire film. By the same token, the film sets up a clear connection between Shoeless Joe's pain and that of the Negro League players, since both were exiled from professional baseball and suffered heartache because of it.

It's hard to understand how the critics could have missed all this. The most logical explanation, especially in light of the way they disregard Terence Mann's character, is that they are less interested in balance than condemnation. Or perhaps the racial connections are never stated explicitly or extensively enough for their liking, since they are only alluded to through these brief references to baseball symbols and the Civil Rights movement. We agree that it would have been good to see the Negro Leagues more integrated into the story, but calling for post-facto changes to a successful narrative is always dicey; at some point you either accept the current narrative structure and work within it, or you end up calling for a substantively different story. For example, it would have been possible to include shots of Negro League players alongside Smokey Joe Wood, Mel Ott, Gil Hodges, and the other ghost players that are seen playing on Ray's field. And it would have even been easy to show Jackie Robinson with the ghost players, especially since in real life Robinson played on the Dodgers with Gil Hodges, one of the ghost players that does appear on screen. Then again, making these additions could have been highly problematic from a narrative perspective. As the story stands, Terence goes off into the cornfield in pursuit of Jackie Robinson, Ebbets Field, and racial healing, an ending that retains the film's sense of quest and mystery. If Terence had found Jackie Robinson and the Negro League players on Ray's field several scenes earlier, he wouldn't have needed to cross over into the cornfield at the end, and the film would have lost much of its tension in the later scenes. A few scenes earlier, on the drive back to Ray's house, Terence says to Ray, "Well, now I know what everybody's purpose here is—except mine." Not knowing what is in store for Terence keeps the film moving right to the end. Thus, even making a seemingly small change, like adding a shot of Jackie Robinson, risks violating the integrity of the narrative.

In fact, if you messed too much with the current structure of *Field of Dreams*, if you made the underlying connections too explicit, the film would lose its mysterious, unconscious symbolism, one of the hallmarks of myths, blockbusters, and narratives in general. Ebbets Field is a good example, and not just in the racial sense already discussed. Ebbets, like any good, polyvocal symbol, stands for many things. Ebbets was the home of the Brooklyn Dodgers, whose fan base was mostly working-class, especially by comparison with their rivals from across town, the New York Yankees. The Dodgers were perennial underdogs, losing so many critical games to the Yankees and others that they simply became known as "dem bums." But the ultimate heartbreak occurred when the Dodgers relocated to Los Angeles in 1958, and Ebbets Field was torn down a few years later. In a game that revolves around going home, the Brooklyn fans had their home destroyed. Ever since, Ebbets Field has been shorthand for pain—the pain of the working class and of African-Americans, and, more generally, the pain of the underdog, the feeling of loss, and the inability to return home. With all these powerful associations, the placement of Ebbets Field in the film creates the possibility for powerful emotional viewer identification across racial lines.

Field of Dreams therefore contains a strong, central African American character, swirls around a history of racial injustice, and offers hope for racial healing—not too shabby for a 1980s Hollywood blockbuster. Perhaps the film could have created an even more effective treatment of race, but critics should have given it more credit for what it did accomplish in this regard.

Other critics complain that the film reflects conservative 1980s values. Caroline Cooper says this film is "in many ways a typical product of the Republican decade of Reagan and Bush as described in some key critical studies: it is an escapist fantasy; it sentimentalizes the nuclear patriarchal family; it bears features of the father-son melodrama; and—more generally—its values are highly conservative" (1995: 164). Boose claims the ghost players are like Vietnam Vets, who must be vindicated so that the father-son ritual of warfare can be continued in American society (1993: 95–9).

These critics raise some good points and we do not deny that their readings are plausible. For example, this text contains possible confirmation of conservative, capitalist values (e.g. making money off the field). Then again, one could find in it a critique of heartless capitalism and a celebration of non-violence and racial unity. One could also note that nostalgia for a lost era of baseball is not necessarily conservative; as we argued in reference to *The Godfather*, nostalgia for lost worlds can present a strong social critique and call for change, "a way to break with the hegemonic corrupt present by asserting the reality of a radical alternative" (Clifford (1986: 114). Perhaps these latter possibilities explain why *Field of Dreams* was the second all-time favorite film of Democratic President Bill Clinton (Cooper 1995: 163). But whether we're talking about Bill Clinton or anyone else, we can only determine the way individuals and specific groups interpret a text through ethnographic research. *Field of Dreams* would be a great candidate for such a study of audience responses, including the way responses vary by race, class, gender, and region.

Our reading, in fact, has stressed ambiguity and ambivalence, in both baseball and *Field of Dreams*. If there's anything to this reading, the one thing we can safely predict is that the social tensions that created *Field of Dreams* will go into extra innings.

NOTES

1. Bill Simmons, The Sports Guy, "Straight to the Sports Guy's Heart," http://proxy.espn.go.com/espn/page2/story?page=simmons/030815, accessed August 20, 2008.
2. See "Best Movie Tearjerkers Ever: The Top 25," www.ew.com, accessed February 4, 2009.
3. See the farm's website (www.fieldofdreamsmoviesite.com), an ethnographic analysis of visitors to the farm (Fruehling Springwood 1995), and a documentary about the farm: "A Diamond in the Husks," on the Bonus Features of *Field of Dreams: Two-Disc Anniversary Edition* (2004). In this documentary, Becky Lansing, one of the owners of the farm, describes seeing "a big strapping, 50-year old man" on his hands and knees at the field's home plate, "crying his heart out." As she starts to cry herself, she adds, "He had something to say to his dad. And people say it—not only this man, but people say it every day out here."
4. Geertz's essay has been enormously influential, but also the subject of many critiques. For our purposes, the most important lessons of Geertz's essay are that sport can be treated as ritual and that doing so requires attention to seemingly trivial components of the ritual.
5. In anthropology, "liminality" refers to the transitional stage of rites of passage, after the period of separation and before the period of reaggregation. In the liminal stage, the ritual subjects no longer have their former social status, and they have not yet acquired the new status that the rite is intended to provide. Marines who haven't left basic training, or the bride and groom who haven't yet kissed in the church and said "I do," are in liminal states—neither civilian nor soldier, single nor married, they're temporarily stuck in-between. Similarly, a ball hit in foul territory is caught between two states, a dead and live ball. Obviously the term liminal is being used here anthropomorphically.
6. Although Shore does not focus on foul territory, our analyses are clearly complementary. Our analysis also dovetails with Healy and Healy, who see baseball's lines as representing social tensions. But their analysis differs in important ways; instead of analyzing foul territory, they focus on the tension between "civilization" and nature, and, when they do briefly consider social control, they look at it in terms of Puritan religion and "human nature itself" (1993: 122).
7. An exception is the pitcher, who, in the American League, gets replaced at the plate by the designated hitter. The designated hitter has gradually gained acceptance, but the weight of baseball's language is still against him; he's technically not a baseball "player," since he doesn't "play" defense in the field. See Shore (1996: 83).
8. Quoted in Bob Cauttero, "Pals Talkin' Baseball," www.rideforlife.com/archives/001023.html, 2004, accessed August 8, 2004. Andrew Knipe's comments were sent as an email to Ed Randall, who read the comments on his radio show under a segment known as *Andy's Major League Rants and Chants*. Since Andy was suffering from ALS (Lou Gehrig's disease) at the time, his email was composed with a medical headset, eyeing letters one at a time on a computer screen and then clicking a computer mouse with his still-sensate index finger. Andy died before this chapter was finished, so we took the liberty of fixing a few typos that he never had the energy to correct in his original email.
9. Wogan (2001) argues that Anderson's account instantiates a long-standing Western dichotomy between orality (as emotion) and print (as cognition). Taken by itself, though, Anderson's point about unisonance still stands, just as you can accept Durkheim's point about "collective effervescence" without being a structural-functionalist.
10. Thanks to Erica Blum-Barnett, a former student of Wogan's, for this point. Blum-Barnett made this point in a 2008, post-graduation note, following up on a point she had made in class in relation to Marx.

11. In a 1994 poll, Iowans selected *Field of Dreams* as the artistic representation they were "most proud of as an Iowan," with 30% selecting *Field of Dreams* out of six possible representations (21% selected the next-closest category, the musical *The Music Man*). See *Des Moines Register*, Iowa Poll, May 2, 1994.

12. Boose is closer to the mark in her critique of the film's gender roles, but here, too, she doesn't seem interested in fair-mindedness. While calling Ray's wife, Annie, a "1960s version of Donna Reed" (1993: 98), she fails to mention possible exceptions, such as the way Annie took on the whole town in a galvanizing speech against censorship.

4 *THE BIG LEBOWSKI:* BOWLING, GENDER, TEMPORALITY, AND OTHER "WHAT-HAVE-YOU'S"

What happens when we remove chronology as the dominant organizing model for talk about the past?

David Samuels, *Putting a Song on Top of It* (2006)

We take up this chapter ten years after the release of *The Big Lebowski* (1998). While this film didn't do extremely well at the box office, it has gained increasing popularity over time and has already had a major cultural impact. Clark Collis (2008) notes that *The Big Lebowski* (TBL, henceforth) is "ensconced at the high table of classic cult films," with a devoted following willing to buy multiple special editions of the DVD, and serious fans who have created an annual "Lebowskifest," where they present multiple screenings, costume contests, and special guest appearances. *Entertainment Weekly* placed TBL 15th on its list of "The Cult 25: The Essential Left-Field Movie Hits Since '83."[1] Especially for younger audiences, TBL is a cultural phenomenon, just as *The Rocky Horror Picture Show* and *This is Spinal Tap* were for previous generations, and it may very well stand the test of time. TBL's cult popularity is what we intend to examine in this chapter, employing several different anthropological angles.

Released in 1998, TBL is set seven years earlier, on the eve of what is now referred to as the First Gulf War. While many movies project the viewer back in time to an identifiable period—the 1950s, the Great Depression—TBL sets its scene in a near past, "the early Nineties," as the cowboy-narrator of the film (Sam Elliot) identifies it. Is this a closing of the nostalgia gap, or what some might call "nostalgia for the present"? We will argue that time is, in fact, central to this movie and to an understanding of its central character, Jeffrey "The Dude" Lebowski (Jeff Bridges).

But what makes The Dude a "man," to paraphrase a line from the movie? While all of the films we discuss deal with questions of proper or "hegemonic" masculinity, TBL makes gender central, setting up, and knocking down, a variety of dominant versions of American masculinity, questioning the very notion that there might continue to exist a dominant "masculinity model." TBL deals with time and gender in ways that we will suggest are highly amenable to anthropological discussion.

We then take up the question of the film's quotability. Even scholars of the film seem unable to resist quoting from it in the title of their essays: "This Aggression Will Not Stand" (Comer 2005), "The Dude Abides" (Williams 2001), "No Literal Connection" (Martin-Jones 2006), "What Makes a Man, Mr. Lebowski?" (Kazecki 2008), not to mention our own title. The enduring popularity of the film, as we will see, seems to be bound up with its quotability. While *The Godfather*, *Jaws*, and *Field of Dreams* have all left their mark on American popular culture in a handful of choice quotations, TBL seems to take quotability to an even more extreme level, as if the film exists in order to be quoted; indeed, many fans cite quotability as the key reason for their love of it.

In what follows, we will try to bring together these different aspects of the film— time, gender, quotability—in one coherent analysis, without leaving out "a lot of in's, a lot of out's, a lot of what-have-you's." And did we mention that it's a film about bowling?

"About" may be too strong a word, since TBL seems to defy plotting. As Collis (2008: 35) puts it, the movie "concerns" Jeffrey "The Dude" Lebowski, "a perennially Zen '60s burnout who deals with every drama life throws at him by smoking pot or going bowling." These dramas are set in motion when thugs mistake Lebowski for an L.A. millionaire of the same name, come to his apartment, threaten him, and urinate on his rug. The Dude tries to get compensation for his soiled rug by going to see the other Jeffrey Lebowski, the eponymous Big Lebowski (David Huddleston). When The Dude's request is refused, he steals one of the Big Lebowski's rugs, and then gets caught up in a kidnapping plot involving Big's wife Bunny (Tara Reid). The Dude and his friends spend the rest of the movie trying to recover The Dude's rug and Bunny's ransom money.

The rest of TBL concerns labyrinthine plot twists as The Dude, his sidekick Walter (John Goodman), and friend Donnie (Steve Buscemi) become involved

Figure 4.1 This might be The Dude's rug.
We found it at a store called Village Rugs
in Portland (Multnomah Village), Oregon.

with Nihilist terrorists, the porn industry, a Fluxist-feminist artist and daughter of the eponymous Big Lebowski (Julianne Moore), and a brutally-fought bowling tournament. Film scholars have suggested a number of key themes that TBL is "about," including:

1. The parody and pastiche of traditional Hollywood film genres (Williams 2001; Comer 2005; Kazecki 2008; Tyree and Walters 2007).
2. The challenging of the U.S. military politics of oil and mass consumption (Martin–Jones 2006).
3. A general "Carnivalesque" critique of the social order (Martin and Renegar 2007).
4. A challenge to dominant masculinity models and the "subversive effect of humor and laughter" on said masculinity models (Kazecki 2008: 153; Tyree and Walters 2007).

Figure 4.2 This rug is on Wogan's living-room floor. Sutton tells Wogan that it ties the whole room together.

Given that the scholarship on TBL has come from film studies, it's not surprising that the focus has been on how the movie comments on other movies, or movie conventions and genres, and on questions of whether TBL challenges or reinforces social norms and conventions (Martin and Renegar 2007: 304). We draw from these excellent readings, while giving them our own anthropological spin.

QUOTABILITY, MISCOMMUNICATION, AND METALINGUISTICS

What makes language quotable, and why is this film, in particular, deemed so quotable? There are a number of aspects of language in TBL that need to be unpacked before we can answer this question; we first need to spend a little time getting a feel for the role of language in TBL. Since these exchanges can be quite funny, we hope that readers will be patient with, and take some pleasure from, our extended examples.

First, TBL seems to revel in miscommunication and non-sequiturs. From the opening scene, in which The Dude is beaten up because he is taken for the wrong Lebowski, words seem not to accurately describe or represent, but to lead to confusion, misrepresentation, and misunderstanding. Here are a few representative examples:

1. When The Dude is shown the wall of "little urban achievers," the children supported by Big's charity, he is told, "These are Mr. Lebowski's children, so to speak." The Dude's response—"Different mothers, huh?"—indicates confusion over the use of the word "children," notwithstanding the speaker's cautionary phrase "so to speak."

2. In the exchanges between The Dude, Walter, and Donny, confusion seems to be the rule:

   DUDE: What's your point, Walter?

   WALTER: There's no fucking reason—Here's my point, Dude—there's no fucking reason—

   DONNY: Yeah, Walter, what's your point?

   WALTER: Huh?

   DUDE: What's the point of—We all know who was at fault, so what the fuck are you talking about?

   WALTER: Huh? No! What the fuck are *you* talking—I'm not—we're talking about unchecked aggression here—

   DONNY: What the fuck is he talking about?

   DUDE: My rug.

3. Constant references by Walter or The Dude to famous figures (Theodore Herzl: "If you will it, it is no dream") are almost always either missed or completely misinterpreted, as in the following exchange at the bowling alley:

   DUDE: It's all a goddamn fake. Like Lenin said, look for the person who will benefit. And you will, uh, you know, you'll, uh, you know what I'm trying to say.

DONNY: I am the Walrus. [Donny, seated behind Walter and The Dude, mistakenly thinks they're referring to John Lennon, so he tries to help The Dude complete his sentence by quoting a Beatles song.]

WALTER: That fucking bitch!

DUDE: Yeah

DONNY: I am the Walrus.

WALTER: Shut the fuck up, Donny! V.I. Lenin! Vladimir Ilyich Ulyanov!

DONNY: What the fuck is he talking about?

4. Even The Dude and the Cowboy-Stranger miscommunicate in their brief interactions:

STRANGER: Wal', a wiser fella than m'self once said, sometimes you eat the bar and sometimes the bar, wal', he eats you.

DUDE: Uh huh. That some kind of Eastern thing?

STRANGER: Far from it.

This sort of miscommunication is compounded and highlighted when characters suddenly switch into Italian or German without subtitles (Maude, the Nihilists), or characters speak in heavily accented English (the Cowboy-Stranger, the Nihilists, the Sellers' maid, the man whose car is wrecked), as in this scene at Larry Seller's house:

WOMAN: [answering door] Jace?

WALTER: Hello, Pilar? My name is Walter Sobchak. We spoke on the phone. This is my associate, Jeffrey Lebowski.

WOMAN: Jace?

WALTER: May we, uh, we wanted to talk about little Larry. May we come in?

WOMAN: Jace?

A different type of miscommunication in TBL involves the consistent use of synonyms that are marked as slang or old-fashioned. While the most prodigious use of synonyms is for specific parts of the male anatomy, in fitting with the theme of masculinity in question, there seems to be a poetic play with language for its own sake throughout TBL. The character of Maude Lebowski provides numerous examples:

MAUDE: … without batting an eye a man will refer to his dick or his rod or his Johnson.

DUDE: Johnson?

MAUDE: Do you like sex, Mr. Lebowski?

DUDE: … Excuse me?

MAUDE: The physical act of love. Coitus.

DUDE: A hundred…

MAUDE: Thousand, yes, bones or clams or whatever you call them.

Another example comes when the private detective refers to himself as a "Brother shamus," which leads The Dude to this confused question:

DUDE: Brother Seamus? Like an Irish monk?

MAN: Irish m- What the fuck are you talking about? My name's Da Fino! I'm a private snoop! Like you, man!

DUDE: Huh?

DA FINO: A dick, man!

When a policeman informs The Dude that his car was discovered "lodged against an abutment," The Dude responds: "Oh man—lodged where?!" It is as if even when talking English, characters are communicating in different languages, with "Huh?" and "What the fuck are you talking about?" the most common replies throughout.

Another feature of language use in TBL is that characters often make metalinguistic statements about their language usage, i.e., statements that comment explicitly on one's use of language. Maude, for example, highlights her own language usage with the phrase "to use the parlance of our times" (a phrase repeated by The Dude). In Big's first confrontation with The Dude, he emphasizes his refusal to replace The Dude's rug: "Hello! Do you speak English? Parler usted Inglese?" Walter concludes his interrogation of the mute Larry Sellers with "Fuckin' language problem." He also takes The Dude to task for his use of the word "Chinaman": "...and, also, Dude, Chinaman is not the preferred, uh ... Asian-American, please." And, finally, there are the Nihilists' seemingly redundant statements of "We szreten you!" In all of these cases, the characters directly call attention to their language usage and its potential for misunderstanding and miscommunication.

Despite, or perhaps because of these miscommunications, language has an almost viral character in TBL. That is, once a word or phrase is used, it crops up repeatedly in the dialogue of related or unrelated characters. The most obvious example is the phrase that sets the narrative in motion, Bush Sr.'s threat to Iraq: "This aggression will not stand ... This will not stand!" This phrase is repeated by Walter and then—slightly transformed—by The Dude.[2] Indeed, The Dude seems to draw linguistic sustenance from others' words and phrases, repeating and sometimes mangling them throughout the course of the film. One might see this as part of the problem of miscommunication; as phrases such as the Bush tagline are repeated, they seem to be emptied out of meaning. But, significantly, this repetition is not restricted to the film itself; indeed, it is one of the key features of the enduring popularity of TBL, its quotability. This is pointed out repeatedly in the fan tribute book *I'm a Lebowski, You're a Lebowski* (Green et al. 2007). Jeff Dowd, the real-life inspiration for The Dude, has commented, "People like to repeat the lines of TBL. Because they're such memorable and classic lines. And of course you can use them, as we've seen, in all kinds of other contexts" (Green et al. 2007: 94).

Certainly, the quoting of films is not limited to TBL, as we have noted in regards to our other blockbuster movies. Lines such as "If you build it, he will come," "I'm going to make him an offer he can't refuse," and "You're gonna need a bigger boat" have become so much part of common parlance as to be used without reference to their origins. As Oliver Benjamin, founder of the Dudeism religion/website, puts it: "Today people quote movies like they used to quote literature and the Bible—it becomes part of who you are" (Green et al. 2007: 139).[3] We can surely trace some of this quote-happiness to new technology. While prior to the mass marketing of video recording devices in the 1980s only the most devoted fans of a movie would see it more than a couple of times, now it has become relatively easy to watch a particular movie dozens of times, such as at college-dorm parties organized around the screening of popular movies. This creates a kind of small screen analog to the phenomenon of *The Rocky Horror Picture Show*, in which the point of repeated, collective viewings was to learn the movie line for line. And this in itself provides an interesting comparison to the ways that myths are transmitted in many non-Western societies, as linguistic anthropologist Greg Urban has documented regarding the Shokleng of South America: "the younger performer is locked to the older, more skilled performer, forced to copy syllable by syllable the discourse produced by his elder" (Urban 1991: 103).

But while quoting movies is *one* of the pleasures of viewership, only relatively few movies become treasure-troves of quotations. We doubt that your average moviegoer could quote many verbatim lines from *Field of Dreams*, for example. And while fans quote (or misquote) a number of lines from *The Godfather,* this is a *subsidiary* aspect of the movie, the pleasure of which comes from its narrative. TBL is unusual in that much of its pleasure and popularity comes specifically from quoting it. Green et al. (2007) recount numerous stories in which fans drop lines from the movie at random in order to identify fellow fans of TBL (see also Collis 2008). Indeed, creative quoting of lines from the film seems to be one of the main points of the annual LebowskiFest, now in its sixth iteration. They also note that "The more we watched the movie, the more we found ourselves quoting it" (Green et al. 2007: 2). Fan Johnny Hickman (founder of the "Little Lebowski Urban Achievers" website) says: "Not a day goes by that I don't quote a line of dialogue from TBL. It's great sport amongst we Achievers to find new and inventive ways to drop lines from TBL into everyday situations to amuse ourselves and one another" (Green et al. 2007: 154–5). This quotability defines TBL as a "cult" film.

LINGUISTIC ANTHROPOLOGY AND QUOTABILITY

A brief tour of recent work in linguistic anthropology will help illuminate the quotability of TBL. Indeed, questions of miscommunication, metalinguistics, and quotability have been at the heart of recent developments in the field. A number of linguistic anthropologists have drawn on the studies of Mikhail Bahktin to call for a rethinking of the way we conceptualize language's relationship to society and time. Bahktin's basic insight was that the speech of each individual person is not created by that individual in isolation, but is "shaped and developed in continuous and constant interaction with others' individual utterances ... Our speech, that is, all our utterances ... is filled with others' words" (Bahktin 1986: 89). Linguistic anthropologists have developed a vocabulary to analyze this basic linguistic truth. They write of "entextualization" as the process "of rendering discourse extractable, of making a stretch of linguistic production into a unit—a *text*—that can be lifted out of its interactional setting" (Bauman and Briggs 1990: 73). Indeed, they argue that most language use takes the form not of applying grammatical rules to construct wholly new sentences, but of learning "chunks" of prefabricated texts or phrases (Mackenzie 2000: 173). If all utterances are made up of such "chunks ... in varying stages of solidification, susceptible to varying degrees of free play and reformulation" (Barber 2007: 30), the conscious poetic or "performative" use of language accelerates this process, focuses attention on the utterance itself. That is, by "put[ting] the act of speaking on display (Bauman and Briggs 1990: 73), a performance facilitates entextualization and subsequent recontextualization in other contexts. While linguistic anthropologists generally focus on oral performances, we would argue that movies like TBL serve a similar role to oral narratives in non-Western societies: they also put speaking on display in a public context, allowing for entextualization and quotability.

Greg Urban, for example, has examined what he sees as the different forces at work that either "accelerate," thereby reproducing, or "dissipate" a particular piece of oral performance,[4] seeing all culture as made up of the "inertial" and the "accelerative." He argues that any text will be subject to random alteration as "part of the entropic forces of the universe at work on culture as it moves through the world" (Urban 2006: 77). We see this in TBL, where "This aggression will not stand" turns into, in The Dude's words, "This will not stand, man." Urban suggests that, to counteract such slippage, the "microdesign" features of texts stress the importance of replication, as in a Cherokee myth that focuses on "the need for precise copying" and the problems that arise when this does not occur. Will Straw adopts Urban's approach in order to look at the way in which movies have both inertial and accelerative elements: "by pushing these prototypes into an engagement with more contemporary themes ... these films fulfill an accelerative function. They renew the familiar by bringing it into an engagement with the new and unfamiliar" (Straw 2005: 184). This is precisely what happens at the LebowskiFests where rewards are given to those who are able to reproduce and recontextualize lines from TBL at appropriate moments, bringing the traditional into engagement with the new and thus renewing TBL itself. As Green et al. state in their series of "Rules to Live By," "Always remember interesting turns of phrase that you hear so that you can employ them in completely unrelated situations later and convincingly sound as if you know what you're talking about" (Green et al. 2007: 19). Within the film itself, one way to understand the miscommunication is as an example of the consequences of the failure to properly copy previous texts (like Urban's Cherokee myth):

DUDE: … just stay away from my fucking lady friend, man.

DA FINO: Hey, hey, I'm not messing with your special lady.

DUDE: She's not my special lady, she's my fucking lady friend. I'm just helping her conceive, man!

But clearly not all movies become entextualized in this way, even though the technology of VCRs and DVD players allow for the kind of repetition described by Urban for Shokleng myths. So this raises a new question: what makes TBL special in this regard? We would argue that there are two factors, and that they are interrelated. One is that metalinguistic statements and miscommunication within the film draw attention to language *as language*, thus highlighting signifiers, at the expense, one might say, of meanings. While in some societies the kind of ambiguity that results from these linguistic practices might be celebrated (see below), in American society this is not typically the case; the dominant U.S. language ideology demands referentiality and meaning. When, for example, The Dude and Walter's quoting of Lenin leads Donny to intone, "I am the Walrus," such speech acts challenge a dominant language ideology of referentiality. Thus, the constant refrain of "What the fuck are you talking about?" represents a metalinguistic demand to strip language to its reference, to privilege denotation over connotation, to tell me what you mean (*God damn it!*), just as "Shut the fuck up!" acts as a futile attempt to suppress such ambiguity.

The second factor underlying the extreme quotability of TBL is its humor. Funny lines, by their nature, lend themselves to entextualization: to decontextualization and recontextualization in new and (in)appropriate contexts. And TBL is, indeed, a very funny movie. But here, again, language is critical. Much of the film's humor is a direct result of the miscommunications we have been discussing; we might suggest that miscommunication is the verbal equivalent of slapstick—one or multiple characters falling on their collective behinds.

THE MAN FOR *WHICH* TIME?

But the humor of miscommunication in TBL has two other dimensions that we have not yet explored, and which we believe are useful in understanding other aspects of the film, particularly the notion that The Dude is "The man for his time." That is, our observations lead us to a consideration of two other aspects of TBL which make it interesting and unusual: notions of temporality and masculinity. Once again, we find contemporary anthropological theory useful in untangling and reconnecting these aspects of TBL.

A key piece of the recent Bahktin-inspired approach in linguistic anthropology is a rethinking of the temporal dimensions of language. Rather than seeing language as a static, atemporal code, anthropologists recognize that language contains multiple temporalities (see Hanks 1989: 113). This idea is perhaps best developed in David Samuels' (2006) ethnography of performance among San Carlos Apache. Samuels argues that there is a strong sense of history on the San Carlos Apache reservation, but one not particularly tied to notions of linear chronology. Instead, a temporally open past of "back then" is continually being called into present consciousness, particularly through the use of quotation. Echoing Bahktin, he notes that linguistic signs are rife with ambiguity, "increasingly difficult to pin down and know because they are always humming with the trace overtones of other meanings, other implications, other usages" (2006: 15). Samuels observed that "successive speakers blend their words with those that have come before, almost literalizing Bakhtin's observation that each speaker's words are only half his or her own" (2006: 69). The suggestion is that this ambiguity is celebrated by San Carlos Apache, who use it to make the past "audible in the mouths of the present" (2006: 39). Samuels develops the concept of "feelingful iconicity" to explore the way that linguistic familiarity can create particular moments in which one has the feeling that one is once again living in a past time. But he argues that it is not simply a Bahktinian perspective on language practice that sensitizes him to such a use of quotation. Rather, he is following the explicit values of San Carlos Apache, in which "citation and repetition are placed in such high relief; in which the speech of others is so prominently and deliberately displayed in one's own speech; where so much communicative energy is spent in reenacting, reanimating, and reperforming other people's utterances" (2006: 73).

Thus, for San Carlos Apache, this sense of the present as made up of multiple pasts (what we will refer to, henceforth, as polytemporality) is explicitly created through the linguistic practices discussed above: entextualization, quotation and the viral circulation of language chunks, ambiguity (miscommunication), and metapragmatic framing. For example, San Carlos Apache engage in a joking frame called "throwing words" (Samuels 2006: 69), in which the point is to mix one's talk with the talk of co-present others, with that of other Apache from the past, and with phrases from mainstream popular culture. The phrase "*tah nnii,*" roughly translated as "you might say," is used to index this Bahktinian double-voicing, where one enters into the "thoughts and voices" of another (2006: 80). "*Tah nnii*" might be used to preface quotations of others and to draw on pop-culture phrases, such as "I've fallen and I can't get up," "You can't have my Bud Light," and "Where's the beef?", that pull people out of the frame of the present through a linguistic evocation of the past.[5] Samuels argues that San Carlos Apache identity is not based on a notion of linguistic or cultural purity, but on an explicit valuing of the ability to mix codes or blur boundaries, much like the mixing of languages we saw in TBL. The value or meaningfulness of talk is linked, for the Apache, to the skill by which such recontextualizations of phrases are performed, the effect being to suggest other possible temporalities that "hum" in the speech of the present moment. San Carlos Apache constantly treat speech as suggestive of other possibilities, "shining lights down roads not taken and underscoring the instability of ... signification" (2006: 83). Similarly, TBL uses quoted speech to creatively index and mix temporalities.

UNPACKING POLYTEMPORALITY

However, polytemporality is not just a linguistic phenomenon; by broadening out the concept, we can tie this discussion of language into some of the broader themes of TBL. In the past twenty years there has been a flurry of scholarly interest in the cultural shaping of historical consciousness, or people's experience of temporality. Whether framed in terms of "the invention/imagination of tradition," the "anthropology of time," nationalist uses of the past, or local counter-memories, anthropologists and those in related disciplines have been exploring the way time is used as a resource in social struggles and quests for identity—gender, class, ethnicity, and/or other.[6] Sutton's work (1998, 2008) on the Greek island of Kalymnos, for example, focused on how the past was used as a resource in modern Greek consciousness in explicit discourses and in daily practices, such as the naming of children after grandparents or the throwing of dynamite bombs at Easter. Sutton contrasted this with the ways that the past is often dismissed in American mainstream culture, where those who hew too closely to what is labeled as the past—styles, ideas, practices—are in danger of being condemned, as in the dismissive and telling phrase "That's history."

Kath Weston develops a similar view of Western historical consciousness, but focuses particularly on gender and sexuality, and on the conscious, ideological work that is done to place people and events in different temporalities:

One does not automatically "see" events in temporal dimensions. There is a kind of work ... involved in any attempt, however "confused," to cast a molten world into the contours of time. Although the specific practices vary tremendously from one social location to another, temporalities generally require some method of delineating and ordering artifacts, events, what have you, into sequenced frameworks... People explain current circumstances with reference to arrangements that they believe prevailed "back in the day..." (Weston 2002: 92–3)

Weston's "what have you" isn't meant here to echo The Dude's confusion, but, rather, to suggest that we tend to assign temporalities to everything in our world, from people and objects, to styles and events.[7] Weston usefully suggests that the world doesn't come with temporalities already assigned, and that a process of delineating or ordering is involved. She argues that in the United States there is an "allegiance to modernity" (2002: 108), consigning past styles, identities, and the older generation itself to "backwardness."[8] Her goal is to upset such narratives of progress through a less unilinear understanding of temporality. For example, she focuses on the figure of the Old Butch in lesbian lore as a way of examining how historical consciousness becomes "anchored" in bodies which "become integral to the production of gender" (107). In contemporary lesbian narratives, the "Old Butch enters as a living fossil, less dinosaur than one of those mysteriously still extant creatures like the dragonfly or the opossum that have managed to endure since antiquity while others have gone the way of time" (107). While the fact of the Old Butch's continuing existence is seen by young, contemporary modern lesbians as an anachronism, Weston argues that we need a much more fluid concept of historical temporality to evade the flattening of history, as well as the elisions of memory by modernity's stark contrast between the contemporary and those that represent the "discredited" past.[9]

Some anthropologists have argued in a similar vein that we need to think of the present not as an even temporal plane, as it was conceived in earlier generations of functionalist, structuralist, symbolic, and interpretive anthropology.[10] Instead, the present is a palimpsest, displaying multiple layers of different temporal processes and different temporal understandings. This was a view that, to Sutton, as he continued his research on history and memory in Greece, seemed more and more appealing. While taught as a graduate student to see the present moment as temporally *systematic*, he began to increasingly recognize the different temporal trajectories of various aspects of the "present" in Greece. He contrasted, for example, two food traditions on the island of Kalymnos: the use of tomatoes to make sauces for most staple dishes, and the use of boiled wheat (*kollivo*) for memorial ceremonies for the dead. While both were vital aspects of the present, considered longstanding traditions, the latter had been practiced (of course in changing forms) for over 2000 years, and the former for less than 200. Such disjunctures were apparent in all aspects of life, as the Kalymnian islanders often recognized. For example, they recognized that their local dialect, while containing many words from Turkish and Italian occupations of the island over the past 600 years, also contained verb forms from Ancient Greek that were no longer part of standard modern Greek. Language, once again, is an illustration *par excellence* of ideas about polytemporality.

Other anthropologists have also explored and theorized similar notions about time. C. Nadia Seremetakis, also working in Greece, suggests that we conceive of this phenomenon as the "non-contemporaneity of the social formation with itself." She argues that social change does not occur all at once; some things change, while others remain the same (a very different view from the structuralist assumption that changes necessarily alter the entire system). This unevenness "preserves and produces non-synchronous, interruptive articles, spaces, acts and narratives" (1994: 12). Combining metaphors from linguistics and archaeology, she suggests the need to excavate these multiple layerings of the present, or to provide an etymology of the present. Bruno Latour (1993: 75) similarly argues for such multiple temporalities, or polytemporality as part of every society, even if modern Westerners try to deny this, labeling the "exceptions" as backwards or anachronistic. He writes:

> I may use an electric drill, but I also use a hammer. The former is thirty-five years old, the latter hundreds of thousands. Will you see me as a DIY expert "of contrasts" because I mix up gestures from different times? On the contrary: show me an activity that is homogeneous from the point of view of … modern time. Some of my genes are 500 million years old, others 3 million, others 100,000 years, and my habits range in age from a few days to several thousand years.

Michael Taussig also suggests that the present has this quality of multiple temporalities; although we may not be consciously aware of them, they continue in the use of words and gestures with complex histories:

> The tongue remembers, but you do not. Life moves on while all around you lie the traces of lost eras, active in the present, hanging on the wall, covering the windows, not to mention the couch on which you sit or the dress you will wear tonight. *Damask.* My dictionary exudes 15th through 19th centuries meanings:

the color of Damask Rose; the color attributed to a woman's cheeks; a blush; rose-water distilled from Damascus roses; a rich silk fabric woven with elaborate designs and figures ... (2008: 4)

We have already seen how this notion of polytemporality plays out in the language of TBL. But it also helps us understand some of the larger thematic elements of the film. Film and Cultural Studies scholars have pointed to an apparent contradiction: the Coen brothers are mixing movie genres from different times and different films, while at the same time insisting that they set TBL in a particular historical moment, 1991, on the eve of the First Gulf War (Williams 2001: 11–12; Martin-Jones 2006: 136 ff.). This is only contradictory, however, within the standard view that particular times are synchronic wholes. This perception of historical purity and homogeneity also explains the compulsive attempt in movies set in a particular period to get all the details historically accurate and to avoid anachronisms. This is also the view promoted by TV shows, such as VH1's *We Are The 80s*, which suggest that each year and decade can be characterized and condensed not just into a few top songs and musical styles, but into the commodities and other styles remembered as new at that time. Weston refers to this phenomenon as "the packaging of U.S. history into decades, the better to retail all manner of retro styles and nostalgia" (2002: 110). In such a view, there is no room for multiple temporalities, except as throwbacks to the things left behind by modernity's advance. TBL captures a very different view, in which the present is made up of multiple, coexisting characters, period details, and architectural styles representing different time trajectories. It is true that at times characters attempt to place each other definitively in the past: Big tells The Dude, "Your revolution is over, Mr. Lebowski! Condolences! The bums lost!" and the police chief intones at The Dude, "What are you, some kind of sad-assed refugee from the fucking Sixties?" Even The Dude himself tells Walter in frustration: "You're living in the fucking past." The characters partake in what Weston describes as modernity's obsession with "then" and "now" temporalities and claims of "progress." However, the "present" enacted by TBL is considerably more complex. Just as language is polytemporal in TBL, suggesting multiple, coexisting time frames (as opposed to, say, films that stress their adherence to *current* slang, e.g. *Dude, Where's My Car?*), so for the characters, props, and backgrounds of the movie. At any given time, 1960s burnouts coexist with Reaganite Republicans, Vietnam vets with techno-pop artists, even old cowboys with "Sam Spade" gumshoes. While much of The Dude's character and apartment refer to the late 1960s (including the poster of Nixon bowling), the

Googie architecture refers to the 1950s (Comer 2005), while the Beach Blanket Bingo scene at Jackie Treehorn's house echoes the early 1960s. Once again, it is not simply that different characters stand for different eras, but different characters blend eras and exhibit different temporal trajectories. As the directors note, TBL is "set ... very precisely in 1991 ... All the characters refer to the culture of thirty years ago, they are its aftermath and its mirror... It's a contemporary movie about what's become of people who were formed and defined by that earlier period" (cited in Kazecki 2008: 157).

Walter, for example, uses his experience in Vietnam as a constant reference; one could say that he *represents* the 1970s. But he also corrects The Dude for using the word Chinaman: "Chinaman is not the preferred, uh ... Asian-American, please," thus drawing from the so-called politically correct discourse of the time in which the movie is set. Walter is also deeply insistent on his adopted Jewish faith. In response to The Dude's criticism of him, Walter responds: "Three thousand years of beautiful tradition, from Moses to Sandy Koufax—*You're goddamn right I live in the past!*" Walter fits perfectly the notion of polytemporality: some of his habits are a few days old, some 20 years old, some 3,000 years old. And the seeming contradictions in his gender postures reflect these different temporal trajectories: the Rambo-like Vietnam vet, the fan of the 1960s show *Branded*, the devout Jewish-Catholic, the cringing ex-husband and dog-minder, the defender of rules and ideologies. All of these aspects mix uneasily but believably in Walter.

POLYTEMPORAL, NON-HEGEMONIC MASCULINITIES

The concept of polytemporality, finally, illuminates one aspect of TBL given much attention by Film and Cultural Studies scholars: the portrayal of gender. The goal here has been to determine the relation of TBL to dominant masculinity models in earlier Hollywood films and in U.S. society more generally (see, especially, Cornwall and Lindisfame 1994; Kazecki 2008; Martin and Renegar 2007). Cornwall and Lindisfarne (1994: 3), for example, argue that hegemonic masculinities in different societies "define successful ways of 'being a man'; in so doing, they define other masculine styles as inadequate or inferior." They suggest that comparative analysis can reveal the "diversity of meanings" of masculinity, so that "the idea of 'being a man' can no longer be treated as fixed or universal ... [but, rather,] fluid and situational" (Cornwall and Lindisfarne 1994: 3).

Elizabeth Traube's analysis of 1980s Hollywood movies, discussed in the Introduction, is also germane here, as she shows the way in which dominant masculinities are reinforced (if not without contradiction) in these films. Indeed, she suggests that these movies are obsessed with questions of manhood, that they amount to a project of "remasculinization in the wake of the Vietnam War," while at the same time recognizing "competing versions of manhood and specific audiences of men, differentiated by class, race and generation" (Traube 1992: 19). She shows, for example, how the Rambo films exploit a white, working-class resentment (the same resentment played on by Reagan) of a middle-class elite that had "feminized" the nation with its values of abstraction, rationality; its use of language to hide "reality;" and a passivity or non-violence that restrained American men from "winning" in Vietnam (Traube 1992: 49 ff.). Other 1980s films, in Traube's analysis, serve to redeem the masculinity of the "creative class" of managers and aspiring younger generation capitalists (e.g. *Nothing in Common, Ferris Bueller's Day Off*).

Traube's anthropological contribution is to draw on Lévi-Straussian myth analysis in revealing the tensions and mythical reincorporation of oppositions (she notes how Rambo and other male heroes in these movies—*Mr. Mom*, for example—often incorporate the feminine into their masculinities, obviating the need for women). But despite these contradictions and tensions, Traube's argument suggests that there is indeed a dominant, or at least several competing dominant, masculinities at play in these texts. The same could be said for the movies we analyze in this book: the generational drama of sons and fathers and racial healing in *Field of Dreams;* the class conflict between the masculinity models of Quint and Hooper, mythically resolved in the character of Brody in *Jaws*; or the concrete *vs.* abstract masculinities represented by Don Corleone and Michael in *The Godfather.* The fairly muted critique of capitalism in all of these films could be fruitfully seen in terms of a Traubian analysis of dominant masculinities and their ethnic, racial, and class-based dimensions.

By contrast, in TBL we enter new terrain. Here, there is no dynamic of dominant and alternate masculinities, but, rather, a polyphony of multiple masculinities that are each set up to be definitively knocked down. The film is certainly full of men threatening the masculinity of other men: from the opening scene in which one of the thugs pees on The Dude's rug, to bowling rival Jesus Quintana's boasts that he will "fuck you in the ass," to The Dude's ubiquitous castration fears (shown in his dreams, as well as in the prevalence of large scissors in Maude Lebowski's art work), and epitomized in the Nihilists' promise to "cut off your Johnson." Each of these threats, however, rings hollow. Quintana is revealed as a pedophile who must walk through his neighborhood giving door-to-door apologies, while the Nihilists are shown up as cringing weaklings, crying "It's not fair" in the final confrontation scene. More significantly, characters that appear to make claims to manliness are also fully revealed in all of their vulnerability. Donnie is the best bowler on the team, but otherwise portrayed as sickly and an object of scorn for Walter and The Dude, who are constantly telling him to "shut the fuck up."

Walter is another good example. His over-the-top commitment to rules leads him to pull a gun on a competitor for crossing the line while bowling, which suggests that he is a typical male action-hero, steeped in the lore of Vietnam, and nostalgic for the kind of up-close violence that we saw in *The Godfather*. As he says at one point, "I had an M16, Jacko', not an Abrams fucking tank. Just me and Charlie, man, eyeball to eyeball." Walter also draws on President Bush Sr.'s boast to "draw a line in the sand," and pushes The Dude to seek retribution for his peed-on rug. It is Walter who destroys what he mistakenly thinks is Larry Seller's new car with a baseball bat, screaming "This is what happens when you fuck a stranger in the ass!" He comes closest to an unrestrained, Rambo-like masculinity of action based on presumably justified revenge. However, Walter's schemes almost always misfire; hence he is a failed action hero. Moreover, his vulnerability is constantly on display, particularly in his relation to his ex-wife. He still nominally practices Judaism, even if his conversion was apparently at his ex-wife's behest, and he cares for his ex-wife's lap dog while she goes on vacation with her new boyfriend. Indeed, his attack on Smokey for going "over the line" seems like an attempt to reestablish his manhood after explaining why he has to look after his ex's dog. Walter himself breaks the proper rules of masculine conduct by attacking the crippled Big Lebowski and biting the ear off of one of the nihilists (a reference to Mike Tyson's boxing infraction (Kazecki 2008: 155), and by displaying a sensitivity—about The Dude's rug, about the use of the term "Asian American" rather than "Chinaman"—not typically associated with aggressive masculinity.

Finally, the Big Lebowski is shown as a paragon of a certain type of productive manhood: he is *Big*, after all, as well as rich, and living in a mansion with a trophy wife. He excoriates The Dude's unproductive laziness, while touting his own accomplishments, "challenges met, competitors bested, obstacles overcome ... I've accomplished more than most men, and without the use of my legs." However, since he is in a wheelchair, it is suggested that he is impotent (Williams 2001: 8). It also turns out that he has inherited (not earned) his fortune, which his daughter manages for him. Each male character in TBL displays such contradictions. The Dude himself, as most critics have noted, is an anti-hero, seemingly most in control in his cool and smug responses to authority and power (getting his head dunked in a toilet or being lectured by the police captain). Otherwise, he is passive throughout the film; "he is always one step behind his counterparts" (Kazecki 2008: 151), only acting through the promptings of others (Big, Maude, Walter). He's constantly getting peed on, or fearing castration, and his one sexual "conquest" turns out to have been planned by Maude so that she could become pregnant. Even his signature drink of choice is feminizing: the White Russian, "with its hint of sugar and mother's milk" (Tyree and Walters 2007: 60). Similarly, the Cowboy's seeming paragon of masculinity from the past is also undercut by his choice of sarsaparilla rather than alcohol, and his focus on aesthetics ("I like your style, Dude") which some critics have interpreted as a sexual come-on (Tyree and Walters 2007).

The only characters in TBL depicted consistently as typically masculine are the women: Bunny, who seems to know how to get what she wants, and Maude, who is portrayed as always in control, who takes pleasure in using the word "vagina," and who "exploits" The Dude so that she can get pregnant (cf. Tyree and Walters 2007: 75 ff.). Thus, TBL shows us a world of post-dominant masculinities, a world where the ambiguities and contradictions of the "Men's Movement," hinted at in the earlier films we discussed, are now on full display. This is a world where gender is performed from one context to the next, and characters constantly struggle with the question of "What makes a man?" (as the Big Lebowski asks The Dude). The airy abstraction that the Big Lebowski offers—"Is it being prepared to do the right thing? Whatever the price?"—seems much less convincing than The Dude's response: "That, and a pair of testicles." But this is not essentialism. (Later, when The Dude worries about the Nihilists' threat to cut off his "Johnson," Donnie responds, "What do you need that for, Dude?") Rather, it suggests that men are simply those with testicles, that masculinity itself is not only "situational and fluid" in Cornwall and Lindisfarne's terms, but is basically impossible to define, rather than some performed abstraction on display in TBL. In fact, keeping with our discussion of language in this chapter, we would argue that the pastiche of polytemporal references to masculine styles undermines the very possibility of a core true masculinity. With so many references to previous masculine styles and posturing on display in TBL, echoing through the filter of past movie and TV references, how can any claim to masculinity not ring hollow? At the same time, there is something profoundly true in TBL's portrayal of a polytemporal world where no Rambo, Reagan, or other figure is made to stand as a synecdoche for the imagined truth of masculinity.

MASCULINITY, POLYTEMPORALITY, AND ... BOWLING

"What the fuck are you talking about?" and "Shut the fuck up, Donnie" act not only as a futile restatement of the dominant linguistic ideology in the face of a reality that clearly escapes it, they are a futile restatement of dominant masculinity models in a film in which each gender performance seems to communicate across different temporalities and to hum with other possibilities, and other possible words, that undercut the gender performance as soon as it is asserted. Just so, the term "Dude" has multiple referents and histories. It seems to have been first used in the late nineteenth century as a challenge to masculinity, as "a pejorative akin to 'city slicker'" (Williams 2001: 7), or a "dandy" (Kiesling 2004: 284). It was linguistically "accelerated," to use Urban's term, in the 1980s by the film *Fast Times at Ridgemont High* (1982), where it became synonymous with "slacker." Indeed, in parallel to the conflict between The Dude and Big, Kiesling argues that the term "dude" developed as a protest against the wealth-accumulating masculinity of Reaganism (2004: 299), and as a term of masculine-cool solidarity.[11]

We would argue that this masculine solidarity provides a kind of anchor amidst the chaos of multiple polytemporal masculinities, and The Dude a kind of stabilizing element. Indeed, it's as if the movie pulls back from the implications of its own insights. In some ways The Dude himself is the least polytemporal character in TBL: from his *Credence Clearwater Revival* tapes, to his signature drink, he surrounds himself with objects that still represent the Sixties and that seemingly suggest that he is, indeed, stuck in the past. He is also the character that seems most befuddled by the language use of others (though he does, as we've shown, adopt many of these phrases which at first confuse him). While The Dude's existence in 1991 is still polytemporal, a reminder, once again, that not everyone *in* the Nineties was *of* the Nineties, his continuity in itself suggests a comforting stability, just as other things that remain unchanged through time can satisfy our desire for continuity.[12]

Critics and fans of the film note the importance of the phrase "The Dude Abides" in the narrator's final lines: "The Dude abides ... I don't know about you, but I take comfort in that. It's good knowin' he's out there, the Dude, takin' 'er easy for all us sinners. Shoosh, I sure hope he makes the finals." "Abide" is another one of those words that sticks out, performatively speaking, especially so closely linked to the final comment about bowling. Its dictionary definition is relevant here: (1) to remain stable or fixed in a state, (2) to continue in place.[13] The word "abide" suggests the comfort that we are to take in the stability of bowling. Interestingly, just a year or so before the Coen brothers filmed TBL, sociologist Robert Putnam published an article entitled "Bowling Alone," using solitary bowling as an image of the possible fraying of U.S. society, the public sphere, and what Putnam described as "social capital"(1995: 65–78).[14] But TBL does not envision such a fate for its characters. Amidst all the miscommunication and "fucking language problem(s)," a state of polytemporality in a society which, unlike San Carlos Apache, does not value temporal ambiguity, the phrase "let's go bowling, Dude" stands as a balm even in the worst of times. The comfort of the bowling alley, surrounded by friends and a set of familiar rules, is held out as a reconciliation similar to that suggested in *Field of Dreams* between Ray and Terence Mann. The Sixties activist (co-author of *the original* Port Huron statement) and the Vietnam vet, an image for two of the many divergent historical trajectories and divergent masculinities that coexist in the present moment, are brought together in a game that involves much clearer lines and simpler rules than baseball (though these lines, too, can be crossed). Bowling, the simple framework of which involves setting them up and knocking them down, in a limited number of combinations, resembles a functionalist ritual, the repetition of which provides the comfort that promises a Durkheimian social glue on a society that would otherwise spin apart in too many divergent directions. Setting them up and knocking them down.

NOTES

1. See http://www.ew.com/ew/gallery/0,,20221982_10,00.html. Accessed April 21, 2008.
2. Martin-Jones (2006) suggests that it is repeated as well by Bush Jr. in the context of the second war in Iraq.
3. Some anthropologists—such as Bloch (2005); Krasniewicz and Blitz (2002); Urban (2001)—might treat this phenomenon with the language of "memes." Krasniewicz and Blitz, for example, trace what they call the meme of Arnold Schwarzenegger through his films, popular culture phrases, viewers' dreams, and metaphor prototypes, arguing that the ability of a meme to "morph" and to detach itself from its original context is key to its replicatory power: "A meme that disconnects from its source but continues to evoke that source becomes, in effect, universally available for situations and expressions unencumbered by its original use but still spreading the meme of its origin" (2002: 37). While we share sympathy with this approach, we fear that the language of memes carries too much additional baggage and tends to treat culture as individual units completely detachable from the larger context in which they circulate.
4. Urban's discussion is part of a larger argument which makes a basic distinction between oral "cultures of tradition" and written "cultures of modernity" (Urban 2001). We have difficulty with this distinction, finding it too close to the problematic Lévi-Straussian notion of "hot" and "cold" societies.

5. As Samuels develops this argument, he shows that music works in similar ways, through "feelingful iconicity" to evoke past times.

6. For reviews of some of this vast literature, see Cole (2006).

7. William Ayers, a staple of the 2008 presidential campaign because of his activities in the Weather Underground and alleged "ties" to Barack Obama, illustrates the concern to be associated with contemporaneity rather than with the past. Commenting on the media's association of him with "'60s radicals," he exclaimed: "I am so much a guy of right now. OK, I lived in the '60s. I apologize" (Overby 2008).

8. Once again, this echoes Latour's argument that "Modernizing progress is thinkable only on condition that all the elements that are contemporary according to the calendar belong to the same time. For this to be the case, these elements have to form a complete and recognizable cohort... This beautiful order is disturbed once the quasi-objects [i.e., mixed temporalities; see below] are seen as mixing up different periods ... or genres... Then a historical period will give the impression of a great hotchpotch" (1993: 73).

9. We are simplifying a more complex argument about the relationship of gender, temporality, and political economy, for which we refer the reader to Weston's complete text (2002).

10. Many anthropologists have insisted on this singular, flat temporality to combat what they fear is the "Othering" of non-Westerners, that is, consigning *contemporary* hunter-gatherers, or even Western rural peasants, Muslims or other groups, to an earlier stage of human history (see Fabian 1981). However, this is a problem only insofar as we don't recognize that *all groups and all individuals* are polytemporal, as Latour argues.

11. Key accelerators here would be the TV show *Teenage Mutant Ninja Turtles* and films, such as *Dude, Where's My Car?*

12. Annette Weiner (1991) has analyzed what she calls *inalienable possessions,* those objects which endure and come to represent stability and continuity, and indeed the identity of a group. Sutton has argued elsewhere that inalienable possession plays an important role in families through their inheritance and their representation of continuity (Sutton and Hernandez 2007). While The Dude's possessions (the rug, the Credence Clearwater Revival tapes) can be seen in this light, we are also suggesting that The Dude himself is a kind of inalienable possession for fans of TBL.

13. *Webster's New Collegiate Dictionary* (1979), Springfield, MA: G & C Merriam.

14. As Putnam puts it, "The most whimsical yet discomfiting bit of evidence of social disengagement in contemporary America that I have discovered is this: more Americans are bowling today than ever before, but bowling in organized leagues has plummeted in the last decade or so... The broader social significance ... lies in the social interaction and even occasionally civic conversations over beer and pizza that solo bowlers forgo" (1995: 70).

5 *THE VILLAGE*: EGALITARIANISM AND THE POLITICAL ANTHROPOLOGY OF THE POSSIBLE

> It is not that we are somehow opposed to the idea of the "common good" but that we are just not sure that such a thing could work in practice without creating pernicious consequences
>
> Christopher M. Duncan (2005: 49)

> Basically, if you're not a utopianist, you're a schmuck—Jonothon Feldman
> (cited in Graeber 2004: 1)

What might it be like to live in a society without leaders or vast inequalities of wealth and power? How would such a society be organized? After the Revolution, will we still have nightmares?

Questions such as these are not much part of mainstream, popular discourse in the early years of the twenty-first century, a time when progressive thinking seems to embrace the pragmatic rather than the utopian, and imaginations are geared more toward undoing the destruction to the environment, economy or healthcare system that the past 30 years have wrought. Times like these might make even thinking that another world is possible seem frivolous or worse. Anthropologists might have a different take on this question, however, as anthropology has consistently expanded ideas of what is possible in human social organization. How might these issues play out in considering a mainstream movie that confronts us with "another world"?

In previous chapters we have argued that the popularity of certain movies makes them ripe for a cultural analysis—that if they fascinate, they can tell us something about the wider issues at stake for the people whom they fascinate. In this chapter we come at the film *The Village* (2004) from a different direction. M. Night Shyamalan, writer and director of critically and commercially successful films like *The Sixth Sense* and *Signs,* released *The Village* in 2004 to lukewarm, sometimes even hostile, responses from critics and moviegoers.[1] *The Village* stands out as the least popular of the films discussed in this book, making it seem strange as a choice for an analysis of blockbusters. But box-office failures and blockbusters are flip sides of the same coin; both can tell us something about American society. We are going to make the case that the relative failure of *The Village* reveals a certain set of American assumptions about small-scale societies, assumptions that were out of sync with this movie's premises. Given that few would doubt that movies often ask us to imagine other worlds of possibility (Caughey 1984), we argue that previous reviews of *The Village* reveal the ways that alternative political and social possibilities are imagined in the contemporary United States.

We should disclose at the outset that we *liked* this movie. As anthropologists, perhaps this is not surprising, given that the subject of *The Village* is, indeed, a village, the classical site of anthropological research. We believe this setting makes the film useful ground for an anthropological perspective.

SYNOPSIS

The movie is seemingly set in the late-nineteenth century, in a small community founded by refugees from "the towns." The inhabitants have left the towns because of the greed, violence, and individualism that they and their families witnessed there. In the opening scene, the village has been hit by the death of a young child, but otherwise people's concerns focus on everyday matters and young love is in the air. They gather communally for an outdoor dinner, at tables weighed down with food, where one of the village elders, Edward Walker (William Hurt), offers a "grace," to no particular god: "Thank you for this time we have been given."

Hurt's words sound more like a plea, however, as shortly afterward we hear a howl coming from the woods, the sounds of "Those We Don't Speak Of": menacing creatures, apparently living in the woods, who have reached a stand-off with the villagers, neither side trespassing into the other's land. The boundary is marked by color: the creatures' totemic color is red (violence), the villagers' yellow (fear).

Any sign of redness is removed from the village. The boundary is tested by villagers straying into the woods or by boys daring each other to go near the woods at night. But more recently the creatures have begun, it seems, to make incursions into the village, leaving small dead animals in their wake.

Although it is not clear at the beginning who the protagonist is, there are a number of characters of particular importance. Edward has two daughters, both budding young women: Kitty (Judy Greer), who seems carefree and frivolous in comparison to her more serious and intense sister, Ivy (Bryce Dallas Howard). Ivy is blind, but this does not seem to impede her self-confidence, or stop her from taking a leading role in educating the village children. She is in love with an intense young villager, Lucius Hunt (Joaquin Phoenix), and good friends with a mentally handicapped man named Noah (Adrien Brody), who also has feelings for her. When, in an act of jealous rage, Noah stabs Lucius, Ivy must test her love by breaching village rules to retrieve medicine from the forbidden "towns" and save Lucius's life.

At this point the major twist is revealed: the towns, it turns out, are actually the contemporary United States, and we are not in the nineteenth century. The villagers are living amidst a huge nature preserve in the Pennsylvania woods, bought and paid for by Edward Walker's father, with guards to make sure that no stray nature seeker from the twenty-first century stumbles into this hidden village. The evil creatures were invented by the village elders dressed in fancy costumes: "We have met the enemy and he is us," in the words of the classic comic strip *Pogo*. The elders had their own memories of the violence of the towns, having met through a support-group for relatives of murder victims. However, their children, born in the village, had not experienced violence firsthand. The elders invented the creatures in order to provide their children with a visceral experience of violence that would lead them to reject any desire to abandon the village and go to the towns.

OUT OF SYNC

This film—and the final twist, in particular—often provoked bitter disappointment among critics and viewers. So what went wrong? Why did a film created by talented actors and an accomplished director not only fail to make it to blockbuster status, but actually stir up hostility? And what can this tell us about American culture?

We believe that the relative unpopularity of *The Village* was rooted in Americans' "either/or" conceptions of small-scale societies. In the popular imagination, such societies are either charming, harmonious communities, or cauldrons of repression and narrow thinking. Popular images of small-scale societies come in two sizes: happy, peaceful communities, as in the Garden of Eden, or backward hell-holes, as in Thomas Hobbes's "war of all against all," the Salem witch trials, and Shirley Jackson's short story *The Lottery* (Suraf 2004). The basic problem was that Shyamalan's movie didn't conform to either side of this binary opposition. Instead, it presented a considerably more complex image, one much closer to what anthropologists have found in studies of actual small-scale societies. The movie presented a small-scale society that is peaceful and cooperative, but, at the same time, plagued by violence and social control. Due to their cultural conceptions, viewers were not prepared to have it both ways.

Critics were especially disappointed by the creatures of the woods, "Those We Don't Speak Of." Both positive and negative reviews noted that the allegorical nature of the film could be taken in multiple directions, but the overwhelming tendency was to read it as a post-9/11 story about what happens when you control people through fear (i.e., with the creatures). One reviewer points to the overlap in leaders' names: Walker, the name of a town elder, is also the middle name of then President George W. Bush. This reviewer says, "...the film depicts a loss of civil liberties, irrational fears, a phony red-alert monster and unilateralism," and refers to the elders' use of the creatures as "Orwellian fearmongering" (PFS Film Review 2004). Reviewer Jeff Overstreet notes, "... *The Village* explores the way that the Powers That Be exploit fears in order to keep their people in line," though he suggests that the village itself might be taken to represent "the Christian church, a political party, a lifestyle, a family, America, or humanity in general."[2] Patrick Collier, in a scholarly consideration of the narrative structuring of the film, comes to a similar conclusion: "*The Village* places its viewers in the position of deceived citizens, allows us to recognize the deception, then asks us to consider whether, all things considered, we really want to know, or would be happier living in a protected ignorance carefully sustained by a power elite" (Collier 2008: 273). Collier further argues that democracy is a sham in the village, covering over the "benign dictatorship" of Edward Walker (2008: 286). Another reviewer is less nuanced, referring to the inhabitants of the village as "xenophobes ... neurotics, psychotics and otherwise imbalanced folks ... led by elders who apparently swam in the same gene pool that burped up Jim Jones and David Koresh" (Anderson 2004).

Most reviewers, then, saw these creatures as an intolerable form of social control by which the elders duped the younger generation into staying in the village. The premise of these criticisms seems to be this: with so many social problems solved, why is the Village still plagued by "Those We Don't Speak Of"? After all, why would one even need such an ideology of Otherness in an egalitarian society? After the "revolution," wouldn't everyone simply accept the superiority of the utopia they had constructed?

At first glance, you wouldn't think images of social control would be so objectionable, since *every* society, even a "democratic individualistic" one like the U.S., employs various means of social control to influence the behavior of its members. In the U.S. such means include the education system, organized religion, the police and penal system, the mass media, and the various layers of government. There are also government organizations, such as the CIA, FBI and the NSA, which monitor and influence all sorts of legitimate citizen activities, and have done so consistently throughout the post-Second World War period. Finally, there are ideologies that identify particular evils, either within the society or threatening it from outside: communists, terrorists, and extremists of various stripes. By comparison, "Those We Don't Speak Of" seem rather quaint and mild. So what's the problem?

Granted, part of the anger here derives from Shyamalan's failure to conform to a certain genre expectation about the form that must be taken by such plot twists. But we would argue that the main problem is that the complexities of *The Village* do not conform to popular conceptions of utopia. Utopia has been seen as the inverse of the corrupt, unequal society, a "state of nature" for Rousseau, where the "goodness of man" could be expressed, or as a withering away of the state in Marx, where each would give according to his abilities and take according to his needs. Most Western utopian thinking has been romantic in its insistence that the current social order can and will be replaced by a close-to-perfect society, where the unconscious, or the mythic world, reflects the tangible everyday world. There are no bad dreams in Marx's communist society or Rousseau's state of nature. The problem was *The Village* violated these expectations; it was plagued with bad dreams: "Those We Don't Speak Of."

Even worse, *The Village* violated notions of the Garden of Eden. In fact, utopian images of the future society, such as Marx's vision, are often rooted in this ur-text. One of the great ironies of intellectual history is that Marx saw himself as a rational scientist opposed to religion, which he famously called the "opiate of the masses," yet he created a theory that replicated Christian millenarianism. In Marx's vision, the second coming will be a secular return to first times, the state of equality that existed in the age of hunter-gatherers—in other words, the Garden of Eden, before people were tainted by knowledge of private property, exploitation, and other sins.

But you don't have to read Marx or Rousseau, or practice Judaism or Christianity, to envision utopia with biblical undertones. Edenic imagery has been especially important in structuring the way Americans see small-scale societies—hence the romanticized imagery that most foreign tourism is built on. While some of this imagery has been corrected with more complicated notions, the urge to see other societies as Gardens of Eden persists, and for good reason: it satisfies a longing to escape the alienation of Western society.

The contemporary importance of the Garden of Eden template can be seen, for example, in *The Gods Must be Crazy* (2004 [1980]). This film conforms to popular notions of utopia and, partly for that reason, has enjoyed tremendous popular success. It romantically (and inaccurately) portrays the !Kung as living in pure harmony, without any private property or conflict. The narrator flatly states, "They must be the most contented people in the world. They have no crime, no punishment, no violence, no laws ... no police, judges, rulers or bosses." This idyllic state suddenly changes, though, when a Coke bottle gets dropped on !Kung territory by a white man flying overhead in an airplane. As a coveted object, "a real labor-saving device," the bottle leads the !Kung into conflict for the first time. The Coke bottle is clearly a symbol for Western technology and consumerism, but also something else deeply resonant in American culture: the apple and the serpent that gave Adam and Eve knowledge of sin and got them expelled from the Garden of Eden. In fact, before the Coke bottle's arrival, the !Kung didn't even view snakes as bad, as the narrator explains: "They believe that the gods put only good and useful things on the earth for them. In this world of theirs, nothing is bad or evil. Even a poisonous snake is not bad. You just have to keep away from the sharp end. Actually, a snake is very good. In fact, it's delicious. And the skin makes a fine pouch." After the Coke bottle arrives, though, the !Kung start to use the bottle to cure snake skin, and fighting ensues, because there's only one bottle to go around. In other words, the Coke bottle, like the snake and apple in the Garden of Eden, ruins everything.

The tremendous success of this film against all odds—we can't think of another popular film starring African hunter-gatherers—must be partly attributed to the way it conforms to the familiar story of the Garden of Eden.[3] By contrast, *The Village* asked viewers to engage with a more complicated story of small-scale society, and thereby put itself at a disadvantage.

As if all this weren't bad enough, *The Village* violated fundamental American notions of power, which are based on the assumption that every society needs a state government or other central organized authority. Americans have been raised in a nation-state system and take the presence of a state for granted. When asked what rites of passage make one an adult in American society, college students most often point to state-run "rituals," such as getting a driver's license, voting for the first time, graduating from high school—in other words, having the government grant them certain adult privileges (Wogan 2004b: 3). The state gives and takes, like God or your parents. This state-centered perspective makes it hard to imagine what life might be like for those without central government.

To put all this in perspective, we will examine what anthropologists have actually found when looking at small-scale societies without a central state. Such findings contain remarkable similarities with *The Village*, and since anthropologists, even after a century of professional existence, have been largely unsuccessful in communicating these findings to a general public, they will give some sense of what *The Village* was up against, why it was so out of sync with public expectations.

POWER IN THE VILLAGE

The most striking thing about the community depicted in *The Village* is that it is egalitarian; there is very little power to go around, and no sources of authority outside of the council of elders. This society is radically different from the U.S.

While individual families seem to own their homes, there is no division of labor in the village, no one works for anyone else, and much of the labor, such as preparing the village-wide meal, seems to be collectively shared. Also, there is no money, nor social classes, nor any identifiable gender hierarchy. The council of elders is divided equally between men and women, and there are none of the restrictions on women's speech, movement, or behavior that typify most systems of small-scale gender inequality. Women on the council take a leading role in discussions and decisions, and do not defer to men, or even to the founder of the town, Edward Walker. There are no elected officials or political parties. The one authority in the village, the council of elders, has no more than an advisory role; this council neither metes out punishment nor makes laws, as is shown in a scene in which Lucius, with considerable contrition, admits to having breached the boundary and gone into the woods. Mentally disturbed Noah shakes his finger excitedly at Lucius and shouts, "Punished!" But, in fact, the council of elders does not rebuke Lucius, and Walker comforts him, suggesting he should not feel guilty; indeed, he praises him for his bravery. Thus, the village might be considered a gerontocracy. But of what sort? In an elaborated gerontocracy, which is often accompanied by male dominance, older men control the resources of the community, and may even control the availability of marriageable women (Meillasoux 1981). This is clearly not the case in *The Village*, where the elders have no special monopoly of resources, nor any power to enforce their decisions. There is no institutionalized system of punishment or jail, apart from the "quiet room" for children (and Noah).

Nor do elders determine their children's marriage choices. We are led to understand that marriage is not a social strategy as it is in many class-based societies where nuptials are arranged for the purposes of forming alliances between families or for class mobility. Here, Kitty simply seeks out the approval of her father, who offers advice but defers to her choices.[4] If we call this a gerontocracy, it is only of the mildest sort, with elders assumed to have more wisdom than the young, but only exercising it in an advisory capacity.

Perhaps most striking, given the resemblance in dress and diction of the members of the village to an early American community, no church exists in the village. Notwithstanding scenes of marriage and funerals, there is no church building. We don't even see evidence of a religious ideology. No one talks about sin, although characters do discuss the importance of controlling their feelings. Nor is there a clergy that restricts the behavior of women in the village (Walker himself is a teacher), another typical source of inequality in many societies.

In short, there is no organizational hierarchy in any recognizable sense in the village. Given the usual two choices, the village has clearly gone the way of the Garden of Eden (at least in the early scenes), rather than the "war of all against all." So how does this village compare with anthropological studies of actual egalitarian societies?

ANTHROPOLOGICAL STUDIES OF EGALITARIAN SOCIETIES

Much of the anthropological literature on egalitarian societies actually parallels the village of Shyamalan's imagination. For example, in Eleanor Leacock's classic account (1981) of the Montagnais-Naskapi, a Native-American group in Canada's Labrador Peninsula, we see the crucial importance of the principle of autonomy or freedom from control of individuals by leaders. As much as there were leaders among the Montagnais-Naskapi, they tended to have minimal power. The chiefs were good talkers, but had no formal power. All of this is thoroughly documented in the diaries of seventeenth-century French Jesuit missionaries who were trying to convert the Montagnais-Naskapi. One Jesuit, Father LeJeune, described the situation as follows:

> They [the Montagnais-Naskapi] imagine that they ought by right of birth, to enjoy the liberty of wild ass colts, rendering no homage to anyone whomsoever, except when they like. They have reproached me a hundred times because we fear our Captains, while they laugh at and make sport of theirs. All the authority of their chief is in his tongue's end; for he is powerful only insofar as he is eloquent; and, even if he kills himself talking and haranguing, he will not be obeyed unless he pleases the Savages. (cited in Leacock 1981: 49)[5]

The Montagnais-Naskapi were further characterized by a flexible division of labor, with male and female roles loosely structured around hunting and childcare. But women could join in with hunting, and men could perform childcare. Public and private spheres were not distinct; there was little sense of men going out to work, and women staying home to perform household chores. Leacock (1981: 133) sums up her research in a way that could be used to describe Shyamalan's village as well: "…economic dependency linked the individual directly with the group as a whole … and … decisions were made by and large by those who would be carrying them out."

Similarly, while there is some gender ideology in the village—Ivy asks Lucius if it bothers him that she is a "tomboy," and it is the boys who dare each other to go near the woods—this ideology does not translate into male authority. Women on the village council are not only shown debating men; they mete out the council's decisions to the villagers. And it is Ivy, of course, who braves the woods, while her male companions are too afraid and turn back.

Another example of a strongly egalitarian society is the Inupiat of Alaska, documented by anthropologist Barbara Bodenhorn. Believing that larger structures of authority are the result of authoritarian family relations, they have constructed a society where biological parents have little sense of authority or "ownership" over children. Thus, children are allowed to decide, from the age of about five, whether to continue to live with their parents, or be "adopted" by a family that they feel more suited to: "Individuals are free to move within families as well as across space, preventing interdependent actors from becoming dependent relatives" (Bodenhorn 2000: 146).

Among the !Kung San of South Africa, Richard Lee discovered that all food is shared among the group, no matter who has hunted it (gathered food is generally shared less widely). However, the !Kung recognize the possibility that some hunters may be better than others, so they deliberately insult each hunter's offering to the group: "...we ... speak of his meat as worthless. This way we cool his heart and make him gentle" (Lee 1998: 30). In all of these examples, structures of authority that we take for granted in the United States and other Western societies are brought into question by societies that value individual autonomy to a much greater degree.[6]

Finally, many of these societies are able to fulfill human needs without a grinding regimen of labor typical of modern "time-poor" societies. Marshall Sahlins playfully dubbed this "the original affluent society," arguing that it lacked notions of scarcity deeply embedded in the contemporary West, and thus did not produce society members condemned to the unhappy lot of having desires that will always outstrip their means: "It is not simply that hunters and gatherers have curbed their materialistic 'impulses'; they simply never made an institution of them" (Sahlins 1972: 13–14).[7] Instead, they can satisfy their wants with relative ease, leaving much more time for social pursuits. Similarly, while there are certain desires that must be controlled in *The Village* (discussed below), characters are not shown as dissatisfied with their material circumstances, nor do they display any wish to acquire material possessions or to raise their status through acquisition. They are, as Sahlins put it, spared the "ordained tragedy, with man the prisoner at hard labor of a perpetual disparity between his unlimited wants and his insufficient means" (1972: 1).

In sum, this village closely resembles the egalitarian societies that anthropologists have studied. Given these similarities, as well as Americans' tendency to romanticize small-scale societies, it's understandable that *The Village* would call forth expectations of a Garden of Eden, a small isolated community living in harmony, like the !Kung.

Moreover, anthropological findings about the egalitarianism of small-scale societies are likely to have filtered into public consciousness at some level. In fact, anthropologists have often been accused of romanticizing egalitarian societies, and certainly their work has often been interpreted this way by an American audience eager to find what they're looking for in remote tribes. *National Geographic*, a primary vehicle through which Americans have learned about the anthropology of small-scale societies, has certainly promoted this romanticized image of harmonious, traditional societies.[8]

A good example here would be the Tasaday, a small "stone age tribe" that was supposedly discovered for the first time in the early 1970s in the Southern Philippines. They were celebrated as the "gentle Tasaday," and said to be so peaceful that they didn't even have a word for war. Their status as a valid scientific discovery was cemented by anthropologists' publications and photographs in *National Geographic*. Later, the Tasaday were found out to be a hoax, but their rise to fame illustrates the ongoing strength of the Garden of Eden model. As Jean-Paul Dumont argues (1988), the Tasaday were just the latest anthropological instantiation of such images of harmonious tribes, and they had their polar opposite in images of violent, "savage" cultures, including the Vietnamese and Yanomamo of Venezuela. However much anthropologists might resist this binary opposition, it remains a powerful filter through which their work gets viewed.

This either/or view did not prepare the film audience for *The Village*, especially "Those We Don't Speak Of." The public was expecting to see one side or the other of the binary opposition, not both sides in the same society. As noted earlier, critics and viewers were especially disturbed by the creatures in the film, seeing them as negative social control. But it turns out that here, too, the film was actually quite close to empirical anthropological findings about egalitarian societies, though these findings have been much less likely to make it past the Garden of Eden filter.

COUNTERPOWER

David Graeber's book *Fragments of an Anarchist Anthropology* (2004) is particularly useful here, since it synthesizes the findings of a large body of anthropological research on egalitarian societies. Also, his points, though written with other ends in mind, directly address the question of why the villagers need the monsters in the woods.

Graeber frames his argument in terms of "counterpower." In analyses of societies with a strongly hierarchical or unequal power structure, counterpower refers to those small-scale institutions that resist the power of the state to impose its will on the people, such as local self-governing communities, radical labor unions, or revolutionary church movements. Graeber suggests that a parallel exists to these institutions in societies without states or other forms of hierarchical power:

> It [the argument of Marcel Mauss and Pierre Clastres] suggests that counter-power, at least in the most elementary sense, actually exists where the states and markets are not even present; that in such cases, rather than being embodied in popular institutions which pose themselves against the power of lords, or kings, or plutocrats, they are embodied in institutions which ensure such types of person never come about. What it is counter to, then, is a potential, a latent aspect, or dialectical possibility if you prefer, within the society itself.

> This at least would help explain an otherwise peculiar fact; the way in which
> it is often particularly the egalitarian societies which are torn by terrible inner
> tensions, or at least, extreme forms of symbolic violence. (Graeber 2004: 25)

Graeber examines cases from widely divergent parts of the world. The Piaroa of South America, for example, place an enormous value on individual autonomy and "are quite self-conscious about the importance of ensuring that no one is ever at another person's orders." Yet they also see their culture as the creation of "an evil god, a two-headed cannibalistic buffoon" who, along with other "insane, predatory" gods, fights constant invisible battles (Graeber 2004: 26). In other words, egalitarian societies like this generate rich imaginative worlds which are in some ways the inverse of the power situation that actually exists in everyday life. These imaginary worlds work not simply as a functionalist release of tension, but also as a constant reminder of the negative alternatives to society as currently constituted.

Many other such examples could be adduced. Peggy Sanday (2002), for example, describes the Minangkabau of Sumatra, Indonesia, with whom she has lived and carried out fieldwork over a twenty-year period. The Minangkabau are well-known in the anthropological literature for their unusually strong gender egalitarianism (see Blackwood 2000; Tanner 1974). Sanday describes a particular village in west Sumatra where the central value is decision by consensus and there is no concept of domination of one sex by another. Strikingly, there was no violence against women, and not a single case of rape within the village in the past fifty years. Even "roughness" in male behavior was not tolerated. In the single case she recorded of wife abuse, "The problem was resolved by sending the husband back to his mother's house" (Sanday 2002: 239).[9] Yet Sumatran myths and legends, set in the world before the constitution of the current society, describe raw violence and chaos. Myths describe a "male-centered world, entirely absent of women, ruled by death and destruction. The men who inhabit this world are as ugly and unappetizing as anything that can be imagined. Unruly and uncontrolled, they do not steal out of need but merely to attract men's souls from their bodies" (Sanday 2002: 43).

The parallels between what anthropologists like Graeber and Sanday describe and "Those We Don't Speak Of" are remarkable. Cross-culturally, it seems that a relatively peaceful and harmonious society, where power and hierarchy are not allowed to flourish, tends to produce its opposite in a fantasy dreamworld, a constant reminder of why people live this way and what would happen if they didn't.

That the elders in *The Village* control the knowledge of the true nature of the creatures is also consistent with anthropological research on small-scale societies, in which young members do not gain access to the secret knowledge of the group until they are initiated into adulthood. The actual "belief" in this knowledge, or the simple acceptance of it because it serves group purposes, is ambiguous in many societies (Needham 1968; Taussig 1998). This ambiguity is captured in the film in that the creatures are not pure inventions, but are based on legends and rumors long in circulation about the woods. As Edward Walker notes, the actions of Noah Percy "have made our stories real" (see below).

Some romanticization notwithstanding, most anthropologists, living day-to-day in these societies, are generally aware of the stresses and tensions that make up social relations in them.[10] As Barbara Bodenhorn (2000: 143) notes of the egalitarian Inupiat: "It is hard work. Having to construct and reconstruct one's social world on a daily basis can be stressful stuff. People develop ulcers wondering if they are 'getting it right.' But they have no doubt that it is real."

Graeber (2004: 31) makes a compelling argument here, so we cite him at length:

> We suspect all this turbulence stems from the very nature of the human condition. There would appear to be no society which does not see human life as fundamentally a problem. However much they might differ on what they deem the problem to be, at the very least, the existence of work, sex, and reproduction are seen as fraught with all sorts of quandaries; human desires are always fickle; and then there's the fact that we're all going to die. So there's a lot to be troubled by. None of these dilemmas are going to vanish if we eliminate structural inequalities (much though this would radically improve things in just about every other way). Indeed, the fantasy that it might, that the human condition, desire, mortality, can all be somehow resolved seems to be an especially dangerous one, an image of utopia which always seems to lurk somewhere behind the pretensions of Power and the state. Instead, as we've suggested, the spectral violence seems to emerge from the very tensions inherent in the project of maintaining an egalitarian society.

In other words, getting rid of hierarchy does not solve all social and personal problems; tension and conflict seem rooted in the human condition. Some anthropologists have been more focused on conflict than others, but few, if any, would deny that conflict exists at some level. Likewise, one of the village elders who lost his seven-year-old son to disease in the first scene of the movie declares: "Sorrow will always find you" (the villagers have no source of modern medicines such as antibiotics). The villagers are also well aware of the need to make choices, even to suppress certain desires; the fact that the village is not driven by notions of the sinfulness of the flesh does not mean that it is sexually liberated. Pleasure is encouraged, as we see in the community feasting and dances. Even in ordinary chores, there seems a certain joy, as Ivy and her sister practically dance while sweeping the porch of their house. At the same time, control is important: "Sometimes we will not do things we want to do so that others will not know that we want to do them," Ivy intones. Indeed, the love between Ivy's father and Lucius's mother remains unspoken, acknowledged late in the movie but never acted on, since the community comes first. Put simply, there are trade-offs in any society, even the most well-structured. The elders' rejection of capitalism, the state, and modern life and all its inequalities has made the village possible. But the use of the creatures to convince the next generation of the wisdom of their choices is also the source of the tension and conflict that animates the film.

CHANGE AT WORK

The above-cited block quote from Graeber further suggests that *every* society contains the possibility of change, for better or worse.[11] At some point, that nightmare fantasy world may no longer preserve the society, and if unchecked, may contain the seeds of the society's destruction (see also Graeber 2004: 30). Indeed, Shyamalan puts us in the midst of a crisis in the village on a number of levels. One of the elders (or perhaps the disturbed Noah) has been going around at night, in the costume of the creatures, killing small animals and leaving them out to terrorize the villagers, acts which are not authorized by the village council. This "terrorism" fits nicely with the notion of spectral violence, and suggests that gerontocratic control is far from absolute. Indeed, once the scary creatures have been released, they are no longer fully controlled by their creators. As a result, even the elders who know the truth come to fear the consequences of their creation. This could make them careful about how they use it, and thus stop the gerontocracy from becoming less benign.[12]

Much more problematic and critical, however, the first act of violence by one villager against another occurs when a jealous Noah stabs Lucius on hearing of his engagement to Ivy (Noah admits to his crime simply by pointing to his bloody hands and repeating, "Bad color! Bad color!"). As a result of this, Edward Walker must choose whether or not to reveal the true nature of the creatures to his daughter

Ivy so that she can travel to the towns to bring back antibiotics to save Lucius. While this decision is sanctioned by Walker's wife (she insists that Walker himself must not go because he has taken an oath never to return to the town, but implicitly suggests that Ivy, who has not taken it, may go), it raises dissent among the council of elders, partially because it was taken without consulting them, and partially because it flouts the founding rules of the community. Walker's response is that since they have founded the village to avoid the violence of the towns, it would be a crime to let Lucius die unnecessarily. More tellingly, perhaps, he frames his argument in terms of the possibility of the reproduction of the community: "Do you plan to live forever? It is in them that our future lies; it is in Ivy and Lucius that this way of life will continue." He then poses his decision in terms of choice and risk: "Yes, I have risked; I hope I am always able to risk everything for the just and right cause." Note how this impassioned speech contrasts with his silent acknowledgement that he loves Lucius's mother, but will never be able to act on that love. Some passions must be controlled for the greater good. He is, in fact, not willing to "risk everything" for the pursuit of his individual passion for her, even though in reference to Ivy and Lucius he claims that "the world moves for love."

In other words, the perpetuation of an egalitarian community takes as much work as its transformation. Ivy makes the trip to the towns, and, as a result of her encounter with one of "Those We Don't Speak Of" (Noah again, bent on killing her, but who is himself killed) comes back more convinced of the necessity of preserving the village. Just after the elders have confirmed their commitment to continuing the village, Ivy arrives with the medicines and asserts her own commitment to it with a simple "I'm back, Lucius."

The community is shown to be a dynamic entity, a just society that is not self-sustaining or timeless, all of which flies in the face of popular images of "stone-age societies, living outside the flow of history." While the notion that no societies are outside history has become a tenet of contemporary anthropology, the related notion that social reproduction takes as much *work* as social change is counterintuitive and needs to be constantly reemphasized (see Connerton 1990; Sahlins 1985; Sutton 1998).

In this, the film ran up against another bedrock American notion: small, happy societies do not need to change. Once again, the film was closer to anthropological findings than popular images.

SOME POSSIBLE OBJECTIONS AND ALTERNATIVE READINGS

Our analysis is meant to be suggestive, not airtight. Having read other interpretations and shared our analysis with colleagues and friends, we have heard or been led to anticipate several possible objections to our reading.

The first objection is that not everyone can buy a thousand acres of woodlands and then hire guards to make sure that no one goes into their private reserve. While this is obviously true, we would also note that *The Village* is an allegory, not a full-blown political strategy for action in this world. Either way, the image of the private reserve is not as unrealistic as this criticism makes it sound. Many contemporary thinkers imagine confronting state power in the modern world in a similar way. As Graeber suggests, anarchist thinking and political movements have moved away from the more classic radical political thinking by which the oppressed seize power from the state and turn that power to good purposes (the classic dictatorship of the proletariat). Instead, they find more and more ways to act as if this objectionable power were irrelevant to everyday life, forming autonomous communities that do not engage in destroying state power. Compare *The Village* to the movie *V for Vendetta*, which is certainly revolution in the older mold of overthrowing the government by blowing up lots of stuff. By contrast, Graeber suggests that when anarchic experiments are successful, they, like the village, exist off the radar screen of the modern state and its media apparatus. They take multiple forms and do not have to be remote communities located far from the reach of the state (those with which anthropologists are most familiar). They may include experiments in worker-owned factories, direct democracy groups, cooperatives of various sorts, alternate currencies or systems of barter (or "lets"), which can exist in the midst of the most modern urban environments. The state and the media typically ignore the existence of such "anarchic spaces" (Graeber 2004: 83), assuming that if they do exist, they are remote in space and in time, i.e., stone-age communities that remain untouched by the modern world. *The Village* provides a perfect metaphor for such spaces—distanced in space by the forest border and removed in time by playing at being a nineteenth-century community.

A second potential objection to our reading is considerably more serious. Critics ask: why is the village so homogenous? Couldn't this community be built across lines of race and ethnicity? Why not have some African-American families in the village? In other words, these critics say, the village resembles a white, gated community, with all its problems (see, for example, Duncan 2005). We largely agree with this criticism. The village's similarity to a gated community is patently clear: remove the historical costumes and the expansive woods, and this could look like any American gated community. The lack of racial diversity is a serious problem with *The Village*, perhaps a failure of imagination on Shyamalan's part. We can only guess at the justifications he might give. Perhaps he might argue that keeping the village "all white" added to the illusion that this was an early colonial community. But this response does not really seem satisfactory; in its colonial guise, the village could have included Native Americans, and in its nineteenth-century guise, African Americans.[13] The absence of non-white characters remains, we believe, a strong argument for reading *The Village* as an allegory for a contemporary gated community. And while we personally don't like to think of the village this way, we recognize that others may. Again, empirical research is needed, to know where individual viewers place the movie in their own political landscapes.

However, such a reading would also have to deal with major inconsistencies. Above all, if Shyamalan wanted to build "a repressed dystopia"—what one critic compares to *Brave New World*, *Farenheit 451*, and *The Lottery*—why would he create a community that celebrated daily life and ritual occasions, lacked religious dogma, and displayed gender equality clearly out of keeping with any historical models? In other words, if the village has some undertones of a gated community, this does not in itself amount to the final word. This particular gated community has many positive social aspects, though they may be hard to see for those in the habit of treating gated communities as a dirty word. In fact, trying to escape urban violence, as the villagers do, is not necessarily a racial commentary; plenty of inner-city violence is perpetrated by white Americans in the contemporary U.S., and no mention is made of race in the film when the villagers describe their reasons for leaving the city.

But even if race isn't explicitly mentioned, is it symbolically represented in the character of Noah Percy? Clearly Noah represents anti-social violence, so his character is worth considering in detail.

Noah is portrayed as a full-grown adult suffering from an unspecified type of congenital mental retardation. Although he is an active part of the community, he is not a fully participating member. He is the one character who seems attracted to the creatures, he claps his hands when the creatures are heard howling, and has been going into the woods regularly without permission, breaching the cardinal rule of the community. In an early scene he is shown trying to pick fights with some of the younger boys, for which he is told off by Ivy. He repeats her mandates like a child who has been reprimanded—"No hitting, no hitting"—less, it seems, with a sense of guilt than with fear of punishment (being sent to the quiet room). And, of course, all these transgressions lead up to his later stabbing of Lucius and attempt to kill Ivy in a jealous rage.

So does Noah represent the "true" nasty underside of all this politeness and equality, the violent human nature that makes this utopian experiment inevitably doomed? Some would say yes, especially those who assume that human nature is inherently violent, and that stateless society is a "war of all against all." But we think Noah fits better with anthropological findings on egalitarian communities. As noted above, these communities require work; they are not effortless, perfectly harmonious utopias. Keeping with the anthropological literature, it's possible to see Noah as representing the difficulty, at least for a few individuals, of internalizing the basic rules of respect for the autonomy and personhood of others ("no hitting, no hitting") that makes such an egalitarian community possible. In fact, the village treats Noah with a high level of tolerance and affection for as long as it can, just as we find in the treatment of eccentrics in small-scale societies (e.g. Widlok and Tadesse 2005). But just because there are people like Noah, a few uncooperative members who require special attention, does not mean that the whole enterprise is doomed; otherwise, human history would not be so full of egalitarian communities.

Noah is an anomaly, the only character who takes pleasure in the misfortune of others (e.g. when thinking that Lucius will be punished by Edward Walker). Importantly, his violence and attitudes are *not* reflected in the behavior of other characters. There is no cruelty in the everyday interactions of the village, but, rather, a shared sense of communality and a *joie de vivre* in their everyday routines and regular rituals (communal meals, wedding dances, and picnics on the lawn). Ivy and her sister Kitty express no sense of jealousy or competition: Ivy comforts Kitty when her declaration of love is rejected by Lucius, and Kitty later rejoices when Ivy admits that she and Lucius are in love. The elders may disagree with each other, but never express disdain or belittle one another. No one attempts to gain power and control over others; autonomy, though not referred to as a principle of village life, is clearly the bottom line. Even the "dare" where one adolescent boy is egged on by his peers to go at night and stand with his back to the woods for as long as he can is shown to be a good-natured ritual with barely a hint of cruelty. And for all the narrative play in *The Village* (Collier 2008), there is no narrative distance from the characters whereby we are to judge their actions and decisions as inauthentic or insincere. As Duncan (2005: 27) notes, "When the elders rise up and vote to continue [the village] we rise with them." In the wider context of life in the village, Noah's actions stick out like a sore thumb. In the actions of other characters, we don't see any suggestion that Noah reflects the nasty, violent subconscious of the village as a whole, so his presence does not necessarily signal its inevitable demise. Indeed, by the end of the film, Noah's threat has been contained, and the village appears poised to endure.

However, Noah obviously plays an important role in the film, and his presence could suggest, by extension, that such communal living is always in danger. Perhaps some viewers will infer that Noah represents the threat of urban racial violence, after all. But if this were the case, they might notice that the film also creates an image of racial harmony, since the villagers accept and incorporate Noah: he is loved by his parents and looked after by his friends until the time of his violent act. And given that Shyamalan's next film, *The Lady in the Water*, plays on similar utopian themes while celebrating a multi-racial, multi-cultural vision of the U.S., it seems unlikely that he would promote a racist vision in *The Village*, associating violence and mental incapacity with the racial Other. Still, in *The Village* Shyamalan may have inadvertently created a film that resonates with viewers who connect race and violence with gated communities. Viewer perceptions, not directorial intentions, are what matter most in this type of analysis.

None of the commentators on the film so far has noted the parallels with egalitarian communities that we've been tracing here. We assume that most viewers have, likewise, not seen these parallels, and there's a simple reason for that: anthropologists, even after more than a century of professional existence, have not had much impact on American conceptions of small-scale societies. Anthropological findings notwithstanding, Americans largely maintain a binary image of small-scale society as one of two extremes—Rousseau or Hobbes, pure romantic good or pure repressive corruption—and *The Village* doesn't fit into this straight-jacketed, Manichean view.

Contrast *The Village* with the contemporaneous film *Dogville*, which depicts a small U.S. town sometime in the past. *Dogville* is also clearly allegorical, not a realistic town, but a stage set with minimal props and references to the classic *Our Town* (Parks 2004). The plot focuses on the townspeople's reactions to "Grace" (Nicole Kidman), a woman on the run from mysterious bad guys. Although at first the townspeople take her in, they soon demand more and more from her in exchange for protecting her. The allegory here is clear: the small town (or village) is a hell of corruption and immorality, merely cloaked beneath a veneer of pleasantness (even the character who "falls in love" with Grace soon attempts to use his protection to extort sexual favors). Overstreet (2004) sees *The Village* as comparable to *Dogville*, noting that "both stories explore the way that those who live sheltered lives in order to escape the evils of the world will find those evils growing in their own gardens." Perhaps on the surface this parallel holds up, but the two movies take this in such obviously different directions that we find this comparison rather shocking ... though perhaps not surprising. In the wake of what many critics have seen as the failure of Western mainstream political thinking to imagine alternatives to neoliberal global capitalism (Huyssen 1994; Hudson 2003), moral corruption is the only allegory that we recognize. It is all that we believe that small towns or villages (where presumably small-mindedness rules) might have to teach us.

Small-scale has always been the hallmark of anthropology, but we have done less than a perfect job of conveying what life in small-scale societies is really like. In mainstream discourse, the small-scale is either the site of a primitive Eden, or a fishbowl of human corruption. *The Village* exists between these extremes: a living, breathing community where ideologies exist and where "sorrow will find you," yet a place where there's a chance to improve community life. Persuading others that a world like this might be possible, and that we might learn something about it by looking at anthropological research, is an urgent task for our times.

NOTES

1. Despite poor reception by the critics, *The Village* still did well at the box office, probably based on Shyamalan's previous successes. Shyamalan's more recent *The Lady in the Water* and *The Happening* have been even less successful than *The Village* in terms of critical reception and popular appeal.
2. See http://lookingcloser.org/2007/12/village-the-2004/, accessed 2/1/2006.
3. For anthropological analysis and critique of *The Gods Must Be Crazy*, see Gordon and Douglas (2000), Tomaselli (1990, 1992, 2002, 2006), and Volkman (1986, 1988). Although these authors analyze the film's romanticized imagery (among other problems), none specifically discusses snake symbolism. For comparisons between this and other films, see Chapter Six, as well as Wogan's article "Audience Reception and Ethnographic Film: Laughing at First Contact" (2006).
4. It is not clear why Ivy's mother doesn't play a larger role in their family life; her character is not well developed.
5. As Graeber notes more generally, "the position [of chief] was so demanding, and so little rewarding, so hedged about by safeguards, that there was no way for power-hungry individuals to do much with it" (2004: 22–3).
6. Not all examples of egalitarian societies are non-European. Anthropologists and historians have also demonstrated the way some European societies of the Middle Ages—lacking states and prior to the growth of organized religion—showed considerable evidence of lacking any organized class or gender hierarchy (see Federici 2004; Muller 1985). And, for a different anthropological view of hunter-gatherers, see Friedl (1975), who, against a backdrop of intense egalitarianism, finds a slight advantage for men in terms of public gifting of meat. See also Ortner (1996).

7. For a reassessment based on contemporary evidence, see Solway (2006).
8. In a 2006 Pew poll, 18 percent of respondents said they subscribe to *National Geographic*, making it one of the most-read magazines in the U.S. by a wide margin. By comparison, 10 percent said they subscribe to *Newsweek*. This poll was conducted by the Pew Internet and American Life Project and published on November 21, 2006. For more discussion of public perceptions of anthropology, see Chapter Six and Lutz and Collins (1993).
9. Sanday does not make this claim lightly, as she has done extensive research on rape in other cultural contexts (Sanday 1990).
10. See, for example, Janet Siskind's tender portrayal of the strengths and strains of an Amazonian egalitarian society in her classic *To Hunt in the Morning* (1973).
11. Graeber's argument makes clear that the concept of "counterpower" is not a retread of functionalist views that mythology simply serves to preserve the current social order. See also Ortner's interesting reassessment of her earlier work, in which she argues that egalitarian societies contain gender hegemonies, but also contain alternative possibilities inherent in the system that potentially could lead to male dominance (Ortner 1996). At another level, one might suggest that this dreamworld works similarly to the hegemonic aspects of movies in the U.S. as described by Traube, although in this case the hegemony that is being defended is an egalitarian one, rather than a hierarchical one. But one could also say that, as with movies that offer images of other possible social relations—as in *Field of Dreams* and *The Godfather*—every imagined dreamworld exists in tension with the "actual" world of the societies that create such dreamworlds.
12. Thanks to Leonidas Vournelis for this suggestion.
13. This race critique holds up much better in this case than it does for *Field of Dreams*, which shows considerably more complexity than critics acknowledge.

6 *JAWS*: KNOWING THE SHARK

Obviously the shark in *Jaws* (2005 [1975]) instills fear, but fear of what, besides the visceral fear of sharks and the ocean depths? What social anxieties does *Jaws* play on, and what does the shark symbolize? These are the questions addressed in this chapter.

If people just wanted to be scared by big animals on screen, by now we would have had scores of blockbuster films about angry bears, marauding cougars, and other frightening animals, but we haven't, and few films have stood the test of time as well as *Jaws*. This film is said to have ushered in the era of blockbuster movies, and it remains popular more than thirty years after its release. The Bravo television network ranked *Jaws* number 1 on its list of "The 100 Scariest Movie Moments," and the American Film Institute put it at number 2 on its list of "100 Most Heart-Pounding American Movies."[1] Clearly, *Jaws* tapped into something in American society.

JAWS SYNOPSIS

Jaws is set in a small oceanside town that depends for its survival on the summer tourist business. The town suffers a series of vicious shark attacks, and it is inferred that the perpetrator is a single shark. After some debate about how to handle these attacks, three men set out to search for the shark in the deep seas: police chief Brody (Roy Scheider), marine biologist Hooper (Richard Dreyfuss), and fisherman Quint (Robert Shaw). Eventually the shark shows itself, and the men try to kill it through various means. Although the shark is unusually strong and kills Quint, Brody finally manages to blow it up by shooting an air tank lodged in its mouth.

PREVIOUS INTERPRETATIONS

Of the many published interpretations of *Jaws*, the most fruitful for our purposes are those that view the shark as an Asian wartime enemy of the U.S., namely, the Japanese in the Second World War and the Vietcong in the Vietnam War (Rubey 1976; Torry 1993; Willson 1977). According to these provocative interpretations, the shark represents an Asian enemy soldier, and the film toys with anxieties and guilt about American wars with Japan and Vietnam.

For example, Robert Torry (1993: 33–4) has noted the following parallels between the film and some common perceptions of the Vietnam War:

1. The shark, like the Vietcong, is an unseen enemy, hidden from view, striking in sudden attacks and then disappearing again. In fact, the movie came out just as the Vietnam War was winding down and the U.S. was gearing up for its bicentennial celebration in 1976 (hence the Fourth of July setting of the film).

2. Civilians and soldiers in Vietnam were hard to distinguish, and, similarly, two young boys in the movie almost get shot while swimming with a fake shark fin.

3. Just as some would say politicians restrained the military in Vietnam with rules of engagement, the Mayor and City Council restrain Chief Brody.

4. Parallels can be drawn between harsh treatment of Vietnam veterans by American civilians and fisherman Quint's description of the USS Indianapolis navy disaster, in which Second World War servicemen were abandoned at sea and left to fend for themselves.

Quint's description of the Indianapolis disaster provides a crucial link to the other wartime subtext, the Second World War. Given the importance of this description for our analysis, it is worth quoting at length:

> Japanese submarine slammed two torpedoes into our side, Chief. It was comin'
> back from the island of Tinian Delady. Just delivered the bomb, the Hiroshima
> bomb. Eleven hundred men went into the water. Vessel went down in twelve
> minutes. Didn't see the first shark for about a half an hour. Tiger. Thirteen
> footer. You know how you know that when you're in the water, Chief? You tell
> by lookin' from the dorsal to the tail. Well, we didn't know. 'Cause our bomb
> mission had been so secret no distress signal had been sent. [Laughs.] They didn't

even list us overdue for a week. Very first light, Chief, the sharks come cruisin'. So we formed ourselves into tight groups. You know, it's ... kinda' like 'ol squares in the battle, like you see on a calendar, like the battle of Waterloo. And the idea was the shark comes for the nearest man, and then he starts poundin' and hollerin' and screamin'. Sometimes the shark go away, sometimes he wouldn't go away. [Quint's comments here on the shark's eyes and a dead buddy are omitted, but discussed later.] ... Noon the fifth day, Mr. Hooper, a Lockheed Ventura saw us. He swung in low and he saw us. A young pilot, a lot younger than Mr. Hooper. Anyway, he saw us and he come in low. And three hours later a big fat PBY comes down and start to pick us up. You know that was the time I was most frightened? Waitin' for my turn. I'll never put on a lifejacket again. So eleven hundred men went in the water: three hundred and sixteen men come out, and the sharks took the rest, June the 29th, 1945. Anyway, we delivered the bomb.

Quint's references here—the A-bomb, the Japanese submarine, the shark attacks—strongly suggest that the *Jaws* shark represents the Japanese wartime enemy of the U.S. In fact, Quint describes events that literally took place during the Second World War. Quint's speech is historically accurate, right down to the name of the ship, the secret A-bomb mission, the Japanese submarine, the shark attacks, and the grisly loss of hundreds of lives at sea.[2] Not only do these historical references make the shark-Japan equation explicit, but they add to this scene's emotional power. Robert Shaw said the main reason he accepted the role of Quint was so that he could do the Indianapolis scene, while director Steven Spielberg said it was his favorite scene in the whole movie, and at least four different people, from screenplay writers to Shaw, had a hand in writing it.[3] As one critic put it, "*Jaws* without the Indianapolis speech would be like Hamlet without 'To be or not to be'" (Andrews 1999: 142).

More specifically, critics have pointed out that this scene gives the film an emotional charge by stirring up American guilt over the bombing of Japan. Dan Rubey argues that "the shark represents fears of retribution for the bombing of Hiroshima (and perhaps for our role in Vietnam as well) growing out of feelings of guilt and doubts about the justifiability of our actions" (1976: 22). According to this argument, the shark is "an image of the viciousness of our own society in war" (1976: 22).

Coming at this equation from the other side, Willson (1977) suggests that the shark represents the *enemy's* viciousness: specifically, Japanese submarines, as filtered through U.S. wartime propaganda and submarine movies. For evidence, Willson draws parallels between the shark and a Japanese submarine:

> The citizens of Amity are obviously in a war with an uncivilized, un-Christian enemy. Indeed, the scene in which the shark throttles a young boy on his rubber raft and bathers head frantically for shore conjures up memories of similar scenes of chaotic running for cover in movies about the raid on Pearl Harbor ... an equally dastardly "sneak attack." Also, the use of floating drums to mark and slow the shark duplicates the visual equivalent of depth charges when they are launched against a sub ... The air tank [in the shark's mouth] looks, moreover, like a torpedo. (1977: 32)

Like Torrey and Rubey, Willson draws precise parallels between the shark and perceptions of an Asian wartime enemy.

Whether about the Second World War, the Vietnam War, or both, these authors have convincingly demonstrated that *Jaws* draws on American wartime experiences with Asian countries. Of course, whether and how these war meanings resonate with contemporary audiences is an open question, requiring ethnographic study of specific audiences and their varied reactions. And as attitudes toward both wars change, the meanings of this film must change as well. For example, polls have shown that American attitudes toward the bombing of Japan have evolved significantly over time, with younger generations increasingly expressing regret over this decision (Asada 2007). Perhaps this creeping regret, as well as a Manichean counter-reaction to the Vietnam War's images of the "bad Asian," explain why *National Geographic* saw a sudden spike in positive articles about Japan from 1967 to 1978 (Lutz and Collins 1993: 130).

In the next chapter, we will consider these complicated, changing reactions in more detail, based on our own ethnographic work with college students, and propose methodologies for the study of audience responses to *Jaws*. For now, though, we will bracket these ethnographic questions, and, instead, offer a tentative, first-step interpretation—what Caton (1999: 21) would call *a plausible reading*—of the film's ongoing popularity. We widen the focus beyond Vietnam and the Second World War *per se*, to show how *Jaws* raises broad questions that still resonate with contemporary audiences.

THE EYES OF THE OTHER

Let's return to Quint's speech about the Indianapolis, specifically the middle section omitted from the earlier block quotation. After describing the "poundin'" and hollerin' and screamin'" of the shark attacks in the Pacific, Quint gives the following, chilling description of the shark's eyes and his own experience with death:

> Sometimes that shark, he looks right into you, right into your eyes. You know the thing about a shark? He's got lifeless eyes, black eyes, like a doll's eye. When he comes at 'ya, doesn't seem to be livin'. Until he bites 'ya and those black eyes roll over white, and then, ah, then you hear that terrible high pitch screamin', the ocean turns red. Spite of all the poundin' and the hollerin', they all come in and rip you to pieces. Y'know by the end of that first dawn, lost a hundred men. I don't know how many sharks, maybe a thousand. I don't know how many men … they averaged six an hour. On Thursday mornin', Chief, I bumped into a friend of mine, Herbie Robinson from Cleveland. Baseball player, bosom's mate. I thought he was asleep, reached over to wake him up. Bobbed up and down in the water, just like a kinda' top. Up ended. Well … he'd been bitten in half below the waist.

The first thing to note is that Quint's description of the shark's eyes as lifeless is strikingly similar to the American stereotype of the "inscrutable Asian" (see Figure 6.1).

Figure 6.1 Great white shark. Even in this photo of an actual shark, the eyes seem somewhat unreal, as Quint suggests. Photo taken by pnicoledolin and distributed by Shutterstock.com.

In fact, this parallel (which the critics have not noted) is what first caught our attention and caused us to think about the film's resonances with America's recent wars.

An entire stereotype has been built around this superficial physical difference, the Asian epicanthic fold in the eyelid. As in other racist stereotypes, a trivial physical difference stands for sweeping Us-Them contrasts between two cultural groups. During the Vietnam War, American soldiers sometimes self-identified as "round eyes," as opposed to the "slant eyes," a derogatory term for the Vietnamese. Within this view, Asian eyes connoted a lack of human emotion, or the hiding of emotions behind an unchanging facial expression. As General William Westmoreland famously put it in an interview about the Vietnam War, "Well, the Oriental doesn't put the same high price on life as does the Westerner. Life is plentiful; life is cheap in the Orient."[4] Though Westmoreland was later criticized for making this statement, especially given the U.S. military's disregard for the human cost of war, it is of a piece with a long-standing stereotype of Asians, i.e., the "yellow peril," heartless kamikaze soldiers, Japanese laughing at funerals, etc. (Dower 1986).

The irony is that the Japanese generally place special importance on the eyes as cues to emotion. For example, when using email or other "keyboard communication," Americans type :) to mean a smiley face, but the Japanese communicate this same meaning with an emoticon that emphasizes the eyes rather than the mouth: (^_^) (Hutson 2007: 15). This simple example reminds us that we're dealing with stereotypes here, not cultural facts. But stereotypes are long lived. As one commentator notes, Asian stereotypes have been embodied more recently in images of the ruthless Japanese businessman: "The villainous Samurai warmonger—inscrutable, robotic, and threatening—is recast, in his modern-day equivalent, as the inscrutable, militant business man..." (Okja Cobb 1989: 89).[5] For that matter, *Jaws* perpetuates an inaccurate—but, again, tenacious—stereotype of sharks as vicious killers. In reality, the number of shark attacks on humans is extremely small; more people have died from wasp stings than attacks by great white sharks.

In fact, Hooper, like Quint, describes the shark in a way that tallies with this stereotype of the emotionless, relentless Asian soldier: "What we are dealing with here is a perfect engine, an eating machine." The 1975 trailer for the film emphasized precisely the same machine-like qualities: "There is a creature alive today who has survived millions of years of evolution without change, without passion, and without logic. It lives to kill, a mindless eating machine. It will attack and devour anything. It is as if God created the devil ... and gave him jaws."

However, we need to look at Quint's comments about the shark's eyes from a broader perspective, especially since many viewers may no longer be familiar with the wartime Asian stereotype, much less adhere to it. Quint is describing, more generally, the instability of knowledge of the Other, the shift in perspective that comes with both distance and closeness. At one extreme, there is knowledge from afar: knowing the cultural Other through stereotypes, mediated images, and illusions. At the other extreme, there is knowledge up close: physical and emotional intimacy, looking right into the eyes of another person, recognizing that person's humanity and individuality. Quint shows he is trying to wrap his mind around the seemingly contradictory blend of these two extremes in a single moment, right before the shark kills its victim. Quint's description of his confusion over the dead bosom's mate ("I thought he was asleep") even creates a mirror image of this problem, where the question is: how can someone seem alive yet be dead? Or, more broadly stated, what is the relationship between life and death?

Note that Quint first mentions the way the shark "looks right into you, right into your eyes." Since Westerners often speak of the eyes as the window into the soul, we can interpret this sort of gaze "right into the eyes" as an image of human, intercultural understanding. "Intercultural" is the correct term, if we assume that the shark represents a human Other, though of course the shark raises questions about human-animal understanding as well (Drummond 1995). As philosopher Emmanuel Levinas stressed, only by looking at the face of the Other can we begin to engage and know him.[6] What Quint still cannot fully understand, though, is how this soul-piercing being could simultaneously seem utterly impersonal and un-real: "You know the thing about a shark? He's got lifeless eyes, black eyes, like a doll's eye. When he comes at 'ya doesn't seem to be livin'." This is a perfect image of cultural knowledge at a distance: the view of someone looking at another person through the distorted lens of cultural stereotypes. From this perspective, the cultural Other seems like a doll, a caricature of a human, not even a living creature. But then Quint once again switches back to his initial view of the palpable reality of the shark: "Until he bites 'ya and those black eyes roll over white, and then, ah, then you hear that terrible high pitch screamin', the ocean turns red."

Thus, Quint sees the shark as both real and unreal, alive and dead, intimately familiar and frighteningly remote. Quint resembles soldiers who first describe hating the enemy soldier, when the enemy is only known through movies and propaganda, and then suddenly recognizing, when they "see the white of their eyes" and are about to pull the trigger, that this enemy is a 17- or 18-year old boy, a human being, just like themselves. At that moment, dehumanization suddenly confronts the irreducible humanity of the Other; distance and nearness collide like two magnets, but it's unclear which end of the magnets to hold on to, whether they should repel each other or snap together.

Moreover, these epiphanies capture a more general, troubling question faced by anybody experiencing another society: how to know the Other? Or put differently, how to integrate indirect, distanced knowledge of the Other with direct, up-close knowledge?

GETTING TO KNOW THE OTHER AND THE ANTHROPOLOGIST

Interactions with the *Jaws* shark go through stages that chart the general process of getting to know cultural Others, which is why you don't have to be a war veteran to appreciate this movie. If you have ever tried to know another (sub)cultural group—whether as a transnational migrant or ethnic minority, as the co-worker of someone from another subculture, or as an anthropologist or businessperson—the following stages of intercultural understanding in *Jaws* should sound familiar:

1. Hear reports about Others, see signs of their presence, not sure what to make of it all (the townspeople in *Jaws* were not sure if the first death was even caused by a shark, then speculated about what kind of shark it was).

2. Start to see a pattern in the Others' actions, start to understand the Other, but from a distance and with an exaggerated Manichean view of the Other as all good or all bad, as in common media representations of other cultures (Bird 1996; Gordon and Douglas 2000; Pack 2000, 2001; Tomaselli 1990, 1992, 2002, 2006; Traube 1992; Volkman 1986, 1988) (the townspeople start to see a pattern in the shark attacks; they label the shark a malicious killer).

3. Move into the Other's own environment, to get to know him or her better (Brody, Quint, and Hooper search for the shark in its own environment, the open seas).

4. Interact more directly with the Other, starting with brief, close-up glimpses (first sightings of the shark).

5. Increase understanding, leading to new questions (starting to understand the exact size and nature of the shark, but mysteries arise, such as why it

comes back at the boat and why it doesn't slow down even with two barrels attached to it).

6. Try to get as close as possible to the Other through immersion in his or her home (Hooper lowers himself into the water in his shark cage, to get within a few feet of the shark).

7. The Other resists total understanding (the shark keeps trying to escape, and kills Quint).

8. Arrive at a deeper level of understanding (Brody kills the shark).

Granted, there are no standardized, precise stages of intercultural understanding in real life, but, as a rough approximation, these filmic stages do match up well with this process, especially within cultural anthropology. Stage 6, for example, in which Hooper gets into the shark cage, is remarkably similar to anthropology's central methodology, participant-observation. For a neophyte anthropologist seeking a Ph.D., participant-observation usually means living in the culture under study for two years, speaking the local language and eating the local food, often living with a family: in other words, getting in the water with the shark, even reaching through the bars and touching it, and then having it smash through your last defenses.[7]

But is the Other really like a shark? Is it fair to compare shark killers with those who learn about other societies?

The minimal response is to say that *Jaws* continues to draw in contemporary audiences because the film struggles, as they do, with problems of intercultural understanding. For people today, who often want to understand cultural Others yet often and necessarily do so from a distance through mass-media representations, *Jaws'* struggle for intercultural understanding probably resonates well. It helps, too, that the symbolism is so well hidden, since issues like stereotypes and war are always emotionally loaded. At least this interpretation is worth considering as another hypothesis for ethnographic inquiry into audience responses.

But is there more to it? Again, what about all that violence?

KILLING THE OTHER

Anyone who has ever tried to understand another society will probably bristle at the suggestion that, in doing so, they are killing that society, metaphorically or otherwise. Anthropologists will likely resist this interpretation, if they haven't already thrown this book on the floor. Most develop genuine affection for the people they study, likening their experience to that of an apprentice or child. Indeed, it's almost impossible not to develop warm feelings when you live together in close quarters with other people for extended periods of time. Anthropologists usually come to feel deep affection for at least some of the people they study—certainly that has been our experience in our fieldwork in Greece, Ecuador, and Mexico. So how could affection be equated with destruction?

The best way to answer this question is to take a close look at Hooper, since he represents a cultural anthropologist.[8] To be clear about the level of analysis, we're not trying to decide whether Hooper is a good anthropologist. It's always tempting to evaluate a film according to this deficit model, evaluating whether the film really "gets" what anthropologists do and then complaining when it doesn't. Although this approach might be psychologically satisfying, it misses a research opportunity. Instead, the goal should be to use feature film as a window into public perceptions of anthropologists, as Richard Chalfen does (2003).[9] From this perspective, the question becomes: how might audiences understand Hooper's participation in the killing of the shark, and, by extension, the anthropologists' murder of their own subjects?

Although professional anthropologists rightly lament their discipline's low profile (see our chapter on *The Village*), most Americans are aware of anthropology at some level. For example, an impressive 81 percent of respondents to a 1994 poll said they were interested in "the peoples of the world," and they undoubtedly assumed that some scientists study such peoples. By comparison, when asked if they were interested in "anthropology," the affirmative response was almost cut in half, dropping to 44 percent. In other words, just because Americans resist anthropology's scientific title doesn't mean they're not interested in its subject matter.[10] And this discrepancy isn't limited to anthropology. In this same poll, 77 percent of respondents said they were interested in "plants and trees," but only 39 percent said they were interested in "botany," and the study concluded that "In most cases, people showed more interest in the sciences when they were not referred to in the technical, scientific term."[11] A publishing editor recently confirmed this conclusion when she told author Ruth Behar that they should cut the word "anthropology" from her book's promotional blurb, explaining that "...we need to reach the general reader, and *any* reference to an academic discipline is a turn-off. They say it's toxic. They've done studies" (Behar 2009: 106, emphasis added). So while the public resists the term "anthropology" and probably can't easily name anthropological scholars or studies, this doesn't mean they're not aware of anthropology's work at some level.

The public has often learned about anthropology, without necessarily using that term, through one particular source: *National Geographic*. Since the early twentieth century, this magazine has been synonymous with exploration of remote, far-away societies, in other words, anthropology, at its intersection with scientific adventure, like the character Indiana Jones in *Raiders of the Lost Ark* and its sequels (more below). In the 1980s, the Magazine Research Institute estimated that a whopping 20 percent of adult Americans read the *National Geographic*, and they called it "America's favorite magazine" in terms of reader numbers, satisfaction, and loyalty (Lutz and Collins 1993: 221). A 2006 Pew poll had similar findings, with 18 percent of respondents saying they subscribe to *National Geographic*.[12] And although these readers are mostly "white," an estimated 43 percent never received a college degree, indicating a certain level of class diversity (Lutz and Collins 1993: 222).

Not coincidentally, *Jaws* includes a reference to *National Geographic*. After Hooper says the shark is an eating machine and that the shark proportions on a billboard's graffiti are correct, the Mayor says, "Love to prove that, wouldn't ya? Get your name into the *National Geographic*." This instantly recognizable reference to *National Geographic* shows how plausible it is, in the public imagination, to link Hooper with anthropology. In fact, starting in the late 1950s, *National Geographic* began to cover exploration of the sea, alongside its more traditional coverage of exotic peoples in far-away places (Angeletti and Oliva 2004: 270). So whether Hooper worked as a marine biologist or cultural anthropologist, his results would appear in the same magazine, showing how easily sharks could be associated with other societies in the popular imagination.

Hooper also fits common American stereotypes of the scientist: he's somewhat unaware of social rules (for instance, eating Brody's left-overs, in shades of the Absent-Minded Professor stereotype); he's passionate about his subject (a bedrock of all scientist stereotypes); and he does his research in the field rather than a laboratory or university (consistent with most fiction films about biologists and anthropologists, as Weingart (2003: 285) shows). In a survey done at a major undergraduate university, most students said they imagined an anthropologist would wear glasses and dress in a casual, "outdoorsy" style (Bird and Von Trapp 1999: 9). On both counts, Hooper fits the bill. He's so scruffy and casually dressed when he shows up in Amity that Chief Brody doesn't even realize he's the scientist the town requested from the Oceanographic Institute. Richard Dreyfuss, the actor who plays Hooper, also has a face, physique, and mannerisms that conform to public expectations of a scientist's appearance, which is presumably why Dreyfuss was later cast in *Krippendorf's Tribe* as a cultural anthropologist (more below).

But these are the more superficial aspects of the anthropologist/scientist stereotype. What about the killing? Would it make sense to the public that someone who studies sharks would willingly kill one, and that anthropologists might do the same with their human subjects?

Strangely enough, the answer is yes. Hooper conforms to a long-standing stereotype of the Inhuman Scientist who sacrifices human attachments and feelings to an obsessive pursuit. As Rosalyn Haynes says in her survey of popular images of scientists, "Of all the charges against the scientist in literature, none has been leveled more frequently or more vigorously than that of aloofness and emotional deficiency" (1994: 212). Haynes demonstrates that this stereotype of the Inhuman Scientist shows up from the Enlightenment through the contemporary period, from Mary Shelley to Aldous Huxley and Frank Herbert (2003: 211–35).

Just so, Hooper is passionately devoted to his subject and free of human attachments. There is no mention of Hooper having a family life, close friends, or romantic relationships. At the beginning of the film, he says that he was just getting ready to leave for Australia to do "pure research, eighteen months at sea," apparently without any concerns about disrupting ongoing human relationships.

Hooper specifically resembles the inventors of the atomic bomb, who were widely perceived to be more concerned with the scientific challenge of their project than its moral implications. Haynes puts it this way:

> The atomic scientists working on the bomb during World War Two and then the Cold War gave added weight to this stereotype with their documented declarations of unconcern about the human cost of their inventions ... for the impersonal scientist inevitably shades into the amoral scientist. In a world of mathematical necessities, ethics are irrelevant. For our generation, this figure encapsulates the most common of all attributes ascribed to scientists in literature and film—inhumanity. (2003: 250)

The connection with *Jaws* is obvious. Given Quint's association with "the Hiroshima bomb," Hooper is like Robert Oppenheimer or Edward Teller, lead scientists in the invention of nuclear weapons. Indeed, Hooper also creates a bomb that decimates the Other: the air tank that finally blows the shark to pieces. Though Brody ultimately pulls the trigger and, as Drummond cogently argues, mediates between Quint and Hooper (1996: 222–6),[13] his role doesn't preclude Hooper's resemblance to a nuclear scientist. While neither Hooper, Oppenheimer, nor Teller pulled the trigger, they all lent their scientific knowledge to a mission to kill the Other.

However, Hooper is not a megalomaniacal, mad scientist; he's no Dr. Strangelove. Hooper is closer to Oppenheimer, who later advocated arms control, than Teller, who took more hawkish positions. More to the point, Hooper is like the anthropologist who helps the military find their target. Hooper particularly resembles the anthropologists who were involved in the Study of Cultures at a Distance Project—social scientists who researched and wrote about the Japanese and Germans for the U.S. government during the Second World War. More recently, anthropologists have assisted the military in the wars in Iraq and Afghanistan. For example, Raphael Patai's book *The Arab Mind* (1973) has been widely read by U.S. military personnel and implemented in the torture of Iraqi prisoners, and Yale-trained anthropologist Montgomery McFate has been working for supposedly more humane purposes with the military in Iraq and the Human Terrain Team in Afghanistan. Most people can't name these anthropologists, and they are probably not aware of anthropologists' opposition to such military use of their knowledge, but they understandably assume that the military works with such experts.

Hooper is not portrayed as a villain or an anthropologist who only wants to torture and kill the enemy Other. Hooper displays great affection for the Other; he's likeable, affable, and a bit absent-minded—a quality that often wins over the public, as in the famous photo of Einstein's funny face and messy hair. Still, Hooper's amiable traits don't necessarily get him off the hook. He seems like a cross between the Inhuman Scientist and another stereotype identified by Haynes: the Helpless Scientist, who loses control of his invention (2003: 252). Many years after the Romantics, this stereotype of the Helpless Scientist is alive and well, due to the fact that recent scientific discoveries constantly seem to spin out of control and raise troubling ethical issues. As Haynes says, "actual events have often outstripped fiction in presenting such an outcome [a runaway scientific discovery]. In the media, atomic power, robots, germ warfare, genetic engineering, in-vitro fertilization and other scientific discoveries have gotten away from their creators and led to unforeseen consequences" (Haynes 2003: 252).

The bottom line is that the public might find it believable that Hooper would participate in the shark's destruction. By extension, the public might imagine an anthropologist killing the very people he or she studies, as hard as that might be for anthropologists to imagine.

It gets even worse: Hooper doesn't just kill the shark with his air tank; he kills it by robbing the shark of its mystery.

MYSTERY AND MEASUREMENT

The shark, as an elusive, rare creature of the deep sea, is clearly a symbol for mystery and wonder. Indeed, scientists still know relatively little about sharks. It's no co-incidence that Melville saw mystery in a similar animal, Moby Dick, whose "mask" Ahab wanted to strike through.

Yet Hooper's primary goal as a scientist is to literally *measure* the shark's size, in other words, to strip away the shark's mystery. Hooper is almost as obsessed with scientific measurement as Ahab was with vengeance. In the first half of the movie, nearly every comment Hooper makes about a shark he sees is an assessment of its size:

1. "It's a man-eater, it's extremely rare for these waters, but the fact is the bite radius on this animal is different than the wounds on the victim." [Said about the shark caught by the town fishermen.]
2. "Now why don't you take a long close look at this sign? Those proportions are correct." [Said about the Amity billboard drawing of a shark.]
3. "That's a twenty footer!" [Said upon the first sighting of the shark at sea.]
4. "I need to have something in the foreground to give it some scale. [Said while Hooper is taking a photo of the shark, and asking Brody to go to the end of the pulpit.]

In each of these comments, Hooper is the quintessential scientist: measuring, pinning down precise dimensions. Hooper's obsession with measurement leads us to the heart of the public's ambivalence about science. From this viewpoint, Hooper is reducing the world's mysteries to measurable, solvable problems. "Reduction of individuals to statistical units" is one of the hallmarks of the Inhuman Scientist stereotype, as is "Elevation of an objective perspective as being essentially closer to reality than a subjective viewpoint" (Haynes 1993: 213). Hooper again fits the Inhuman Scientist stereotype.

This stereotype has deep roots. Even people who do not fully subscribe to it, and even people who do not begrudge science's unprecedented power over the entire planet, still take comfort in knowing that science can't explain certain things in the universe, such as why two particular people fall in love, God's will, the essence of Beethoven, why some dreams apparently come true, or what extraterrestrials look like. These mysteries have become a final refuge against the ubiquity of science, and they give some people comfort, like delighting in the thought that a tribe in the Amazon still resists the "modern world." From this perspective, Hooper's measurements threaten one of the final refuges from science—the shark.

Readers might be tempted to dismiss the entire science *vs.* mystery formulation as a faulty dilemma, preferring to believe that for every mystery solved by science, hundreds more get opened up. Personally, we share this view, and we're guessing that you, our readers, do as well, since you're still reading this dissection of movies down to their innermost parts. Yet we know that others believe that the "magic of movies," like the shark or the meaning of a sunset, should be left alone, and we recognize that this "pro-mystery" view has to be treated sympathetically and relativistically.

Recent national polls give some sense of the depth of these mixed feelings about science. 59 percent of respondents agreed that "scientific research has created as many problems as it has solutions," 37 percent agreed that "science makes our way of life change too fast," and 49 percent said that "scientific research today doesn't pay enough attention to the moral values of society." At the same time, roughly half of the respondents took the opposite side on each of these questions, and, in another poll, 89 percent said that "developments in science help make society better."[14] Clearly science stirs up strong ambivalence.

To take a more concrete example, consider anthropologist Elizabeth Bird's study of U.S. supermarket tabloids (1992). On the one hand, Bird shows that the tabloids consistently celebrate "anti-science mysteries," such as paranormal experiences, medical miracles, monstrosities, and UFOs (Bird 1992: 48–63). As one tabloid writer said, "It gives them [the readers] a lot of comfort to know there's something else up there..." (Bird 1992: 99); or as one reader put it, "You know that there's no such thing, but in a sense you wish that there was, you know" (Bird 1992: 122). Readers feel "a distrust of science as representing 'them'—the faceless people who control the country. Some readers, in comparing their tabloids with other news sources, complained that scientists, politicians, and experts talk in language they do not identify with, and dismiss experiences they consider important" (Bird 1992: 126). However, Bird also shows that readers expect stories to be supported by a scientific expert or authority, and they do not simply accept everything they read; instead, they often prefer to dance on the line between truth and imagination (Bird 1992: 119–24; cf. Bird 2003: 171–2). In short, Bird locates complicated, ambivalent attitudes toward science among tabloid readers.

Far from a lunatic fringe phenomenon, the tabloids had a combined estimated readership of 50 million people per issue in the early 1990s. As one editor said, "[I]f a national television show had 50 million viewers it would be regarded as an enormous success" (Bird 1992: 33). Not every viewer of *Jaws* reads the tabloids, and tabloid circulation is now much lower than it was in the early 1990s, but many presumably still share the tabloid readers' longing for a world where wonder, mystery, and enchantment still exist, if only in small, fleeting moments, like the sighting of a shark.

From this perspective, Hooper's obsessive measuring and studying of the shark represents science's attempt to understand and catalogue every last inch of the globe: the equivalent of killing Jaws. Hooper's measurements also resemble the military and politicians' obsession with body counts during the Vietnam War—mathematical precision misapplied to an ultimately unquantifiable mystery. In Vietnam, too, the lines between life and death were blurred every time military officers claimed they had to burn down a village to save it.

This morbid mixing of life and death is most concretely manifested in the scene of Hooper doing an autopsy on the tiger shark: when he cuts open the shark that had been killed by the local townsmen to see if it still contains the remains of any of the victims in its digestive tract. This scene reminds viewers that Hooper examines sharks inside and out, dead and alive. He wants to measure, document, and understand these animals right down to their very entrails—and in this way he takes away their life.

But, again, Hooper is no simple villain. He doesn't kill sharks for animal testing, and he's not an amoral bean counter. When he refers to a shark as an eating machine, he enthusiastically calls it a "miracle of evolution," and when the shark comes after the boat, he shouts with genuine surprise, "He's chasin' us! I can't believe this!" In other words, Hooper views the shark as a living mystery. Similarly, *National Geographic* doesn't just publish measurements; it draws its readers in with mysteries like Jacques Cousteau's deep-sea explorations—a more scientifically acceptable version of the mystery-hawking tabloids. So measurement and mystery, though opposed from one perspective, can be joined together from another.

We've seen this kind of juxtaposition of supposed opposites before in the discussion of the shark's eyes, which seem both alive and lifeless. The film plays in subtle ways with these fundamental tensions—life and death, humanity and stereotypes, mystery and science—so viewers are left with something to contemplate, according to their own subjective and social positioning.

ANTHROPOLOGY AND DEATH

The stereotype of the Mystery Killer applies to Hooper not only as a generic scientist, but specifically as an anthropologist. Anthropologists, after all, continue to study the Other, to extract his or her secrets and publish them for the world to see. Not that most cultural anthropologists revel in numbers, but, like Hooper, they strive to understand their subject with precision and exhaustive detail ("thick description"). The public certainly knows that anthropologists (or whatever such experts are called) try to understand other cultures, just as Hooper passionately studies sharks.

The public is keenly aware of one anthropologist who kills the Other: namely, Indiana Jones. Just as Hooper studies and kills the shark, Indiana Jones masters the secrets of other cultures, and sometimes kills hostile natives. Think of the famous scene where Jones shoots the turbaned swordsman in *Raiders of the Lost Ark*. In a recent poll, viewers voted this their single favorite "Indiana Jones moment" out of *all* the Indiana Jones movies ever made.[15] And consider Elizabeth Traube's critique of Jones' battle with the "bad Other" in *The Temple of Doom*. Traube argues that this sequel "seeks to explain the world in terms of the Other's evil nature," and "evokes in the viewer a strong desire for [the Other's] destruction" (Traube 1992: 33). If Indiana Jones can so readily kill the Other, Hooper can as well, especially when his target is the Other in the guise of a vicious shark that eats people.

This is not a minor example; Indiana Jones is arguably the most famous anthropologist of our time. When 100 undergraduate students were asked to name an anthropologist, Indiana Jones was the single most commonly cited example, with only three students able to name a real-life anthropologist (Bird and Von Trapp 1999: 10; see also Chalfen 2003: 384). And, in a separate online poll, Indiana Jones was voted sixth on a list of the "100 Greatest Movie Characters of All Time."[16] Indiana Jones, as a putative archaeologist, also shades into other popular imagery of anthropologists, again closely associated with death: forensic anthropologists, as featured in the popular TV show *Bones*, and archaeologists, as seen on PBS and the History and Discovery channels. Anthropologists are so used to the Indiana Jones stereotype that they understandably groan when it comes up, but those who dismiss the relevance of Indiana Jones and other popular archaeologists do so at their own peril.

It is worth adding that editorial changes in *National Geographic* correlated rather neatly with the emergence of the *Jaws* blockbuster phenomenon. In the first half of the twentieth century, *National Geographic* made its name by publishing stories of scientific adventures in exotic lands, that is, searches for "lost" and "undiscovered" tribes and customs. But after nearly a half century of such stories amidst the steady onslaught of modernization, readers must have noticed that the supply of pristine tribes and exotic customs was dwindling. At this point, roughly the 1950s, the magazine was forced to seek new sources of wonder, so they started publishing stories about scientific explorations of space and the deep seas (Angeletti and Oliva 2004: 270; Lutz and Collins 1993). *Jaws* came out in 1975, once these changes had a chance to sink in. By this time, *National Geographic* readers sensed that the anthropological paradigm had started to exhaust itself—that cultural mysteries were another endangered species. In other words, *National Geographic*'s trajectory prepared the public for *Jaws*, a film that revolves around a scientist killing off the very mystery that he passionately studies.

As noted earlier, there is real ambivalence here. The public wants scientists to reveal mysteries, but resents them when they do this too well and for too long— the counterpart to the public's complicated relationship with the paparazzi, which are expected to uncover scandalous stories and then resented when they do so. Perhaps viewers of *Jaws* in the 1970s already sensed that the exciting mysteries being explored in *National Geographic* by Jacques Cousteau would one day meet the same fate as the cultural mysteries studied by anthropologists. In any case, *Jaws* plays on ambivalent feelings about science, which partly drives the film's ongoing appeal. Of course, viewers don't watch this film because they want to see a critique of anthropology; nevertheless, anthropology gets caught up in the film's underlying play with ambivalence about science and mystery, as well as Asian wars and intercultural understanding.

The more recent *Krippendorf's Tribe* (1998) indicates that this view of anthropologists as Mystery Killers is still present. *Krippendorf's Tribe* centers around a cultural anthropologist (Richard Dreyfuss, once again) who tries to satisfy a grant foundation and a curious public by dressing up his own kids in "native garb" and passing them off as an undiscovered tribe from New Guinea. Though intended as a farcical comedy and not particularly well received, the film plays off a real stereotype of anthropology as a discipline in which "exotic differences are preferred above all—in a sense, the weirder the better" (Chalfen 2003: 384). According to this perspective, anthropologists, unable to find any more lost tribes, must now fabricate discoveries and study themselves.[17]

Films like *Krippendorf's Tribe*, *Raiders of the Lost Ark*, and *Jaws* arise in the vacuum left by anthropology's low profile in the public sphere. Perhaps better analogs to the anthropologist can be found in films about a traveler, broadly defined as someone who goes on a journey and gets deeply involved in another society. For example, Steven Caton (1999) has argued to good effect that *Lawrence of Arabia* presents an allegory of long-term fieldwork, complete with its messy contradictions and deep involvements. Jonathan Gales and Elizabeth Bird (2005) also argue that the movie *Jerry Maguire* creates parallels to the anthropological encounter and "expeditionary discourse": a standard cultural narrative about the white man who journeys into the world of the Other, only to find redemption for himself and his charge. And Yolanda Van Ede (2007) offers a provocative analysis of Elliot Ness in Brian de Palma's *The Untouchables* as an allegory for anthropological research and the dilemmas of remaining "cool" but not cold, the need to touch and be touched by fieldwork. Clearly, though, these film models are more analogical or metaphorical than literal depictions of anthropology. These authors usefully expand our definitions of mass media representations of anthropology, but, in the public view, there still seems to be minimal association between academic anthropology and these broader models of the traveler, leaving room for stereotypes of the anthropologist as a student of exotic mysteries in far-away places.

It doesn't do any good to protest that these stereotypes are inaccurate, or that anthropologists want to preserve and explore mystery rather than eliminate it.[18] Perception has the final word in this case. And if anthropologists are being honest with themselves, they'll admit that these perceptions have some basis in reality. In point of fact, most anthropologists still heed Clifford Geertz's famous battle cry, to "hawk the anomalous, peddle the strange" (1984: 275). Publications on extreme aspects of the human condition—crack dealers, stolen body parts, unusual rituals— still tend to be given a high billing in anthropology, overshadowing studies of everyday routines. Anthropologists also go off into the field without co-workers. It's not too hard to get from Geertz's "merchants of astonishment" to the public's perception of anthropology as Indiana Jones and the sole adventurer's search for lost tribes and other exotica.

And since anthropologists study the Other with the single-minded intensity characteristic of any scholar, they can seem like scientific crushers of cultural mystery. This view was well articulated by a man being studied by anthropologist Barbara Myerhoff:

> You cannot tell someone, "I know you." People jump around. They are like a ball. Rubbery, they bounce. A ball cannot be long in one place. Rubbery, it must jump.

> So what do you do to keep a person from jumping? The same as with a ball. You take a pin and stick it in, make a little hole. It goes flat. When you tell someone, "I know you," you put a little pin in. (Myerhoff 1978: 41)

Vincent Crapanzano also throws this problem into stark relief in his book *Tuhami: Portrait of a Moroccan*, where he admits to his own anthropological drive to know the Other completely: "He [Tuhami] was, within his terms, giving; and I, with avariciousness supported by my science, was willing to receive. I wanted to possess everything that Tuhami knew and could tell me—and even more. I wanted to know him completely" (1980: 134). Crapanzano also suggests an interesting, counter-intuitive explanation for this drive for complete knowledge: "The push toward such cognition—fusion, really—is motivated, I suggest, by the fear of the very opposite—solipsistic miscognition or de-fusion—which the psychoanalyst would associate with separation" (137). Similarly, Quint oscillates between a sense of the Other's nearness and distance, and presumably Hooper and anthropologists do as well.

To be sure, some have made heartfelt pleas for more recognition of the mystery of the Other (Behar 1997; Crapanzano 1980: 152; Sommer 1991), and anthropology has even experienced a "crisis of representation." However, the public doesn't generally know about these things, and they still (often rightly) see anthropologists as revealers of cultural mysteries.

Furthermore, anthropological publications often seem like murder to the public because they reduce human lives, in all their complex, vivid individuality, to the written word. As noted in our chapter on *The Godfather*, writing has long been associated in Western society with the irretrievable loss of a more authentic, oral life (Clifford 1986; Wogan 2004b). In this view, a human life comes to an end when put on the written page—metaphorically, if not literally, as in stories of women who die once their secret recipes get written down (Sutton 2001: 154–5). As Crapanzano adds, ethnographic writing results in the premature death of an ongoing dialogue and process of discovery (1980: 140).

There are three other reasons why the public likely believes that anthropological writing kills off the human subject. The first is anthropology's inherent typologizing—cataloging people as social types (young male from Society X, newly educated female from Society Y), rather than fully realized, complicated, flesh-and-blood individuals. Although anthropologists now routinely sprinkle interview quotes throughout their accounts and sometimes go into depth on a few individuals, they ultimately still reduce their "informants" to social types and patterns; indeed, doing so remains the discipline's raison d'être. Consider the contemporary anthropological study of dreams, an opportunity for exploration of emotion and real people if there ever was one. If you read these studies, though, you will rarely find moving accounts of how dreams relate to the emotional texture of a real person's life. Instead, you will find typologies of the semiotics and discourse structures of dream interpretation in entire communities, generalizations about the use of dreams in Society X. Through passing remarks in the text, you can tell that these anthropologists got deeply involved with the people they lived with, so you sense how much has been lost in these accounts. Cases like this remind us that anthropological typologizing diminishes the complexity, vibrancy, and mystery of the individual.

Secondly, anthropological writing rarely portrays the ethnographer as a fully real-ized person, notwithstanding increased attention to the ethnographer's positioning. This is a crucial failing because, as revealed in a Book of the Month Club survey, readers expect a good book to contain, above all else, identifiable personalities (Radway 1984; Sutton 1991).

Finally, anthropological writing has been getting even *less* accessible over time. For example, "clarity ratings" on articles in the *American Anthropologist*, one of the discipline's flagship journals, showed a marked decline in the second half of the twentieth century. According to student readers from various colleges across the country, 83 percent of the articles published in the *American Anthropologist* in 1962 were clearly written, yet by 2001 the students found that only 51 percent of the articles were clearly written. This 32 percent decline in clarity is even more remarkable when you consider that the students were much less familiar with the theoretical paradigms of 1962; clarity ratings for 2001 should have gone up, not down.[19] Sutton's assessment of anthropology in the early 1990s still holds true: "for all their innovation, post-modernist anthropologists have failed to buck the trend towards increasing sub-specialization and decreasing audience" (1991: 91).[20] At least to outsiders, such opaque language, which turns real people into incomprehensible jargon, must seem dehumanizing. Non-anthropologists probably feel like Mary Louise Pratt, who famously said, "For the lay person, such as myself, the main evidence of a problem is the simple fact that ethnographic writing tends to be surprisingly boring. How, one asks constantly, could such interesting people doing such interesting things produce such dull books?" (Pratt 1986: 33). Readers like this probably don't see much contradiction in Hooper's willing participation in the killing of the shark/Other.

Granted, changes are underway. For example, Ruth Behar has written poignant anthropological stories in exquisite language; she honors the mystery of the people she writes about; and her books have found a readership outside the usual anthropological circles (Behar 1993, 1997, 2007). Still, it's hard to find anthropologists who write as well as Behar, and few contemporary anthropologists have come close to entering mainstream consciousness. It's not even clear how much anthropology has accepted Behar's humanistic approach, as she herself recently stated:

> I worry because I do not consider my work to be representative of what most anthropologists consider anthropology. I worry about my lack of a sense of authority in this discipline where I reside, still uncertainly, often disloyally, and sometimes, I feel, illegally ... I worry because I know that even though anthropology has changed in the last few decades ... it really has not changed all that much, not enough yet. (2009: 110)

Behar fears that the demands of anthropology and narrative may be fundamentally irreconcilable: "I know I have said that ethnography at its best is just another form of creative non-fiction, but I still often think that one day I will have to stop being an anthropologist in order to write stories that can truly be called literature" (2009: 115). Perhaps the tension Behar identifies comes down to differing stances on mystery and ambiguity: literature instructs writers to "show, don't tell," whereas anthropology expects writers to make their points explicit.

It's hard to say where anthropological writing will end up, but it's certainly telling that almost no graduate anthropology program requires courses on the craft of writing (McClaurin 2009: 129–30). Most anthropologists still seem to buy into a self-serving dichotomy between "the popular and the pompous" (Campbell 1996), not realizing that those anthropologists who do reach broader audiences often use their "popular" writings to develop theoretical ideas (see Sutton 1991).

Like the shark, anthropology is so close, yet so far away: soul-piercing, yet strangely lifeless. Anthropology at the start of the twenty-first century seems to be at a crossroads, just as W.H.R. Rivers was at the turn of the last century. In the early 1900s, Rivers pioneered the anthropological study of dreams and the unconscious, yet he could never quite shake off the waning paradigms of armchair anthropology, evolutionism, and diffusionism. Rivers had deep insight into culture and the human soul, and could have been the founder of modern anthropology, but he, too, could not let go of old ways of thinking.

Anthropology is caught again at a turning point, and it's not clear where it will end up, other than in *National Geographic*.

NOTES

1. For the Bravo list, see http://www.listafterlist.com/tabid/57/listid/9449/Movies/Bravos+The+100 +Scariest+Movie+Moments.aspx. For the American Film Institute list, see http://connect.afi.com/ site/DocServer/thrills100.pdf?docID=250. Both accessed April 3, 2009.

2. In one of its few inaccuracies, the speech gives the impression that all the deaths were caused by shark attacks, whereas many were caused by drowning, hydrophobia, and exposure. Nonetheless, there were by all accounts many shark attacks, qualifying this as one of the worst shark-human attacks in history and a major U.S. naval disaster. For a discussion of the speech's basis in historical fact, see Andrews (1999:138–40).

3. See Andrews (1999:140–3) on Shaw's role and the debate over who did what to the script for the Indianapolis speech. Also, see Spielberg's interview in "The Making of Steven Spielberg's *Jaws*," in the bonus materials for *Jaws*, thirtieth anniversary edition (2005 [1975]). In this interview, Spielberg refers to the speech as his "favorite part in *Jaws*," and discusses its complex writing history.

4. Westmoreland made this statement in a taped interview for the documentary *Hearts and Minds*.

5. It's also important to recognize changes in American society and media images, rather than assuming that nothing ever changes. Some of Okja Cobb's conclusions about Teenage Mutant Ninja Turtles, for example, too easily equate these complicated representations with patterns from the early twentieth century. For a more historically complex treatment, see Asada (2007).

6. While we applaud Wright's application of Levinasian ethics to Spielberg's corpus, we find his treatment of *Jaws* unfairly dismissive. In the one paragraph where he considers *Jaws*, Wright simply says, "Thus, the otherness presented here [*Jaws*] resists any claim of or call for recognition of difference. Instead, the choices made reinforce difference as a source of danger, of repulsion and horror only" (Wright 2008: 54). We believe, to the contrary, that *Jaws* grapples with complicated, Levinasian questions about the Other.

7. This isn't to say the anthropologist has to go off to some far-flung place. Increasingly, anthropologists are as likely to see their field site around the corner as around the world, studying stock market brokers, gay activists, or even other anthropologists. In either case, participant-observation entails deep immersion in a certain cultural world.

8. Quint and Brody, of course, are also trying to understand the shark/Other, but Hooper, as a marine biologist, has made this into a scientific career. And note that we use "societies" throughout to refer to the relevant groups that anthropologists identify in their study, whether defined ethnically, by gender, or other criteria.

9. Chalfen rightly notes that feature films are pedagogically useful as texts that college students can examine for public perceptions of anthropology, as well as for juxtaposition with anthropological films and methods (Chalfen 2003: 387; Chalfen and Pack 1999). Chalfen's main example is *Krippendorf's Tribe*, which is discussed below and also mined for public perceptions of anthropology by Drummond (2000).

10. For example, 20 percent of undergraduates at one college had no idea what anthropology was (compared with only 1 percent for psychology), and, among those who had heard of anthropology, 58 percent defined it as archaeology or physical anthropology, rather than cultural anthropology (Bird and Von Trapp 1999: 9). Cultural anthropology's low profile as a discipline seems causally related to relatively low course enrollments, which, in turn, affect the prospects of the new lumpenproletariat: all those anthropology Ph.D.s enduring unemployment and non-living wages as adjunct, part-time laborers. Granted, other factors are at play here, including a general trend away from tenure-track hiring in all disciplines, but professional anthropologists share at least part of the blame.

11. American Museum of Natural History, 1994, as cited in the Polling the Nations database.

12. By comparison, 10 percent said they subscribe to *Newsweek*. This poll was conducted by the Pew Internet and American Life Project and published on November 21, 2006.

13. As one recent commentator briefly notes, "...Brody uses Quint's old-fashioned M-1 rifle to explode Hooper's air tank lodged in the fish's mouth, melding facets of the traditional and the modern" (Friedman 2006: 165).

14. The poll on science creating as many problems as solutions was conducted by the Virginia Commonwealth Institute, September 30, 2002; the poll on science making life change too fast comes from the National Science Foundation, 1991; and the polls on science and morality and science making society better both come from the Pew Internet and American Life Project, November 21, 2006. For simplicity, "strongly agree" and "agree" answers are combined here.

15. 46% voted this their favorite moment, while the other top five moments garnered less than 20 percent each. See "Favorite Indiana Jones Moment, According to Poll," http://blogcritics.org/video/article/favorite-indiana-jones-moment-according-to/, accessed May 21, 2009. The poll was conducted online by MovieTickets.com in May, 2009, with roughly 2,000 respondents. Part of the appeal of this scene seems to derive from its comical display of Western technological superiority—Jones's hand gun *vs.* the traditional Middle Eastern sword. Such technological displays have a long tradition in Western literature and film, as in *The Gods Must be Crazy* and *First Contact* (see Wogan 2006), as well as *The Godfather* (see our discussion in Chapter Two of the bandleader's contract).

16. See http://www.empireonline.com/100-greatest-movie-characters/default.asp?c=6, accessed May 14, 2009. Apparently Indiana Jones enjoys a similar reception in Great Britain; in a 2001 survey by Britain's *Total Film* magazine, Jones was voted "the top movie hero of all time," even beating James Bond. See http://edition.cnn.com/2001/SHOWBIZ/Movies/01/26/indiana.hero/index.html, accessed June 2, 2008.

17. *Krippendorf's Tribe* seemed to go too far in its portrayal of white people dressing up as Papua New Guineans ("blackface") and its emphasis on sexuality, an apparent hold-over from *National Geographic*'s heyday of bare-breasted women. As one reviewer put it, "the film reaches beyond politically incorrect to patently offensive" (Stack 1998: C-12). And presumably viewers aren't concerned enough with anthropology to flock by the millions to see a send-up of it. But certain excesses aside, the film exemplifies ongoing stereotypes of anthropology, as Chalfen (2003) and Drummond (2000) effectively argue.

18. See Wogan (2006) on the role of wonder in anthropology, especially in relation to images of first contact.

19. Although *American Anthropologist* was never designed for public consumption, its fate gives some sense of overall trends in anthropological writing. For information on this project, including the actual ratings, see www.publicanthropology.org/Archive. We're defining "clearly written" as articles that were given a rating of 4 or 5 on a 5-point scale, with 5 being the highest rating for "clarity." All articles from the two years, 1962 (43 articles) and 2001 (66 articles), were considered, except for obituaries. Perhaps the students gave higher ratings than general readers would have because they were reluctant to admit to their professors, internet readers, and themselves that they had difficulty understanding an article in their own major.

20. For similar, more recent assessments, see Eriksen (2006) and Waterston and Vesperi (2009). And for more on the underlying disconnect between anthropology and the public, see Di Leonardo (1998).

7 CONCLUSION

You're gonna need a bigger boat.
Chief Brody

Did any of the interpretations in this book give you something to think about? Were you surprised when you read about the shark's eyes in *Jaws*, or the foul line in *Field of Dreams*, or the cannoli in *The Godfather*? If so, then writing this book was worth the effort. But if all of our interpretations were ho-hum, then we have failed.[1] It's that simple: there's nowhere to hide with this kind of analysis. You have presumably seen these films, so you can decide whether we have added any insight into them.

This litmus test doesn't just apply to movies. We have tried to shed light on American society and anthropological theory as well, just as any investigation should push into new territory when exploring disciplinary concepts. While anthropologists have been developing notions of polytemporality and entextualization, our chapter on *The Big Lebowski* should have demonstrated how these two things are connected in American society. Or perhaps the chapter on *The Village* revealed something about the nature of American assumptions about small-scale communities.

We prefer to have this book evaluated, then, according to its degree of insight into particular texts and concepts, not whether it provides "a new unified theory of media culture." Our approach doesn't exclude theory; it just keeps it in the service of cultural analysis, rather than sacrificing everything to an abstract, one-size-fits-all theory of culture and mass media.

That said, this book has wider applicability. There is no reason the kind of analysis we have done here cannot be applied to other movies or, for that matter, TV shows and other media formats. *The Seinfeld Show*, for example, offers abundant opportunities for anthropological analysis, since it probes the cultural rules and taboos of American society. Take the episodes that revolve around problems with gift-giving—Jerry giving cash to Elaine for her birthday, or accepting a suit from a guy he doesn't really like, or an astronaut pen from someone who bugs his parents:

these play on some of the same issues that we've discussed here, such as public *vs.* private and societal *vs.* individual tensions in *The Godfather* and *Field of Dreams*.[2] Though it claims to be "a show about nothing," *The Seinfeld Show* probes the cultural logic of just about every aspect of American society. And, of course, there are movies like *The Lord of the Rings* and *My Big Fat Greek Wedding*, and shows like *Friends* and *The Office*. Whether the focus is *Seinfeld* or any other media text, there are only two requirements for this kind of analysis: the text must be popular with some audiences, and the analyst must believe that it's possible to say something culturally interesting about it.

But just because a film achieves blockbuster status does not, *ipso facto*, make it a complex cultural myth, nor does every myth deal with social tensions. We have found that some films are more amenable to analysis than others. Other viewers, however, will see it differently; they might see enormous possibilities in a text that we didn't know what to do with.

These differences remind us that we need to investigate the way specific audiences have responded to specific texts. Anthropology can be particularly useful in this regard. In the last few decades, anthropologists have been particularly successful in bringing ethnographic analysis to bear on media texts, offering fine-grained readings and subtle insights based on long-term fieldwork. Evidence of this burgeoning subfield is found in two edited volumes (Askew and Wilk 2002; Ginsburg, Abu-Lughod, and Larkin 2002), a book-length review (Peterson 2003), and several monographs (Abu-Lughod 2005; Dickey 1993; Mankekar 1999). Many of these studies examine local media texts in non-U.S. contexts, such as television serials produced and viewed in Egypt (Abu-Lughod 2005) and India (Mankekar 1999), while others focus on receptions of U.S. media in other countries (Kulick and Willson 2002; Wilk 2002). In a series of articles, another group of anthropologists has looked at American student responses to ethnographic films (Bird and Godwin 2006; Martínez 1990, 1992, 1995; Wogan 2006), and book-length studies have examined Western audience responses to film and television (Bird 1992, 2003; Crawford and Hafsteinsson 1996). Despite their different empirical foci, these authors all share a commitment to the anthropological study of mass media based on long-term participant-observation and ethnographic inquiry.

This type of ethnographic analysis could be applied with equally good results to the blockbuster films studied in this book. We'd like to think that our interpretations offer useful jumping-off points for such ethnographic investigations, wherever these films have been widely viewed. To give some sense of what such work might look like, we devote most of this chapter to a concrete example: Wogan's examination of student responses to *Jaws*. This work, while still just scratching the surface, shows how complicated and interesting ethnography can get. A secondary benefit is that readers will get an extended example of how film might be used in the teaching of anthropology.

Sutton has also done ethnographic work on audience response—with Greek television cooking shows (Sutton and Vournelis 2009), for example—and his experiences could just as easily be included in this section. However, we will only focus on Wogan's experience, so that we can go into depth on one extended example (as in our other chapters) and maintain our focus on Hollywood blockbusters.

JAWS IN THE CLASSROOM

Since 1999, I (Peter Wogan) have been teaching full-time in the Anthropology Department of the College of Liberal Arts at Willamette University,[3] a selective liberal arts college, located in Salem, Oregon. The particular class in which I taught *Jaws* was titled "Survey of Anthropological Theory," a required course for all Anthropology majors and minors. I used *Jaws* for a unit on French structuralism, taught about halfway through the semester. Analyzing a Hollywood blockbuster seemed like a good way to make Lévi-Straussian myth analysis come to life. Also, film provided a convenient solution to a constant pedagogical challenge: given that anthropologists don't make their field-notes or other "raw data" available to the public, how do you find case material that students can take in original directions (in class discussions and individually written papers), without doing a semester's worth of their own fieldwork? *Jaws*, in particular, seemed amenable to structuralist analysis: three men on a boat, two opposing figures (Hooper and Quint), and a mediator in the middle (Chief Brody). I also specifically chose *Jaws* because I wanted to use Lee Drummond's chapter on this film (1995: 199–240), to illustrate, update, and improve on Lévi-Strauss.

The analysis was conducted over three classes, taught in the fall of 2005, 2006, and 2007. Each of these classes was relatively small, ranging from ten to nineteen students, and run as a seminar, with plenty of discussion and minimal lecturing. The students were sophomores and juniors (plus a few seniors in the 2005 class), about half had taken other classes with me, and they all seemed actively engaged in the course; they did the readings, came to class prepared, and got involved in class discussions. Most of the students were from the West Coast, female (about a

70:30 female:male ratio), "white," and middle class, and all but one was somewhere between nineteen and twenty-two years old.

I started by having students read and discuss summaries, samples, and critiques of Lévi-Strauss. After going through the critiques, we increasingly moved away from Lévi-Strauss's model. Since the students would next be taking the Anthropology Department's field methods course, the idea was to have them not only get to know an important paradigm in anthropological intellectual history, but also to see how theories change, and how they can be applied to novel empirical cases.

Even though most of the students had seen *Jaws* before, we watched it again, to allow a close reading with a fresh anthropological lens. Over several class periods, we watched about thirty minutes of the film at a time, and then discussed what we had seen. To conserve class time, we watched the second half of the film for homework, at a special night screening. During class, students sometimes brought in written homework with their own interpretations of the film. Some discussions were carried out in small groups of three to four students, whose ideas were written up on the board for all to see; class-wide discussions then focused on these student-generated ideas.

Students were encouraged to create their own, original analyses. For this reason, they did not read Drummond until *after* they had come up with their interpretations, and I tried to limit my input to leading the discussions: raising questions, referring to the texts, pointing out contradictions and problems. When the students finally read Drummond, they were pleased to see that they had independently arrived at some of the points he makes (such as the opposition between wealthy Hooper and working-class Quint). At the same time, many found intriguing surprises in Drummond's chapter, especially his point about the correlation between *Jaws'* popularity and the ecology movement. Having something new to add was no small accomplishment on Drummond's part, given that the students had just finished an intense, collective reading of this text. Nor was it a negative reflection on Drummond that the students' own readings tended to diverge from his; this is exactly what you'd expect, according to Drummond's own theory about schismogenesis and the protean nature of American society (Drummond 2000).

It's hard to capture all the different student interpretations, especially since I didn't record most of the class discussions. However, each year I did take written notes at the end of particularly intense class discussions. The below-listed examples from these notes give some sense of how the film resonated with some of my students, as each example is framed in terms of a vexing dilemma that the students found in both the film and American society:

1. How can intellectual knowledge (Hooper/scientist) and traditional, pragmatic knowledge (Quint/fisherman) co-exist?[4]
2. What is the relationship between the finite, known world (land, sun, the color yellow) and the infinite, unknown world (the ocean, color blue)?
3. Can we cheat death?
4. What kind of fear is acceptable, according to American models of class and masculinity?

These discussions indicate aspects of *Jaws* that most spoke to my students. What's particularly noteworthy is that, when left more or less on their own like this, the students did *not* talk about any of the points raised in the previous chapter: Vietnam, Japan, science, and mystery. In all our far-ranging class discussions, these issues were never raised independently by the students.

I myself never even brought up the idea about anthropology and mystery because Sutton and I didn't think of it until we wrote this book. Even the Japan/Vietnam idea didn't occur to us until 2006, when I taught *Jaws* for the second time. While watching *Jaws* with the class that year, I was struck by Quint's comments on the shark's eyes, and started thinking about their implications. I talked through these ideas with Sutton, and started to realize we might be onto something (more evidence for the value of multiple viewings—and good friends). When I did finally mention the Japan/Vietnam interpretation in my 2006 and 2007 classes, most students seemed to find it intriguing and provocative, and some even tried to run with it.

But what should we make of the fact that they didn't come up with these interpretations on their own? Four possibilities present themselves:

1. These are the kinds of interpretations that people don't usually think of on their own, due to repression and/or the unconscious nature of the symbolism.
2. The students were afraid to contradict me. This doesn't usually seem to be a problem in these kinds of discussions, where everything is clearly up for grabs, but it's still a possibility. As disarming as any of us might think we are, it would be naïve to ignore the power dynamics that come with grading and age differences.
3. The students were willing to contradict me, but they couldn't come up with a rebuttal on the spot.
4. My interpretations simply didn't resonate with the students' own lives and perspectives.

It is hard to know which of these explanations, if any, makes sense of the majority of the students' responses, and what this tells us about the students' views of the *Jaws* interpretations given in the last chapter. This difficulty in itself raises interesting methodological questions about how we ever know what others make of a film, so it will not be swept under the rug. We have to discern which explanations work best, and consider the implications of the most knotty methodological problems.

To get some more traction here, it helps to note that these students were decidedly and rather uniformly committed to "multiculturalism" and the helping of others. My sense of this orientation comes from many sources: reading the students' papers and homework assignments throughout the semester; having intense class discussions; talking one-on-one outside of class; seeing how many students went to study abroad, and how many got involved in activist, humanitarian causes on campus (e.g. tutoring local Hispanic and Native American students, participating in service-learning projects, the Vagina Monologues, AIDS awareness, breast cancer fundraisers); hearing about their personal interests and family histories; observing how they reacted to stories of others' suffering; and teaching these same students in other courses. Although every class I've ever taught has had a distinct personality, the commitment to compassion and multiculturalism has been a definite constant among the Anthropology majors I've known at Willamette.

Further evidence for this orientation came from a study I did with two other anthropology classes during the spring of 2004. For this study (Wogan 2006), I used class discussions and written surveys to examine what students found funny in the documentary *First Contact*, on the premise that humor reactions would give more reliable evidence than direct verbal answers. Contradicting earlier studies (e.g. Martínez 1990), the results indicated that the students—especially those in an upper-level class—were sympathetic with the seemingly strange Papua New Guineans in the film, and condemning of the Australian gold miners.

How did this same orientation among my students affect their responses to *Jaws*? First, it made them highly unlikely to gravitate toward the view that Hooper's killing of the shark is like anthropology's killing of the subject. This view would have been the diametric opposite of the way the students saw themselves. At that point in their undergraduate careers, they were especially excited about the possibilities anthropology offered for understanding and getting closer to others, not killing them, as in our *Jaws* chapter. They were also grappling with new anthropological theories, concepts, and findings, a very different experience from that of *National Geographic* readers who have seen cultural discoveries go stale over the years. Finally, they were still consolidating their identities as Anthropology majors. In these circumstances, it would be hard to see themselves as having just joined a group of taxidermists. For that matter, Sutton and I didn't notice the implications of Hooper's role for several years, and even when we did, we initially resisted the comparison between anthropologists' work and Hooper's killing of the shark.

That said, the students' multicultural orientation does support one of the points made in the previous chapter: that viewers identify with the challenges of intercultural understanding, the oscillation between distance and closeness. For these students, eager to know the cultural Other but often painfully aware of their own lack of direct experience with other cultures, this was an ongoing concern that could partly explain their attraction to *Jaws*.

STUDENT PERSPECTIVES ON WAR

When I suggested that *Jaws* could be a commentary on Vietnam and the Second World War, my students seemed to find this idea plausible and interesting, but it was hard to know how much it resonated with their own experiences and emotions. There was good reason to think it did not resonate deeply. After all, these students were born in the mid-1980s, so they would have seen Vietnam and the Second World War as rather remote aspects of U.S. history. These wars are certainly not as close to them as they are to me, and my own experience remains far from that of a Vietnam veteran or older American who watched *Jaws* in the 1970s, while the embers of the Vietnam War were still burning, or someone who grew up with the bloodshed and anti-Japanese propaganda of the Second World War.[5] In fact, some students barely even remembered that Quint mentioned the atomic bomb, and none ever noted that he was referring to something that really happened, the torpedoing of the USS Indianapolis. I am embarrassed to say that I myself hadn't realized that the Indianapolis sinking was a real event until a Vietnam veteran, Sergeant Thomas Vanderhoof, pointed it out to me. On generational grounds alone, then, we have to expect varied reactions to the war subtext in *Jaws*.[6]

Indeed, nation-wide surveys show important generational changes in attitudes toward the bombing of Hiroshima and Nagasaki. The percentage of Americans expressing regret over the bombing has steadily risen, as Sadao Asada notes in a review of polls taken at various times:

(*Year*)

1956: 17% expressed regret over the decision to bomb Japan

1971: 20% expressed regret over the decision to bomb Japan

1991: 39% expressed regret over the decision to bomb Japan

1995: 49% expressed regret over the decision to bomb Japan.[7]

Moreover, these polls show important differences by age. For example, in a 1986 poll, 33 percent of those who were between 21 and 25 years old disapproved of the atomic bombing, but only 12 percent of 40–49 year olds did the same (Asada 2007: 216). These generational differences become even more striking when it comes to college students in the twenty-first century. In a 2006 survey of college students at Miami University in Oxford, Ohio, Asada found that a "total of 70.8 percent of American students favored apologizing to Japan" (Asada 2007: 240).

I never asked my students how many favored apologizing to Japan, but, based on what I know of their attitudes, I suspect that about 90 to 100 percent of them would have said they did. In fact, I didn't ask this question because it seemed like a non-issue. To suggest otherwise would have probably struck the students as disturbing, and since I did not have time to go into a long discussion of wartime issues, I let it go.

My sense, then, was that the war subtext did not generate pressing social dilemmas for most of these students, and, accordingly, did not play a major role in their emotional reactions to *Jaws*. However, I still wasn't sure one way or the other, so I decided to look at another group of undergraduates: one of Sutton's classes at Southern Illinois University (SIU), Carbondale, Illinois. In April 2009, I flew out to Carbondale, presented the "war parts" of our *Jaws* chapter to this class, and solicited their reactions. Although I obviously didn't know this group as well as my own students, this "cross-check" had certain advantages over my Willamette data. Firstly, there was less chance that the SIU students were just going along with my theories for fear of alienating me; their responses were not graded and Sutton had not told the class that the ideas I was presenting were his as well.

More importantly, I got to ask everyone in the class to put down their views in written, quantitative terms, something I never had time to do with my own students. I asked every student in Sutton's class to respond in writing to my interpretations, rating them on a ten-point scale in terms of resonance with their own lives. This survey method brought out group patterns, reducing the risk that my impressions were skewed by a few vocal students in a class-wide discussion. This is advantageous when trying to ascertain the opinions of an entire group, yet anthropologists rarely tell readers how many people they interviewed on a given point, and they seem downright opposed to survey methods, apparently because they are deemed "positivistic." For example, Mark Allen Peterson takes Catherine Lutz and Jane Lou Collins to task for employing reader surveys, complaining that their study is "flawed" in a "significant" and "serious" way because of its "quasi-experimental nature" (Peterson 2003: 142; cf. Lutz and Collins 1993: 217–58). "Quasi-experimental" is a code word here for sociology or psychology—the bad, non-anthropological Other. By contrast, I believe that survey data, as one part of the picture, can be quite useful (see also Bird 1992, 2003).

The class had twelve students, all undergraduates in the Honors program. None of these students was an Anthropology major; instead, they came from various programs, such as Pre-med, Business, and Psychology. The students had all watched *Jaws* on their own, and came to class on the day of my visit with an index card with their answer to this question: what do you think the shark in this film represents? In this 75-minute class, I showed the clip of Quint's speech about the Indianapolis, and presented our interpretation of the shark's eyes and the connection to wars with Japan and Vietnam. I then explained that I was interested in their honest responses to my interpretation, that I wouldn't be hurt or surprised if they didn't agree with it. I asked everyone to take out a piece of paper and write down answers to the following questions: (1) on a scale of 1 to 10, how much (possibly unconscious) resonance do you feel with this war symbolism?; (2) please explain your answer to question 1. After the students had spent about 15 minutes writing out answers at their desks, we had a class-wide discussion, and at the end of class, students handed in their written answers and filled out an "informed consent form," indicating whether their answers and names could be used in this study (all agreed).

The results were interesting. Out of the twelve students, only one mentioned anything about war on her index card (handed in before I began the class). In contrast, 58 percent gave a rating of 7 or higher on the "resonance scale." The other 42 percent gave ratings of 6, 5, or 4, but none went below 4.[8] While not overwhelming, these ratings seemed to confirm that the "*Jaws*-war theory" works with these college students. In fact, these results seemed to fulfill the ideal for any symbolic interpretation: the interpretation does not occur to most people at first, but once someone else articulates it, the majority agrees that it makes sense. If this comparative evidence were valid, it would indicate that the Willamette students accepted the war theory, but just didn't articulate it themselves at first (explanation number 1).

However, the situation is more complicated. The SIU student comments made in the written explanations and class discussions did not indicate a great deal of emotional investment in the war theory. The most common written comment was some version of "It makes sense" (for example, "I can see the connection," or "Until we started talking about it, I honestly made no connection, but now I can see it"), but there were almost no expressions of strong resonance. Even though I stressed that I wanted to know what they personally felt, the students sometimes seemed to be trying to view the film from a 1970s' perspective, agreeing that the war theory is logical ("I can see it") and it works, but for other Americans, not necessarily themselves. For example, several students got distracted by the question of the director's intentions, and one student said, "Putting myself in the '70s, my issue would center…" These examples left me unsure as to exactly how much stock I should put in the ratings. And given their age, it still stood to reason that the Vietnam War and the Second World War would not figure prominently in their viewing of *Jaws* (though some did make the comparison to Iraq).

This experience demonstrated again that college students, like any other group, are not homogenous and unchanging. For example, Jean-Paul Dumont reports that, in the wake of the Vietnam War, college students in the 1970s were likely to see the Yanomamo as violent "savages" yet, by the mid-1980s, the climate had changed so much that students tended to empathize with the Yanomamo:

> Whoever teaches an introductory course in anthropology in the United States might have been struck by the ways in which the students have changed their perception of the Yanomamo, now less intractable savages whom one has every reason to distrust, than individuals with whom one cannot but sympathize. These Indians are, in effect, people who do not let anyone step on their toes and whose aggressiveness is, in the end, justified. (Dumont 1988: 272)

Variations in student reactions can also be attributed to institutional contexts. A large lecture class, especially if it's one where ethnographic film is used as a baby-sitter and not contextualized, is not the same as a small class with a basis in film discussion.[9] By the same token, the context in which the teaching occurs—the goals of the lesson, the teacher-student dynamics—will obviously have an impact.

Although Sutton's teaching methods and student demographics were similar to mine, there were also differences, such as the degree of anthropology coursework among our students, and the pedagogical context for the film discussions. Still, if the SIU results had been more consistent and emphatic, I would have used them for partial confirmation of my own students' responses, especially in light of the advantages noted earlier. Given the mixed results, though, I think the SIU reactions can't be used to prove or disprove the meaning of my own students' reactions at Willamette.

For now, I am still inclined to say that the war interpretation does not work particularly well for my Willamette "Theory" students. Or, rather, the evidence is inconclusive and the issue requires further study. An ambiguous case like this might seem like a strange choice for the Conclusion, where things usually get neatly wrapped up, but it serves an important function, as it reminds us that interpreting audience responses is not a straightforward methodological issue.

But all is not lost. We have seen good evidence for the interpretation about inter-cultural understanding and *Jaws*. And if doubts have been cast on the applicability of the war theory to college-student audiences, that, too, is valuable. Also, when students spoke with people above the age of thirty, they found confirmation for the war theory, as we will see in the next section.

OTHER VIEWS OF *JAWS*

In 2005 and 2006, I used *Jaws* only in class discussions, and then had the students choose other movies (or a Turnerian analysis of ritual symbolism) for their paper topics. In 2007, however, I tried something different. After we had analyzed *Jaws* in class, I asked the students if they'd like to write their papers on interviews about *Jaws*, rather than take up text-internal analyses of new movies. Everyone in the class voted for the *Jaws* option.

Each student had to do at least two interviews (45-minute minimum) with someone over the age of thirty. Most students interviewed their parents, but some interviewed neighbors, or grandparents, or, in one case, a Vietnam veteran from the local VFW. Each student also had to listen to the digital recordings of at least two other student interviews. For their papers, the students had to weave their interviews into an original analysis that revealed something surprising about *Jaws* and American society.

Given the requirement for originality and the fact that we had discussed Sutton's and my war theory in class, the students didn't write about Hiroshima, the shark's eyes, or the Indianapolis. Instead, they wrote about a variety of other topics, including the following: the oil crisis of the 1970s (Mara Engle), survivor guilt (Sarah Kutten), communism (Victoria Moffat), propaganda (Jake Reese), profit (Nelya Drofyak), government secrecy (Katelyn Wright), and the relationship between joy and terror (Jessica Junke).[10]

Not only did many of the students come up with interesting interpretations in their papers, but they elicited moving stories in their interviews. For example, John P. Junke, Sr. told his daughter Jessica about getting a draft deferment because he was undergoing theological training, while his roommate Phil left college, got drafted, and was killed in Vietnam. Also, when asked about his worst childhood fear, Mr. Junke described getting trapped under a box one time and being terrified by the darkness and his sudden loss of control. Another woman described the needless clubbing of a small alligator by men who felt compelled to fight all perceived threats:

> There was a … some kid found an alligator in the river in a little slough off the river. And I mean it had probably been some pet that had been set free some time back. It was a fairly good-sized alligator. And the boy, you know, screamed he found it. He and his mom got it, or got hold of it in one place, and kinda' pulled it up on land. Well, the next thing, they had all these guys come over and start beating the alligator to death. And it was killed by these men with clubs. And the alligator was no threat. There was nothing wrong. They had actually kind of tied it up, and they still beat it to death. It was kind of like, "We're protecting you and it shouldn't be here." (Susan Clanton, interviewed by Kelsey Walsh)

These and other stories, recollections, and opinions were creatively related back to *Jaws* in the students' papers, showing how it's often better to ask indirectly about a movie, rather than hitting interviewees point blank with a question like, "what does *Jaws* mean to you?" The interviews also indirectly supported parts of our war theory. Precisely because they were not explicitly about this theory, it was striking when they did touch on related themes. For example, Mr. Junke was impacted by the death of his friend in Vietnam, suggesting a kind of survivor guilt that could play into war themes. Another student's mother explicitly connected Vietnam with *Jaws*:

> One thing that was very similar between people's reactions to *Jaws* and peoples' reactions to the Vietnam War crisis and the fear of the unknown and all of that … one thing it was OK to do with *Jaws,* the movie, was to scream and yell, to act scared, to be scared, to grab each other. It seemed to be because it was known to be a scary thing; there seemed to be an acceptable level of lack of control of your behavior. (Donette Kutten, interviewed by Sarah Kutten)

These brief examples suggest that the Vietnam War shaped the students' parents' understanding of *Jaws*. And even where these student projects go off in other directions, they demonstrate some of the methodological challenges and possibilities of audience-response analysis.

METHODOLOGICAL RECOMMENDATIONS

Some general points emerge from Wogan's experience. In terms of pedagogy, the usual rules for this kind of teaching apply: go into depth; less is more; hold out for original, surprising insights; create structure and embrace chaos; trust yourself and your students; doubt everything.

As for ethnographic projects on the media, whether about students or not, we would make the following recommendations:

1. Don't always take explicit statements at face value.
2. Use a variety of methods.
3. Come at the situation from indirect angles, such as asking people to draw pictures of the movie (to see what they highlight), or asking for stories about social issues that aren't ostensibly related to the movie (e.g. childhood memories of a scary experience).
4. Immerse yourself deeply in the audience's experience.
5. Be reflexive about the ways that different methods bring out different insights.
6. Examine the many factors that can shape audiences: not only age, race, class, region, and gender, but also institutional setting, group dynamics, and personal background.
7. Delve into emotions, feelings, and life histories, including your own.
8. Do not dismiss surveys.

DREAM PALACES AND BEYOND

On the one hand, we have to attend to the many different factors that influence viewer perceptions, and anthropology's main methodological contribution will continue to be ethnography. On the other hand, ethnography is not a panacea. Neither ethnography nor any other methodology has direct access to what people really think, especially not when it comes to movies. Wogan's mini-ethnography on audience feelings about *Jaws* illustrates that we've entered a complex area filled with inner feelings and impulses, unconscious symbolism, ambivalences, and contradictions. According to recent work in many fields, the individual self is less a unified, coherent whole and more an inchoate amalgam of contradictory, overlapping feelings, motivations, and practices. Thus, to understand what emotionally powerful movies mean to audience members is a tall order, one not easily filled by just saying, "Do ethnography."

Movies are especially likely to stir up complex feelings. They are like giant, moving ink blots, dreams that run through millions of minds at the same time. And the likeness between movies and dreams isn't just metaphorical. In both cases, we recline in the dark while images flicker in front of our eyes and provoke consideration of vexing issues, those pieces of the puzzle that won't quite fit. It's no coincidence that early movie theatres were known as "dream palaces." This vernacular intuition is supported by recent research showing that, in the 1940s, three-quarters of Americans said they only dreamed in black and white, whereas now, after several decades of color television, three-quarters say they dream in color.[11] But if it's possible to show the correlation between color television and color dreaming, it's harder to enter the dream palace, to figure out what movies mean to people at a deep personal and collective level. Doing so is, nonetheless, possible; it just requires a creative mixture of ethnography and other methods.

Good models are Elizabeth Bird and John Caughey, anthropologists who have delved into the ways that fans create intimate imaginary relationships with media figures, not only in dreams, but also fantasies, daydreams, and imaginary friendships (Bird 1992, 2003; Caughey 1984, 1994, 2006). For example, in his study of an informant's imaginary relationship with movie star Steven Seagal, Caughey argues for the value of focusing on the subjectivity of individual viewers:

> ... [It is] illuminating to consider how the character types of a person's favorite
> media realms correspond not only to other figures in the genre but to consider
> also how they correspond to types of figures in the individual's fantasies, dreams,
> and actual social worlds. As Gina's classifications here indicate, the Seagal drama,
> in which the strong figure wreaks vengeance on the villains who have abused
> weak women, provides a satisfying play on a variety of dramas in Gina's actual
> and imaginary social worlds. (1994: 132)

Along similar lines—dreams about movies, flexible methodologies, consideration of the individual—the work of Louise Krasniewicz and Michael Blitz is quite interesting. In the course of researching the cultural impact of Arnold Schwarzenegger's movies, Krasniewicz and Blitz found themselves having repeated vivid dreams about the star. They have recorded over 150 such dreams, which they analyze in terms of Schwarzenegger's ability to "morph" into different forms, and, like a good metaphor or dream, to create connections between diverse and highly personal aspects of our lives. Such dream analysis fits into their study of the way Schwarzenegger's "influence steps off the screen and beyond the box office to become pervasive in every nook and cranny of our lives" (2002: 21). They have traced the ways that Schwarzenegger has become a metaphor for many different cultural values, including power, excellence, persistence, poor speech and acting styles, and the "immigrant experience" (29–30).

Wogan's current research also explores the relationship between movies and dreams. He started an ethnographic project on a Mexican-American video store in Oregon in 2005, naïvely assuming that within a few years he would be able to publish an article or two on audience responses to the store's cowboy (*ranchera*) films. Four years and over 5,000 pages of field notes later, he hasn't published a word on this topic. He has gotten especially caught up in the life of the video store owner, Ranulfo Juárez, hearing not just about the movies this man watches, but also his fears, family dynamics, resentments, hopes, fantasies, and intense, convoluted, spiritual dreams. Wogan now talks with Ranulfo about his dreams on a weekly, often daily, basis, and Wogan, too, has come to dream about the issues they discuss. Ranulfo has a rich fantasy life, not only in relation to *ranchera* films, but also the Incredible Hulk, Bill Gates, and Don Quixote, among others. To capture the complex connections between Ranulfo's life, dreams, fantasies, and perceptions of movies, Wogan is looking for new methods and writing formats—perhaps a cross between life history, memoir, media studies, and anthropology.

While Sutton's current research does not deal specifically with dreams (though he dreams a lot about his research as well), he has been trying to integrate diverse methods into audience and media studies. For example, in a recent publication co-authored with his student Leo Vournelis (Sutton and Vournelis 2009), he explores the way TV cooking shows in Greece have become sources of reflection on, and engagement with, contemporary social issues, as well as a source of nostalgia. A few of these shows are not unlike blockbuster movies in their wild popularity in Greece. Sutton has been particularly interested in not only documenting the comments of his Greek informants about these shows, but has been filming the way the recipes and other cooking practices and devices on these shows are tried out, rejected out of hand, or incorporated into people's everyday cooking repertoires. Through this method, Sutton and Vournelis are able to show that cooking shows connect with culturally shaped memory practices, the ways that informants create a verbal and practical dialogue with the stars of these shows, praising and criticizing their dishes in relation to their own long-established cooking knowledge and practices.

We believe that all of these approaches offer exciting possibilities for an anthropology engaged with movies and other contemporary mass media. We also hope that the analysis continues. After all, there can be no final word when it comes to movies like this.

To hear our additional thoughts and more personal observations, and, most of all, to let us know what you think—about these movies, about our interpretations—please visit our blog: http://blockbusteranthropology.blogspot.com/

We hope to see you there.

NOTES

1. Even if that's the case, we can still say, as McMurphy did after trying to throw the sink through the hospital window in *One Flew Over the Cuckoo's Nest*, "But I tried ... at least I did that."
2. For a copy of this manuscript, "Seinfeld's Anthropology," please visit this book's blog at: http://blockbusteranthropology.blogspot.com/
3. Many people have trouble pronouncing "Willamette" correctly, so Oregonians half-jokingly suggest the following mnemonic aid: "Willamette" rhymes with "Dammit" (as in "will-ammit").
4. For more discussion of this issue in *Jaws*, see Drummond (1996: 222–6) and Friedman (2006: 165). For related discussion of *Rambo*, see Traube (1992: 39–47); and for analysis of practical knowledge in general, see Ingold (2000).
5. For example, many people don't realize that more Vietnam veterans have died from suicide after the war than from combat fatalities during the war.
6. One critic put this temporal dimension in perspective when, in 1975, he wrote, "There used to be a time when *Jaws'* significance would have been apparent to all, when we wouldn't have had to cast about for symbolic meanings to hang on the shark. A few years ago, during the Cold War, the shark would have stood for International Communism, pure and simple" (Biskind 1975: 1).
7. See Asada (2007: 213–6). The wording of the polls varied, but the basic question was the same: do you feel the atomic bombing was necessary?
8. The ratings broke down as follows: one 9, three 8s, three 7s, two 6s, one 5, and two 4s. A rating of 6 seems like a good cut-off point, based on the written explanations that followed. Those who gave ratings of 7 or higher didn't voice major doubts, whereas one of the students who gave a 6 rating immediately added "– and that's a stretch."
9. Compare Bird and Godwin (2006), Martínez (1990, 1992, 1995), and Wogan (2006). I was also reminded of these institutional differences in the course of a roundtable session on "Audience Reception of Ethnographic Film," organized by Sam Pack and me for the American Anthropological Association Meeting, San Francisco, California, November 20, 2008.
10. The other students in the class were Kelsey Walsh, Sheila Kelly, Bekah Hykan, and Stephanie Fleming.
11. See O'Connor 2008: D5.

REFERENCES CITED

Abu-Lughod, Lila (1997), 'The Interpretation of Culture(s) After Television', *Representations*, 59: 109–34.

Abu-Lughod, Lila (2005), *Dramas of Nationhood: The Politics of Television in Egypt*, Chicago: University of Chicago Press.

Aden, Roger C (1999), *Popular Stories and Promised Lands: Fan Cultures and Symbolic Pilgrimages*, Tuscaloosa, AL: University of Alabama Press.

Allison, Anne (2001), 'Cyborg Violence: Bursting Borders and Bodies with Queer Machines', *Cultural Anthropology*, 16(2): 237–65.

Altherr, Thomas L (2002), 'W.P. Kinsella's Baseball Fiction: *Field of Dreams* and the New Mythopoeism of Baseball', in Stephen C. Wood and J. David Pincus (eds.), *Reel Baseball: Essays and Interviews on the National Pastime, Hollywood and American Culture*, pp. 52–62, Jefferson, NC: McFarland and Company, Inc.

Anderson, Benedict (1991), *Imagined Communities: Reflections on the Origin and Spread of Nationalism*, London: Verso.

Anderson, Matt (2004), *It Takes a Village*, Movie Habit (website) www.moviehabit.com/reviews/vil_g004.shtml (Accessed 2/8/2006).

Andrews, Nigel (1999), *Nigel Andrews on Jaws*, New York: Bloomsbury.

Angeletti, Norberto and Oliva, Alberto (2004), *Magazines That Make History: Their Origins, Development, and Influence*, Gainsville, FL: University of Florida Press.

Asada, Sadao (2007), *Culture Shock and Japanese-American Relations: Historical Essays*, Columbia, MO: University of Missouri Press.

Askew, Kelley and Wilk, Richard R (eds.) (2002), *The Anthropology of Media: A Reader*, Oxford: Blackwell.

Bahktin, Mikhail (1986), *Speech Genres and Other Late Essays* (V.W. McGhee, trans.), Austin, TX: University of Texas Press.

Barber, Karen (2007), 'Improvisation and the Art of Making Things Stick', in Tim Ingold and Elizabeth Hallam (eds.), *Creativity and Cultural Improvisation*, pp. 25–41, Oxford: Berg.

Bateson, Gregory (1958) [1936], *Naven, A Survey of the Problems Suggested by a Composite Picture of the Culture of a New Guinea Tribe Drawn from Three Points of View*, Stanford, CA: Stanford University Press.

Bateson, Gregory (1980), 'An Analysis of the Nazi Film "Hitlerjunge Quex"', *Studies in Visual Communication,* 6(3): 20–55.

Battaglia, Debbora (2001), 'Multiplicities: An Anthropologist's Thoughts on Replicants and Clones in Popular Film', *Critical Inquiry,* 27(2): 493–514.

Bauman, Richard, and Briggs, Charles (1990), 'Poetics and Performance as Critical Perspectives on Language and Social Life', *Annual Review of Anthropology,* 19: 59–88.

Beeman, William O (2000), 'Margaret Mead: America's Premier Analyst', in Margaret Mead (ed.), *Studying Contemporary Western Society: Method and Theory,* pp. x–xix, Oxford: Berghahn.

Behar, Ruth (1993), *Translated Woman: Crossing the Border with Esperanza's Story,* Boston: Beacon Press.

Behar, Ruth (1997), *The Vulnerable Observer: Anthropology That Breaks Your Heart,* Boston: Beacon Press.

Behar, Ruth (2007), *An Island Called Home: Returning to Jewish Cuba,* New Brunswick, NJ: Rutgers University Press.

Behar, Ruth (2009), 'Believing in Anthropology as Literature', in Alisse Waterston and Maria D. Vesperi (eds.), *Anthropology Off the Shelf: Anthropologists on Writing,* pp. 106–16, Malden, MA: Wiley-Blackwell.

Bird, S. Elizabeth (1992), *For Enquiring Minds: A Cultural Study of Supermarket Tabloids,* Knoxville, TN: University of Tennessee Press.

Bird, S. Elizabeth (1996), *Dressing in Feathers: The Construction of the Indian in American Popular Culture,* Boulder, CO: Westview Press.

Bird, S. Elizabeth (2003), *The Audience in Everyday Life: Living in a Media World,* New York: Routledge.

Bird, S. Elizabeth and Godwin, Jonathan P. (2006), 'Film in the Undergraduate Classroom: Applying Audience Response Research in Pedagogical Practice', *Anthropology and Education Quarterly,* 37(3): 285–99.

Bird, S. Elizabeth, and Von Trapp, Carolena (1999), 'Beyond Stones and Bones', *Anthropology News,* December: 9–10.

Biskind, Peter (1975), '*Jaws* Between the Teeth', *Jump Cut: A Review of Contemporary Media,* 9: 1, 26.

Blackwood, Evelyn (2000), *Webs of Power: Women, Kin and Community in a Sumatran Village,* New York: Rowman and Littlefield.

Bloch, Maurice (2005), *Essays on Cultural Transmission*, Oxford: Berg.

Bodenhorn, Barbara (2000), '"He Used to be My Relative": Exploring the Bases of Relatedness among Iñupiat of Northern Alaska', in Janet Carsten (ed.), *Cultures of Relatedness: New Approaches to the Study of Kinship*, pp. 128–48, Cambridge: Cambridge University Press.

Boose, Lynda E (1993), 'Techno-Muscularity and the "Boy Eternal": From the Quagmire to the Gulf', in Miriam Cooke and Angela Woollacott (eds.), *Gendering War Talk*, pp. 67–106, Princeton, NJ: Princeton University Press.

Boulanger, Claire (2004), 'American Pie: Good to Eat, Good to Think?' Paper presented at the *American Anthropological Association Meetings*, Atlanta, GA.

Bourdieu, Pierre (1997), 'Marginalia—Some Additional Notes on the Gift', in Alan D. Schrift (ed.), *The Logic of the Gift, Toward an Ethic of Generosity*, pp. 231–41, New York: Routledge.

Bourke, Joanna (1999), *An Intimate History of Killing: Face-to-Face Killing in the Twentieth Century*, New York: Basic Books.

Brown, Keith (1998), 'Macedonian Culture and its Audiences: An Analysis of *Before the Rain*', in Felicia Hughes-Freeland (ed.), *Ritual, Performance, Media*, pp. 160–76, London: Routledge.

Browne, Nick (ed.) (2000), *Francis Ford Coppola's The Godfather Trilogy*, Cambridge: Cambridge University Press.

Burr, Ty (1999), *100 Greatest Movies of All Time*, New York: Entertainment Weekly Books.

Campbell, Alan (1996), 'Tricky Tropes: Styles of the Popular and the Pompous', in Jeremy MacClancy and Chris McDonaugh (eds.), *Popularizing Anthropology*, pp. 58–82, London: Routledge.

Carrier, James (1990), 'Gifts in a World of Commodities: The Ideology of the Perfect Gift in U.S. Society', *Social Analysis*, 29: 19–37.

Carrier, James (1997), 'Mr. Smith, Meet Mr. Hawken', in James Carrier (ed.), *Meanings of the Market*, pp. 129–58, Oxford: Berg.

Carrier, James, and Miller, Daniel (1999), 'From Private Virtue to Public Vice', in Henrietta L. Moore (ed.), *Anthropological Theory Today*, pp. 24–47, Cambridge: Polity Press.

Caton, Steven C. (1999), *Lawrence of Arabia: A Film's Anthropology*, Berkeley, CA: University of California Press.

Caughey, John L. (1984), *Imaginary Social Worlds: A Cultural Approach*, Lincoln, NB: University of Nebraska Press.

Caughey, John L. (1994), 'Gina as Steven: The Social and Cultural Dimensions of a Media Relationship', *Visual Anthropology Review*, 10(1): 126–35.

Caughey, John L. (2006), *Negotiating Cultures and Identities: Life History Issues, Methods, and Readings*, Lincoln, NB: University of Nebraska Press.

Chalfen, Richard (2003), 'Hollywood Makes Anthropology: The Case of *Krippendorf's Tribe*', *Visual Anthropology*, 16(4): 375–91.

Chalfen, Richard and Pack, Sam (1999), 'Why *Krippendorf's Tribe* is Good for Teaching Anthropology', *Visual Anthropology Review*, 14(1): 103–5.

Clifford, James (1986), 'On Ethnographic Allegory', in James Clifford and George E. Marcus (eds.), *Writing Culture: The Poetics and Politics of Ethnography*, pp. 98–121, Berkeley, CA: University of California Press.

Clifford, James (1988), *The Predicament of Culture: Twentieth Century Ethnography, Literature and Art*, Cambridge, MA: Harvard University Press.

Coen, Ethan and Coen, Joel (1998), *The Big Lebowski*. London: Faber & Faber.

Cole, Jennifer (2006), 'Memory and Modernity', in C. Casey and R. Edgerton (eds.), *A Companion to Psychological Anthropology: Modernity and Psychocultural Change*, pp. 103–20, Malden, MA: Blackwell.

Collier, Patrick (2008), '"Our Silly Lies": Ideological Fictions in M. Night Shyamalan's *The Village*', *Journal of Narrative Theory*, 38(2): 269–92.

Collins, James (1995), 'Literacy and Literacies', *Annual Review of Anthropology*, 24: 75–93.

Collis, Clark (2008), 'The Dude and I', *Entertainment Weekly*, March 21, 35–7.

Comaroff, Jean and Comaroff, John L. (eds.) (1993), *Modernity and its Malcontents: Ritual and Power in Postcolonial Africa*, Chicago: University of Chicago Press.

Comer, Todd (2005), '"This Aggression Will Not Stand": Myth, War, and Ethics in *The Big Lebowski*', *SubStance #107*, 34(2): 98–117.

Connerton, Paul (1989), *How Societies Remember*, Cambridge: Cambridge University Press.

Cooper, Caroline M. (1995), '*Field of Dreams*: A Favorite of President Clinton—But a Typical Reaganite Film?', *Literature and Film Quarterly*, 23(3): 163–8.

Corliss, Richard (1989), 'Don't Run: One Hit, One Error', *Time* (April 24): 78.

Cornwall, Andrea and Lindisfarne, Nancy (eds.) (1994), *Dislocating Masculinities: Comparative Ethnographies*, London: Routledge.

Couric, Katie (2008), *The Candidates on Their Favorite Films: CBS Evening News: McCain and Obama Answer Katie Couric's Presidential Questions*, CBS News. Broadcast September 23 (2008), Transcript retrieved on February 14, 2009 at http://www.cbsnews.com/stories/2008/09/23/eveningnews/main4472884.shtml ?source=RSSattr=Politics_4472884.

Crapanzano, Vincent (1980), *Tuhami: Portrait of a Moroccan*, Chicago: University of Chicago Press.

Crawford, Peter Ian and Hafsteinsson, Sigurjon Baldur (eds.) (1996), *Construction of the Viewer: Media Ethnography and The Anthropology of Audiences*, Denmark: Intervention Press, in association with the Nordic Anthropological Film Association.

Derrida, Jacques (Gayatri Chakravorty Spivak, trans.) (1976), *Of Grammatology*, Baltimore, MD: Johns Hopkins University Press.

Di Leonardo, Micaela (1998), *Exotics at Home: Anthropologies, Others, American Modernity*, Chicago: University of Chicago Press.

Dickey, Sarah (1993), *Cinema and the Urban Poor in South India*, Cambridge: Cambridge University Press.

Dika, Vera (2000), 'The Representation of Ethnicity in *The Godfather*', in Nick Browne (ed.), *Francis Ford Coppola's* Godfather *Trilogy*, pp. 76–108, Cambridge: Cambridge University Press.

Dower, John W. (1986), *War Without Mercy: Race and Power in the Pacific War*, New York: Pantheon Books.

Drummond, Lee (1995), *American Dreamtime: A Cultural Analysis of Popular Movies, and Their Implications for a Science of Humanity*, Lanham, MD: Rowman & Littlefield.

Drummond, Lee (2000), 'Last Undiscovered Tribe Exposed', *Anthropology News*, February: 5–6.

Dumont, Jean-Paul (1988), 'The Tasaday, Which and Whose? Toward the Political Economy of an Ethnographic Sign', *Cultural Anthropology* 3(3): 261–75.

Duncan, Christopher (2005), *Community and Culture: Reflections from Contemporary Resources*. Paper Presented at the Marianist Universities Meetings, University of Dayton, Dayton, OH, June 6–9. http://campus.udayton.edu/~amu-usa/pdfs/ duncan_final_paper.pdf. Accessed February 21 2009.

Eriksen, Thomas Hylland (2006), *Engaging Anthropology: The Case for a Public Presence*, Oxford: Berg.

Fabian, Johannes (1981), *Time and the Other: How Anthropology Makes its Object*, New York: Columbia University Press.

Farber, Stephen (1972), 'Coppola and *The Godfather*', *Sight and Sound: International Film Quarterly*, 41: 217–24.

Fausto, Carlos and Heckenberger, Michael (2007), *Time and Memory in Indigenous Amazonia: Anthropological Perspectives*, Gainesville, FL: University of Florida Press.

Federici, Silvia (2004), *Caliban and the Witch: Women, the Body and Primitive Accumulation*, Brooklyn, NY: Autonomedia.

Fernandez, James (1986), *Persuasions and Performances: The Play of Tropes in Culture*, Bloomington, IN: University of Indiana Press.

Ferraro, Thomas J. (1993), *Ethnic Passages: Literary Immigrants in Twentieth-Century America*, Chicago: University of Chicago Press.

Franklin, Sarah (2000), 'Life Itself: Global Nature and the Genetic Imaginary', in Sarah Franklin, Celia Lury, and Jackie Stacey (eds.), *Global Nature: Global Culture*, pp. 188–227, London: Sage Publications.

Friedl, Ernestine (1975), *Women and Men: An Anthropologist's View*, New York: Holt, Rinehart and Winston.

Friedman, Lester D. (2006), *Citizen Spielberg*, Urbana: University of Illinois Press.

Fruehling Springwood, Charles (1996), *Cooperstown to Dyersville: A Geography of Baseball Nostalgia*, Boulder, CO: Westview Press.

Gales, Jonathan and Bird, S. Elizabeth (2005), 'Anthropology at the Movies: Jerry Maguire as "Expeditionary Discourse"', in David Holloway and John Beck (eds.), *American Visual Cultures*, pp. 284–90, London: Continuum.

Geertz, Clifford (1973), *The Interpretation of Cultures: Selected Essays*, New York: Basic Books.

Geertz, Clifford (1984), 'Distinguished Lecture: Anti Anti-Relativism', *American Anthropologist*, 86(2): 263–78.

Geertz, Clifford (1998), 'Deep Hanging Out', *New York Review of Books*, 45(16): 69–72.

Gehring, Wes D. (2004), *Mr. Deeds Goes to Yankee Stadium: Baseball Films in the Capra Tradition*, Jefferson, NC: McFarland.

Ginsburg, Faye, Abu-Lughod, Lila and Larkin, Brian (eds.) (2002), *Media Worlds: Anthropology on New Terrain*, Berkeley: University of California Press.

Gordon, Robert J. and Douglas, Stuart S. (2000), *The Bushman Myth: The Making of a Namibian Underclass*, 2nd edition, Boulder, CO: Westview Press.

Graeber, David (2001), *Toward an Anthropological Theory of Value: The False Coin of our Own Dreams*, New York: Palgrave.

Graeber, David (2004), *Fragments of an Anarchist Anthropology*, Chicago: Prickly Paradigm Press.

Green, Bill, Peskoe, Ben, Russell, Will, et al. (2007), *I'm a Lebowski, You're a Lebowski: Life,* The Big Lebowski*, and What Have You*, New York: Bloomsbury.

Hanks, W. F. (1989), 'Text and Textuality', *Annual Review of Anthropology*, 18: 95–127.

Harbsmeier, Michael (1985), 'Early Travels to Europe: Some Remarks on the Magic of Writing', in Francis Barker, Peter Hulme, Margaret Iverson et al. (eds.), *Europe and Its Other*, pp. 72–87, Colchester: University of Essex Press.

Hart, Keith (2005), *The Hit Man's Dilemma: Or, Business, Personal and Impersonal*, Chicago: Prickly Paradigm Press.

Haynes, Rosalynn D. (1994), *From Faust to Strangelove: Representations of the Scientist in Western Literature*, Baltimore, MD: Johns Hopkins University Press.

Haynes, Rosalynn (2003), 'From Alchemy to Artificial Intelligence: Stereotypes of the Scientist in Western Literature', *Public Understanding of Science*, 12(3): 243–53.

Healy, Dave, and Healy, Paul (1993), 'Half-Cultivated Fields: Symbolic Landscapes of Baseball', in Peter C. Bjarkman (ed.), *Baseball and the Game of Ideas: Essays for the Serious Fan*, pp. 115–22, Delhi, NY: Birch Brook Press.

Herzfeld, Michael (1992), *The Social Production of Indifference: Exploring the Symbolic Roots of Western Bureaucracy*, Oxford: Berg.

Hess, John (1975), '*Godfather, Part II*: A Deal Coppola Couldn't Refuse', *Jump Cut: A Review of Contemporary Media*, 7(1): 10–11.

Hochschild, Arlie Russell (2003), *The Managed Heart: Commercialization of Human Feeling*, 2nd edition, Berkeley: University of California Press.

Howes, David (2003), *Sensual Relations: Engaging the Senses in Culture and Social Theory*, Ann Arbor, MI: University of Michigan Press.

Hudson, Wayne (2003), *The Reform of Utopia*, Aldershot: Ashgate Publishing.

Hutson, Matthew (2007), 'Whatta You Lookin' At? When Reading Minds, the Eyes Have It', *Psychology Today*, 40(6): 15.

Huyssen, Andreas (1994), *Twilight Memories: Marking Time in a Culture of Amnesia*, London: Routledge.

Ingold, Tim (2000), *The Perception of the Environment*, London: Routledge.

Ingold, Tim (2007), *Lines: A Brief History*, London: Routledge.

Jacobson, David (1991), *Reading Ethnography*, Albany, NY: State University of New York Press.

Jameson, Frederic (1979), 'Reification and Utopia in Mass Culture', *Social Text*, 1: 130–48.

Karp, Ivan (1976), 'Good Marx for the Anthropologist: Structure and Antistructure in Duck Soup', in William Arens and Susan Montague (eds.), *The American Dimension*, pp. 37–50, Sherman Oaks, CA: Greenwood Press.

Kazecki, Jakub (2008), '"What Makes a Man, Mr. Lebowski?": Masculinity under (Friendly) Fire in Ethan and Joel Coen's *The Big Lebowski*', *Atenea*, 28(1): 147–59.

Kiesling, Scott (2004), 'Dude', *American Speech*, 79(3): 281–305.

Kinsella, W.P. (1982), *Shoeless Joe*, Boston: Houghton Mifflin.

Kottak, Conrad P. (1982), 'Structural and Psychological Analysis of Popular American Fantasy Films', in Conrad P. Kottak (ed.), *Researching American Culture: A Guide for Student Anthropologists*, pp. 87–97, Ann Arbor, MI: University of Michigan Press.

Krasniewicz, Louise (2006), '"Round up the Usual Suspects": Anthropology Goes to the Movies', *Expedition*, 48(1): 8–14.

Krasniewicz, Louise, and Blitz, Michael (2002), 'The Replicator: Starring Arnold Schwarzenegger as the Great Meme-Machine', in Angela Ndalianis and Charlotte Henry (eds.), *Stars in Our Eyes: The Star Phenomenon in the Contemporary Era*, pp. 21–43, Westport, CT: Praeger Press.

Kulick, Don, and Willson, Margaret (2002), 'Rambo's Wife Saves the Day: Subjugating the Gaze and Subverting the Narrative in a Papua New Guinean Swamp', in Kelly Askew and Richard R. Wilk (eds.), *The Anthropology of Media: A Reader*, pp. 270–85, Malden, MA: Blackwell.

Latour, Bruno (1993), *We Have Never Been Modern* (Catherine Porter, trans.), Cambridge, MA: Harvard University Press.

Leacock, Eleanor (1981), *Myths of Male Dominance: Collected Articles on Women Cross-Culturally*, New York: Monthly Review Press.

Lee, Richard (1998) [1969], 'Eating Xmas in the Kalahari', *Annual Editions: Anthropology 1998/99*, pp. 27–30, Guildford, CT: Dushkin/McGraw Hill.

Lutz, Catherine, and Collins, Jane Lou (1993), *Reading National Geographic*, Chicago: University of Chicago Press.

MacKenzie, Ian (2000), 'Improvisation, Creativity, and Formulaic Language', *The Journal of Aesthetics and Art Criticism*, 58(2): 173–9.

Mankekar, Purnima (1999), *Screening Culture, Viewing Politics: An Ethnography of Television, Womanhood, and Nation in Postcolonial India*, Durham, NC: Duke University Press.

Mann, Glenn (2000), 'Ideology and Genre in the *Godfather* Films', in Nick Browne (ed.), *Francis Ford Coppola's* Godfather *Trilogy*, pp. 109–32, Cambridge: Cambridge University Press.

Martin, Paul, and Renegar, Valerie (2007), '"The Man for His Time": *The Big Lebowski* as Carnivalesque Social Critique', *Communication Studies*, 58(3): 299–313.

Martin-Jones, David (2006), 'No Literal Connection: Images of Mass Commodification, US Militarism, and the Oil Industry in *The Big Lebowski*', *Sociological Review*, 54(1): 131–49.

Martínez, Wilton (1990), 'Critical Studies and Visual Anthropology: Aberrant vs. Anticipated Readings of Ethnographic Film', *Commission on Visual Anthropology* (Spring): 34–46.

Martínez, Wilton (1992), 'Who Constructs Anthropological Knowledge?: Toward a Theory of Ethnographic Film Spectatorship', in Peter Crawford and David Turton (eds.), *Film as Ethnography*, pp. 130–61, Manchester: Manchester University Press.

Martínez, Wilton (1995), 'The Challenges of a Pioneer: Tim Asch, Otherness, and Film Reception', *Visual Anthropology Review*, 11(1): 53–82.

McCall, John (2002), 'Madness, Money and Movies: Watching a Nigerian Popular Video with the Guidance of a Native Doctor', *Africa Today*, 49(3): 78–94.

McClaurin, Irma (2009), 'Walking in Zora's Shoes or "Seek[ing] Out de Inside Meanin' of Words": The Intersections of Anthropology, Ethnography, Identity, and Writing', in Alisse Waterston and Maria D. Vesperi (eds.), *Anthropology Off the Shelf: Anthropologists on Writing*, pp. 119–33, Malden, MA: Wiley-Blackwell.

Mead, Margaret (2000), *Studying Contemporary Western Society: Method and Theory*, Oxford: Berghahn.

Meillasoux, Claude (1981), *Maidens, Meals and Money: Capitalism and the Domestic Community* (Felicity Edholm, trans.), Cambridge: Cambridge University Press.

Meyer, Birgit (2003), 'Visions of Blood, Sex and Money: Fantasy Spaces in Popular Ghanaian Cinema', *Visual Anthropology*, 16(1): 15–41.

Muller, Viana (1985), 'Origins of Class and Gender Stratification in Northwest Europe', *Dialectical Anthropology*, 10(1–2): 93–106.

Murray, David W. (1981), 'American/Indian', *Anthropology and Humanism Quarterly*, 16: 82–8.

Myerhoff, Barbara G. (1978), *Number Our Days*, New York: Dutton.

Needham, Rodney (1973), *Ritual, Belief and Experience*, Chicago: University of Chicago Press.

Nugent, Stephen and Shore, Chris (eds.) (1997), *Anthropology and Cultural Studies*, London: Pluto Press.

O'Connor, Anahad (2008), 'Really? The Claim: Some People Dream Only in Black And White', in *The New York Times, Science Times* section, December 2: p. D5.

Okja Cobb, Nora (1990), 'Behind the Inscrutable Half-Shell: Images of Mutant Japanese and Ninja Turtles', *Melus*, 16(4): 87–98.

Ortner, Sherry (1996), *Making Gender: The Politics and Erotics of Culture*, Boston: Beacon Press.

Overby, Peter (2008), *As Election Spotlight Dims, Ayers the Author Speaks*. NPR Morning Edition, November 18 2008. http://www.npr.org/templates/story/ story.php?storyId=97124808. Accessed December 10 2008.

Pack, Sam (2000), '"The Navajo": Visual and Literary Representations from Inside and Out', *Wicazo Sa Review*, 15(1): 137–56.

Pack, Sam (2001), 'The Best of Both Worlds: Otherness, Appropriation, and Identity in *Thunderheart*', *Wicazo Sa Review*, 16(2): 97–114.

Parks, Robert (2004), Review of *Dogville. The Phantom Tollbooth Website*. www. tollbooth.org/2004/movies/dogville.html. Accessed February 23 2006.

Patai, Raphael (1973), *The Arab Mind*, New York: Scribner.

Peterson, Mark Allen (2003), *Anthropology and Mass Communication: Media and Myth in the New Millennium*, Oxford: Berghahn Books.

PFS Film Reviews (2004), 'The Village', *Political Film Society Website*. www.geocities. com/~polfilms/village.html. Accessed 1 February 2006.

Pratt, Mary Louise (1986), 'Fieldwork in Common Places', in James Clifford and George Marcus (eds.), *Writing Culture: The Poetics and Politics of Ethnography*, pp. 27–50, Berkeley: University of California Press.

Powdermaker, Hortense (1950), *Hollywood: The Dream Factory*, New York: Grosset & Dunlap.

Putnam, Robert (1995), 'Bowling Alone: America's Declining Social Capital', *Journal of Democracy*, 6(1): 65–78.

Puzo, Mario (1969), *The Godfather*, New York: Signet.

Radway, Janice (1984), *Reading the Romance: Women, Patriarchy, and Popular Literature*, Chapel Hill, NC: University of North Carolina Press.

Rubey, Dan (1976), 'The *Jaws* in the Mirror', *Jump Cut: A Review of Contemporary Media*, 10: 20–23.

Rudd, Robert, and Most, Marshall G. (2003), 'Portrayals of Racial Minorities in Baseball Film', in William M. Simons (ed.), *The Cooperstown Symposium on Baseball and American Culture*, pp. 232–43, Jefferson, NC: McFarland and Company, Inc.

Sahlins, Marshall (1972), *Stone Age Economics*, Chicago: Aldine.

Sahlins, Marshall (1985), *Islands of History*, Chicago: University of Chicago Press.

Samuels, David (2006), *Putting a Song on Top of it: Expression and Identity on the San Carlos Apache Reservation*, Phoenix, AZ: University of Arizona Press.

Sanday, Peggy (2002), *Women at the Center: Life in a Modern Matriarchy*, Ithaca, NY: Cornell University Press.

Schein, Louisa (2008), 'Text and Transnational Subjectification: Media's Challenge to Anthropology', in Neni Panourgiá and George E. Marcus (eds.), *Ethnographica Moralia: Experiments in Interpretive Anthropology*, pp. 188–212, New York: Fordham University Press.

Schneider, David (1980), *American Kinship: A Cultural Account*, 2nd edition, Chicago: University of Chicago Press.

Schor, Juliet (1991), *The Overworked American: The Unexpected Decline of Leisure*, New York: Basic Books.

Seremetakis, C.N. (1994), 'Memory of the Senses, Part 1', in C.N. Seremetakis (ed.), *The Senses Still: Perception and Memory as Material Culture in Modernity*, pp. 1–22, Boulder, CO: Westview.

Shore, Bradd (1990), 'Loading the Bases: How Our Tribe Projects Its Own Image into the National Pastime', *The Sciences* (May/June): 10–18.

Shore, Bradd (1996), *Culture in Mind: Cognition, Culture, and the Problem of Meaning*, pp. 75–100, New York: Oxford University Press.

Silverman, Sydel (2007), 'American Anthropology in the Middle Decades: A View from Hollywood', *American Anthropologist*, 109(3): 519–28.

Siskind, Janet (1973), *To Hunt in the Morning*, New York: Oxford University Press.

Solway, Jacqueline (2006), '"The Original Affluent Society" Four Decades On', in Jacqueline Solway (ed.), *The Politics of Egalitarianism: Theory and Practice*, pp. 65–77, Oxford: Berghahn.

Sommer, Doris (1991), Rigoberta's Secrets, *Latin American Perspectives*, 18(3): 32–50.

Stack, Peter (1998), 'Dreyfuss Can't Save Offensive "Krippendorf"', *San Francisco Chronicle*, February 27: C–12.

Straw, Will (2005), 'Pathways of Cultural Movement', in Caroline Andrew, et al. (eds.), *Accounting for Culture: Thinking Through Cultural Citizenship*, pp. 183–97, Ottawa: University of Ottawa Press.

Street, Brian V. (ed.) (1993), *Cross-Cultural Approaches to Literacy*, Cambridge: Cambridge University Press.

Suraf, Adam (2004), '*The Village*', In Review by Adam Suraf.

www.dunkirkma.net/interview/archives/the_village.html. Accessed 2/1/2006.

Sutton, David (1991), 'Is Anybody Out There?: Anthropology and the Question of Audience', *Critique of Anthropology*, 11: 91–104.

Sutton, David (1998), *Memories Cast in Stone: The Relevance of the Past in Everyday Life*, Oxford: Berg.

Sutton, David (2001), *Remembrance of Repasts: An Anthropology of Food and Memory*, Oxford: Berg.

Sutton, David (2006), 'Cooking Skill, the Senses and Memory: The Fate of Practical Knowledge', in Chris Gosden, Elizabeth Edwards, and Ruth Phillips (eds.), *Sensible Objects: Colonialism, Museums and Material Culture*, pp. 87–118, Wenner-Gren International Symposium Series. Oxford: Berg.

Sutton, David (2007), 'Tipping: An Anthropological Meditation', in David Beriss and David Sutton (eds.), *The Restaurants Book: Ethnographies of Where We Eat*, pp. 191–204, Oxford: Berg.

Sutton, David (2008), 'Tradition and Modernity Revisited: Existential Memory Work on a Greek Island', *History and Memory*, 20(2): 84–105.

Sutton, David and Hernandez, Michael (2007), 'Voices in the Kitchen: Cooking Tools as Inalienable Possessions', *Oral History*, 35: 67–76.

Sutton, David and Vournelis, Leonidas (2009), 'Vefa or Mamalakis? Cooking up Nostalgia in Contemporary Greece', *South European Society and Politics*, 14(2): 147–66.

Sutton, David and Wogan, Peter (2003), 'The Gun, the Pen, and the Cannoli: Orality and Writing in *The Godfather, Part I*', *Anthropology and Humanism*, 28(2):155–67.

Tanner, Nancy (1974), 'Matrifocality in Indonesia and Africa and among Black Americans', in Michelle Rosaldo and Louise Lamphere (eds.), *Woman, Culture, and Society*, pp. 129–56, Stanford: Stanford University Press.

Taussig, Michael (1998), 'Viscerality, Faith and Skepticism: Another Theory of Magic', in Nick Dirks (ed.), *In Near Ruins: Cultural Theory at the End of the Century*, pp. 221–56, Minneapolis, MN: University of Minnesota Press.

Taussig, Michael (2008), 'Redeeming Indigo', *Theory, Culture and Society*, 25(3): 1–15.

Tomaselli, Keyan (1990), 'Annoying Anthropologists: Jamie Uys's Films on "Bushmen" and Animals', *Society for Visual Anthropology Review*, 6 (Spring): 75–80.

Tomaselli, Keyan (1992), 'Myths, Racism, and Opportunism: Film and TV Representations of the San', in Peter Ian Crawford and David Turton (eds.), *Film as Ethnography*, pp. 205–21, Manchester: Manchester University Press.

Tomaselli, Keyan (2002), '"...We Have to Work with Our Own Heads" (Angn!ao): San Bushmen and the Media', *Visual Anthropology*, 15(2): 203–20.

Tomaselli, Keyan (2006), 'Rereading the *Gods Must be Crazy* Films', *Visual Anthropology*, 19(2): 171–200.

Torry, Robert (1993), 'Therapeutic Narrative: *The Wild Bunch*, *Jaws*, and Vietnam', *The Velvet Light Trap*, 31: 27–38.

Traube, Elizabeth (1986), *Cosmology and Social Life: Ritual Exchange among the Mambai of East Timor*, Chicago: University of Chicago Press.

Traube, Elizabeth (1989), 'Secrets of Success in Postmodern Society', *Cultural Anthropology*, 4(3): 273–300.

Traube, Elizabeth (1990), 'Reply to Moffatt', *Cultural Anthorpology*, 5(4):374–9.

Traube, Elizabeth (1992), *Dreaming Identities: Class, Gender and Generation in 1980s Hollywood Movies*, Boulder, CO: Westview Press.

Tyree, J.M., and Walters, Ben (2007), *The Big Lebowski*, London: British Film Institute.

Urban, Greg (1991), *A Discourse-Centered Approach to Culture: Native South American Myths and Rituals*, Austin, TX: University of Texas Press.

Urban, Greg (2001), *Metaculture: How Culture Moves Through the World*, Minneapolis: University of Minnesota Press.

Urban, Greg (2006), 'Power as the Transmission of Culture', in Sergei Kan and Pauline Turner Strong (eds.), *New Perspectives on Native North America: Cultures, Histories, and Representations*, pp. 65–97, Lincoln, NE: University of Nebraska Press.

Van Ede, Yolanda (2007), 'From *The Untouchables* Towards Cool Investigation', in Rob van Ginkel and Alex Strating (eds.), *Wildness and Sensation: Anthropology of Sinister and Sensuous Realms*, pp. 275–94, Appeldoorn Antwerpen, Holland: Het Spinhuis.

Verrips, Jojada (2001), 'The *Golden Bough* and *Apocalypse Now*: An-Other fantasy', *Postcolonial Studies*, 4(3): 335–48.

Volkman, Toby Alice (1986), 'The Hunter-Gatherer Myth in Southern Africa', *Cultural Survival Quarterly*, 10: 25–31.

Volkman, Toby Alice (1988), 'Out of Africa: "The Gods Must Be Crazy"', in Larry P. Gross, John Stuart Katz, and Jay Ruby (eds.), *Image Ethics: The Moral Rights of Subjects in Photographs, Film, and TV*, pp. 237–47, New York: Oxford University Press.

Vowell, Sarah (2000), *Take the Cannoli: Stories from the New World*, New York: Simon & Schuster.

Warshow, Robert (1975), *The Immediate Experience*, New York: Atheneum.

Waterston, Alisse and Vesperi, Maria D. (eds.) (2009), *Anthropology Off the Shelf: Anthropologists on Writing*, Malden, MA: Wiley-Blackwell.

Weakland, John H. (1966a), *Chinese Political and Cultural Themes: A Study of Chinese Communist Films*, Studies in Deterrence #14, China Lake, CA: U.S. Naval Ordnance Test Station.

Weakland, John H. (1966b), 'Themes in Chinese Communist Films', *American Anthropologist*, 68(2): 477–84.

Weiner, Annette (1992), *Inalienable Possessions: The Paradox of Keeping-While-Giving*, Berkeley, CA: University of California Press.

Weingart, Peter (with assistance from Claudia Muhl and Petra Pansegrau) (2003), 'Of Power Maniacs and Unethical Genuises: Science and Scientists in Fiction Film', *Public Understanding of Science*, 12(3): 279–87.

Weston, Kath (2002), *Gender in Real Time: Power and Transience in a Visual Age*, New York: Routledge.

Widlok, Thomas, and Tadesse, Wode Gosse (eds.) (2005), *Property and Equality Volume I: Ritualization, Sharing, Egalitarianism*, Oxford: Berghahn.

Wilk, Richard R. (2002), '"It's Destroying a Whole Generation": Television and Moral Discourse in Belize', in Kelly Askew and Richard R. Wilk (eds.), *The Anthropology of Media: A Reader*, pp. 286–98, Oxford: Blackwell.

Williams, Amrys (2001), '"The Dude Abides": Western Influences in *The Big Lebowski*', MS Online at http://www.mit.edu/~amrys/prose/lebowski.pdf. Accessed February 5, 2006.

Willson, Robert (1977), '*Jaws* as Submarine Movie', *Jump Cut: A Review of Contemporary Media*, 15: 32–3.

Winkler, Scott A. (2004), 'Is This Heaven? No, It's Iowa; Or The Avant-Garde in a Cornfield Cures What Ails You', *Journal of Popular Culture*, 37(4): 704–18.

Wogan, Peter (2001), 'Imagined Communities Reconsidered: Is Print-Capitalism What We Think It Is?', *Anthropological Theory*, 1(4): 403–18.

Wogan, Peter (2004a), '"Deep Hanging Out: Reflections on Fieldwork and Multi-sited Andean Ethnography"', *Identities: Global Studies in Culture and Power*, 11(1): 129–39.

Wogan, Peter (2004b), *Magical Writing in Salasaca: Literacy and Power in Highland Ecuador*. Boulder, CO: Westview Press.

Wogan, Peter (2006), 'Audience Reception and Ethnographic Film: Laughing at First Contact', *Visual Anthropology Review*, 22(1): 14–33.

Wogan, Peter (2007), 'Review of *Travels with Ernest: Crossing the Literary/Sociological Divide*, by Laurel Richardson and Ernest Lockridge', *American Ethnologist*, 34(2): 2043–5.

Wolfenstein, Martha (2000) [1953], 'Movie Analysis in the Study of Culture', in Margaret Mead and Rhoda Metraux (eds.), *The Study of Culture at a Distance*, pp. 293–308, New York: Berghahn.

Wolfenstein, Martha, and Nathan Leites (1950), *Movies*, Glencoe, IL: Free Press.

Wright, John W. (2008), 'Levinasian Ethics of Alterity: The Face of the Other in Spielberg's Cinematic Language', in Dean A Kowalski (ed.), *Steven Spielberg and Philosophy: We're Gonna Need a Bigger Book*, pp. 50–68, Lexington: University of Kentucky Press.

FILMS CITED MULTIPLE TIMES

The Big Lebowski (2005), Ethan Coen and Joel Coen, directors, Universal City, CA: Universal Studios.

Field of Dreams (2004) [1989], Lawrence Gordon and Charles Gordon, directors. Two-disc Anniversary Edition. Universal City, CA: Universal Studios.

The Godfather (2004) [1972], Francis Ford Coppola, director. Hollywood, CA: Paramount Home Entertainment.

The Gods Must be Crazy (2004) [1980], Jamie Uys, director. Culver City, CA: Columbia TriStar Home Entertainment.

Jaws (2005) [1975], Steven Spielberg, director. 30th Anniversary Edition. Universal City, CA: Universal Studios.

Krippendorf's Tribe (1998), Todd Holland, director. Burbank, CA: Touchstone Home Video.

The Village (2004), M. Night Shyamalan, director. Burbank, CA: Buena Vista Home Entertainment.

AUTHOR INDEX

SUBJECT INDEX

85500745R00105

Made in the USA
Lexington, KY
01 April 2018